WITHOUT RESERVE

Stories from Urban Natives

WITHOUT RESERVE

Stories from Urban Natives

Lynda Shorten

NeWest Press
Edmonton

First printing 1991
Second printing 1992

Canadian Cataloguing in Publication Data
Shorten, Lynda, 1955 -
  Without reserve
  ISBN 0-920897-01-0

  1. Indians of North America – Alberta – Edmonton
 – Biography. 2. Indians of North America – Alberta
 – Edmonton – Urban residence. I. Title.
E78.A34S56 1991   971.23'3400497022   C91-091465-6

Credits
COVER & INTERIOR DESIGN: Bob Young/BOOKENDS DESIGNWORKS
COVER PHOTOGRAPH: Sima Khorrami
EDITORS FOR THE PRESS: Larry Pratt and Eva Radford
FINANCIAL ASSISTANCE: NeWest Press gratefully acknowledges the financial assistance of Alberta Culture and Multiculturalism, The Alberta Foundation for the Literary Arts, The Canada Council, and The NeWest Institute for Western Canadian Studies.

Printed and bound in Canada by Best Gagné Book Manufacturers Inc.

NeWest Publishers Limited
#310, 10359-82 Avenue
Edmonton, Alberta
T6E 1Z9

Contents

❂ INTRODUCTION

Marcel, addictions counsellor, pipe-carrier, Métis elder: "A book? We don't need another book. What we need is a rock and roll star."

I believe in books. I believe in stories. And so, despite the plea for a rock star, I offer this book of autobiographical stories told by Native people living in a mid-size Western Canadian city at the close of the twentieth century. The stories were spoken into a tape recorder and reduced to print. They are powerful and speak the "truth" about being an urban Native in Canada in a way that is more telling than the most precise of surveys or studies. Their power lies, simply, in the individuals revealed. I am not a sociologist, anthropologist, or statistician.

I am a reporter. More accurately here, I am a walking tape recorder. I did not, in any sense, "write" this book. Rather, I served as the conduit through which these Native people could make their stories known. The method was simple. I did not go looking for anything in particular, not Cinderella stories, not tearjerkers. I simply asked people I met if they would like to take part in the writing of a book. If they said yes, I turned on the microphone.

These stories do not pretend to be a representative sample, such sampling being beyond my ability or intent. They do, however, cover a range of experiences, from that of a fourteen-year-old boy in foster care, to that of an eighty-six-year-old Métis teacher as a girl in residential school. Some of the storytellers are successful by any "white" standard. Some are students. Some are on the street. At least one, now, is back in jail.

Several of the storytellers are Catholic, some evangelical

Christians who dismiss traditional Native spirituality as superstition. Some believe that traditional spirituality, a return to the grandfathers, to the sweat lodges and sweetgrass, is the only hope for all Native people. One calls herself a headbanger, another would rather be black. One feels she found a home in feminism. Some are fiercely proud of being Métis and resent being called Indian. One spoke English as his first language and was forced to learn Cree and French at residential school; some spoke Cree and were forced to learn English. Some speak only English and have no knowledge of any Native language at all.

These people all grew up or live in Edmonton, a northern Alberta city of 568,000 people, 21,000 of whom are "aboriginal," according to Statistics Canada (1986), a city where, as elsewhere in Canada, Natives go to jail in disproportionate numbers, earn less, die younger. Many of the storytellers have lived in a number of urban centres, or move back and forth between city and reserve. Thus, while Edmonton is the location where most of these stories are told, the particular city does not determine the stories' content. What does determine their content is simply the experience of living life as a Native in a Canadian city.

These people are all "urban Natives," too, in the sense that their lives are not reflected in most of the current discourse on Native people. These are individuals without a chief, often without a band or treaty number, people not represented in land claims negotiations or treaty claims; people ignored, for the most part, in discussions about Canada's treatment of its Native population. They show us what should be self-evident: that to talk about "Native people," as though that were in any way an adequate description, is laughable. These people compel us to see them, to listen to them, and to respect them in all their diversity.

I am not Native. I am white, a second-generation Canadian of English and Scottish descent. I struggled with the question of appropriation of voice raised by my involvement with this book. I believe I have neither the right nor the ability to tell the stories of Native people for them. I also believe that if I had been denied the chance to learn what I learned, denied the gift of sharing time with these storytellers, of being taken by them to places I would never otherwise have been, both in the physical world and in a very personal sense – that, for me, would have been a great loss.

If someone like Jimmy Mix or Lisa or any of the others who tell their lives in these pages were denied the chance to have their stories known simply because the person with her hand on the tape recorder was white, that, too, would have been a great loss.

And, to the extent this book gives people, of whatever race, a chance to meet Maggie, Sky, Casey, Jane, that opportunity should not be denied them because I am white.

Having said that, it is undeniable that it was my white fingers on the computer, editing these stories down from hundreds of hours of tapes and hundreds and hundreds of transcribed pages. I had feelings about what I saw and heard, and it would be dishonest to pretend that my editing was in any way "pure."

I have tried, as well as I am able, to be honest with the reader. I have tried to make it clear when it is my perceptions being recorded and when the storyteller has command.

For the rest, I have tried to respect and reflect accurately the voices of the storytellers by interfering as little as possible with the words they used to tell their lives. Any changes were made in the interest of clarity only. In making the stories shorter, I tried to remain true to each teller's spirit and intent, as true as the printed word allows.

Accordingly, different stories take different forms. Lisa's story is told entirely in her own words. With Kicker, where my involvement with him extended over the entire three years it took to complete this project, my perceptions form a larger part of the story because I cannot pretend those perceptions had no influence on the way the story is revealed.

In each case the storyteller told me only as much as he or she chose. I did not attempt to verify the details from other sources, nor did I press them to fill in gaps they were reluctant to discuss. As a consequence the reader may find herself with questions after the story is complete. That is as the storyteller intended.

In all but two cases, the storytellers asked to have their identities protected. Names and other details are therefore changed or omitted. Sky requested anonymity because he believes his individual "ego" is far less important than the fact many of his people have shared his experiences. In other cases, such as those of Maggie and Helen, the storyteller did not want to protect her own identity as much as those of her children. Kicker's concern was with the police, Jimmy Mix's for his family. Casey and Lisa are young and their identities are protected for that reason.

The two exceptions are Dr. Anne Anderson, a respected Métis elder, author and teacher who appears briefly in the story of Grace, and Jane Ash Poitras, a well-known Canadian painter.

Sky, a Sioux pipe-carrier and ex-convict, and Maggie, a Métis social worker, were my guides. They took me into a sweat lodge, to a Sun Dance, to rodeos, to powwows, to Round Dances, to AA meetings, to their offices, into their friends' homes, introduced me to their families. They were generous with their time and generous with their friendship. Without Sky and Maggie there would be no book, and it is to their caring for their people that this books owes its existence.

I also want to thank Rudy Wiebe, Larry Pratt, and Eva Radford, without whom this project would never have gotten off the ground nor been completed. My sister, Patti Wilson, gave me invaluable support and editing advice, as did James Adams, Karen Sherlock and Kathleen Thurber, who is responsible for the title. I also wish to thank my employer, The Edmonton Journal, in particular, city editor Sheila Pratt and editor Linda Hughes for being so generous in giving me time off to work on the book.

✪ JIMMY MIX

SHADES. HIGH TOPS. His Famous Ancestor's bow legs. A head for blondes. An at-ti-tude.

The first time he phones he says, "You looking for a fucking Cinderella story or what?"

Or what.

He signs his name Jimmy Mix, brackets, Canadian.

Jimmy Mix (Canadian) walks the walk. He's been off the street and in Alcoholics Anonymous for two years. One of the bright spots in his new life, he says, is to crack people up. Watch them split a gut. He's snarky. Quick. The kind of big-mouth pretty boy girls harbored a distant and secret crush on in junior high school; cool, too bright, trouble. He smokes constantly, sucking in the smoke like punctuation. He is twenty-three years old.

"I'm up on a lot of people in a lot of ways," he says. "I've been white. Somewhat Indian. I've been rich and really poor." He laughs, more snort than chuckle. "It's a rough road. I should know; I paved it."

He is adept at fitting in, at taking people's measure, calculating how to get what he wants, how to act white, how not to. At the same time, he stays always on the fringes so takes no responsibility, not for a thing, and feels free to criticize, which he does abundantly and with passion. Me. His fellow AA members. The Indians on his filthy-rich "skid-row" reserve. His pill-popping mother. "I call my own mother dorfus," he says. "Her name is Dora; I just kinda elaborated." His white roommate. "Fucking whites who fucked this world up." Himself. Harshly and especially himself.

We meet at my office. He walks in wearing black sunglasses with scratched, mirrored lenses that throw my image back at me.

1

He wears the glasses even though it is December and the sun is dull. He carries a Styrofoam coffee cup from the YWCA across the street; he is thin from constant caffeine, nicotine, and scant attention to food.

The bad bar band down the hall is practising *Satisfaction*. The scritchy-voiced bad-boy singer can't get no, no no no, again and again and again. Above the racket, Jimmy exercises his deep voice like a DJ; his knee pumps up and down and he smokes without end. At the close of the interview he says he has never told anybody all this shit before; he feels sick.

Still, he volunteers to type out his own interview tapes. Later he transcribes those, and others, for pay. He draws ears for the computer and glues them to the sides of the terminal. He calls the computer Ed and makes it a name plate. He moves in his music, tapes labelled "Ever Feel Like Biting Someone's Face Off" and "Acquired Taste" and "Boy Inside the Man." He pins a red plastic sign to the wall that reads, "Why is that what I want and what's not good for me are always the same thing?" He tacks up a photo someone took of him at the top of a mountain. It is taken from behind; you cannot see his face. His arms are stretched out embracing the sky. He looks as though he is ready and, at any moment, will leap joyously off the mountain's edge into thin blue air. He tells me that was the happiest moment of his life.

When he disappears he leaves the photo behind.

He disappears after two months. I hear from him only once. He phones to say he's got problems. His reserve is cutting off his oil payments; his girlfriend has successfully sued for child-support arrears. He's back in a half-way house. He never finished the tapes I paid him for. He's sorry. Then he's gone and I never hear from him again.

One day in the office he tells me, "I was always going to write my own story. I had a title for it and everything. I was going to call it 'Runaway.' "

Jimmy Mix (Canadian). Nowhere to run to. Nowhere to hide.

"CHILDHOOD. Mom and dad were alcoholic. Heavy drinkers. Drugs. And there was five of us kids and, uh, they were out drinking one day and I guess somebody found me and my four sisters in the house alone. Social Services took us and put us in foster homes. Me and my two sisters – an older sister and a younger sister – we ended up on a farm in Ponoka. Missy was just a little baby, about one. I was two and a half.

"My foster mom was Norwegian, my dad German. Christians. We lived there for about nine years. It was good. Lots of love. Normal childhood. School. Clothing. Good food. Cow shit.

"Our mom, our real mom, would pop in once in awhile. I always looked forward to that, seeing my mom. She'd come to visit us once a year. Summertime. The greatest day of my life every summer. For weeks I would just sit there and play with my toys, thinking about seeing mom.

"Never saw my dad. Never saw him until I was about thirteen.

"Then I got a little bit older and things were starting to change for me at home. I was starting to want to play hockey and stuff like that. They were an older couple and didn't want to run into town. So when I was twelve they moved me to an orphanage in Wetaskiwin.

"There was thirty-five kids there. It was a huge place. Just massive. Farm again, more cow shit. I was one of the older boys, so they got me into hockey.

"Hockey." He grins. "I was home. I played for about two or three years. Made the best teams. Really good at it.

"I was a left-winger. I was big then. And mean. Broke a guy's arm once. Just nailed him. Poor guy didn't even see me coming.

"It took me awhile to get over it, the change. Three or four months in the home before I started trying to fit in. There were older boys there, too. Used to fight. We were all tough street orphanage kids, you know. Like we'd have to prove a point, what it was we never knew. Just the thing to do. I think once I found I could beat up a couple of them, I started to fit in.

"I just started growing up. Hockey was there. School was

there. Girls. They were always blonde, too. All of them." He laughs. "I had lots of girlfriends.

"In one sense I was happy, you know, when my foster parents gave me up, because then I could go do something. In another sense it was like leaving mother. Like leaving the nest. There just wasn't a regular environment anymore where there's only three kids, you know, and relatives, and family, holidays, you name it. It was gone. Absolutely gone.

"From that time on I felt like I was always on the outside looking in."

HISTORY BOOKS describe Jimmy Mix's Famous Ancestor as a short, taciturn, bowlegged halfbreed. No looker. But as an Indian scout for the North West Mounted Police in the late 1800s, the books say, he was without equal. He is remembered for many things: among them the fact that in battle after battle – shot dead straight in the face, outnumbered, out-horsed, outrun – he would not die; and for his uncanny, omniscient sense of direction, even when snow blind.

"MY STEPFATHER used to try to tell me that all I needed to know was on their farm. Just the farm. Nothing else. But I was real rebellious. Even when I was a little kid, like around six. I used to do stuff like hang from the rafters in the barn. Just hang there. Thirty or forty feet up. Nobody up there but me. He used to say, 'Don't do that or you'll die and go to hell.' Everything was hell. Heaven and hell. I got real atheistic after awhile. Like, 'If there's a hell, prove it. Let me feel the flames, man.'

"Ya, I guess there was some abuse there. Mental abuse. Physical abuse. Got slapped around a lot. But mostly mental abuse. Like they kept me really boxed in. Shut in. Nothing but the farm. The farm and heaven and hell.

"I used to run away from the foster home when I was nine, ten.

I remember my real mom, she told me she lived out on the reserve; she took us out there once. So I took off on my bike. Set off to go find this place. They caught up with me. Dragged me back home. Put me in a cage so I couldn't get out. It was a playhouse and it had a huge fence around it. It was locked. I couldn't get out. Left me there, for a day.

"What did I want on the reserve? My mom? Ya. Ya, well I think I started realizing I wasn't white. There was something else there, you know, on the reserve. I went out to Hobbema and I remember seeing all these deer, my grandmother showing me all these deer. Walking down the road and she goes, 'It's safe for you out here.' I never forgot that.

"We'd sit in this tepee my grandmother put up. Eat bannock. She had a house and everything, eh, but she always had a tepee out back. Lived the traditional way. Big garden every year. I think my grandmother was the only person who ever liked me. She had these real tough hands, tough and soft at the same time, you know what I mean? Like the paws of a dog. She'd take those hands and rub them over my face and through my hair. I think she liked me because I had curly hair. She'd give me moccasins and stuff. I felt like I was an Indian back in the 1800s. That's what I felt like when I was with her.

"Then when you come out of something as simple as that and go back into a complex world of, 'Don't do this, don't do that, don't do this,' I freaked. I just freaked."

I STUDY a photo of the Famous Ancestor, searching for resemblances. His eyes are smaller, his hair straight; other than the bowlegs there are no obvious physical similarities. He holds a shotgun in his right hand, a beaded bag hangs from his belt. He wears a narrow-brimmed cap, a fringed coat, moccasins. He has an exaggerated handlebar mustache; it almost looks like it was drawn in later in heavy black pen, a joke, a defacement.

The books say the Famous Ancestor drifted from his mother's

people to the white whiskey traders and back again. That he was loyal to the North West Mounted Police, but the Blood were his people. It is difficult to know, they say, where the homely little halfbreed's allegiances stood.

AS THE WEEKS move closer to Christmas, Jimmy starts to call me at home late at night. I can hear him sucking in cigarette smoke, exhaling clouds through his teeth. His DJ voice is ragged. He says he can't sleep.

"There was a time I didn't tell you before. When I was nine. Another time when I ran away. My foster parents caught me. They brought me back. They put a rope around a pole and they tied it around my neck. They brought me my supper out on a plate and set it down in the dirt just far enough away where I couldn't reach it. And I had to eat it like that, tied up like a dog. My stepfather said, 'Just like a dog. Heck, you're not going to be able to go anywhere unless we let you loose.'

"I remember my sisters were sitting there and they were crying, right."

I ask him, "Did you cry?"

I almost cannot hear his answer. "Yep.

"Another time. I was seven. They butchered this pig and they cut off its head and they put it on this pole that was up, and then they told me it was my sister. They were just teasing, eh, but I was only seven years old. I was bawling my eyes out.

"I remember I was about ten. We had this back porch, eh. I remember being out there on the porch, this one night. It was dark. Nobody around. Nothing around for miles. And then I heard this voice. Something said to me, 'Why don't you come down and play with me?'

"I was scared shitless. I was so scared shitless.

"It was a child . . . I don't know what the hell it was. I'm trying to think, like maybe was it a dream that I remembered vividly out of everything else? Or was it real? I don't know. Maybe I just had a really vivid imagination back then. Maybe I was just hoping that something would come along and take me away from there.

"I think my foster parents gave me away because I was just getting too wild. I don't know, I think I was getting close to something. I think I was getting really close to figuring out a few things that are not really kosher in any home. And maybe it was time to let me go.

"I've been thinking about this a lot for the last month, about sexual abuse in that home. And uh, I've been trying to shut it out but it's . . . it's getting very real. And now I'm starting to have a few dreams. About my sisters mostly. I don't think, I don't think that I was sexually abused. Everything that happened to me as a kid, sexually, I remember. I just do. But I remember my older sister, Heather, she was starting to get really rebellious. That puberty thing. She was growing boobs and stuff. Around that time I left."

On the other end of the phone line cigarette smoke is sucked in, blown out.

"There was this other adopted sister in the foster home. I was about four, she was sixteen. I went down to sleep with her, you know, just an innocent thing. And I guess she let me feel her. All over. I didn't understand what was going on. She asked. She didn't have, there really wasn't any talking. She just grabbed my hand and. . . ."

He stops.

"From what I can remember it happened once. I don't know if there was anymore that I can't remember.

"I guess to me at the time that was normal. That was what a family did.

"I remember when I was eighteen, nineteen when my girlfriend Trixie and I split up. I was trying to push her and our baby away because I didn't trust myself. My mind, my thoughts are just sick, man. God. Fuck, it was incredible. I wanted them to just get away from me because I was just a monster. I thought it was just the drugs, and I quit that. But it didn't help.

"I knew then that I didn't want for my daughter what had

7

happened to me. And I thought that I'd be the one to do it. And here I didn't even know what that was.

"By the time I left I hated my fucking stepfather. Just wanted to waste him. I just, just felt like a caged animal sometimes, like my life was like a slave's.

"And I think one of the reasons I hated him the most was that, one night when I woke up he was masturbating at the end of the bed. And there I was. We were just getting up to go to work. Like I was awake and I knew what he was doing.

"My sister was in there, too. I forget which one it was, Missy or Heather. One of my sisters was there.

"I couldn't understand that, you know. It baffled me. Times before, if he did something he'd always give an explanation for it. But he never said anything about this at all to me. He just kinda withdrew.

"That was just before I went to the home. Just a couple of months.

"I can tell you it was one huge mind-fucker. Between the ages of ten and thirteen I was just . . . it was hell, you know. I don't think a twelve-, thirteen year old should be thinking like that. I was thinking about suicide. I was thinking about killing people. I was thinking about cutting his dink off.

"The thing that bugs me about it the most now is I go and visit them once in awhile. They really play up about how much they care about me. And I'm beginning to see that as a bullshit story. What I've wanted to do recently is just approach them, sit them down and say, 'Look, I know what you did that night. I was there. I was awake.'

"You know, I think if everything had went smooth, right now I'd be playing NHL hockey. I'd be in college or university. I wouldn't have a criminal record. I wouldn't have been a drug dealer. You see, I know it didn't change when I went to the street. It had to have changed before that, because the street was comforting compared to where I came from.

"I think about that stuff now. I tell you if I knew I could get away with it I'd kill him. If he pissed me off bad enough now I would kill him."

"SUICIDE. YA. I tried quite a few times actually. In between the ages of about twelve to nineteen. I never had the guts. I knew there was something about me that was better than doing something like that. When I was about twelve I was up on top of one of these towers they have for silage. I was looking down and I thought to myself, 'Fuck, four seconds, buddy, and it would be all over.'

"I was just tired of life. Just tired of being always forced into change. Or just knowing that I was different. There was just so much going on in my head, you know. The only escape I ever had was, I had a girlfriend. She used to make me laugh. And sports. I played a lot of sports."

He pauses.

"I just didn't want to be anyone. I didn't want to be me. I'd go to school, and a lot of times I was a lot superior in a lot of things that kids were trying to do. And they'd go home to their families and I'd go back to this huge fucking orphanage.

"Suicide became very real in there because there were other kids in there that were just, Christ, worse than I was. And I was thinking, 'God, am I going to get like that?' Their minds. Mentally they were just screwed. I seen a few of those kids today and they are still just fucked. Most of them have been in mental hospitals.

"The closest I came to carrying through was a gun. I was eighteen, nineteen. I had a gun in my mouth. I had it in there for about five, ten minutes. I was trying to figure out what the other side would be like, how much pain would I have, would I miss and live, would I have time to take another shot. Right in the middle of fucking downtown Ponoka. Cars driving by and I was sitting with a 30-30 in my mouth. Nobody stopped. Trixie was sitting right there. She just didn't care, she really didn't. I think she would have been happy if I was gone, at the time."

WHEN THE FAMOUS Ancestor was still a baby, his Scots father was murdered, shot in the face through a stockade wicket by a one-eyed Peigan, a case of mistaken identity. The boy was taken in by another Scot, a madman who had killed thirteen unarmed Blackfoot with a cannon blast in retribution for the death of one Black employee. This man was so cruel he once wounded an Indian who was trying to steal a cow, sat down beside the injured man, gave him a pipe to smoke and then shot out his brains even as the Indian begged for mercy. He was so hated his fellow traders tried to murder him. When the attempt failed he fled, abandoning the Famous Ancestor, then five.

And so the Famous Ancestor was handed over to his third and final Scot who, the books say, was a good man, a kindly soul who taught the child many Indian languages, and how to make his way in both the Native and white worlds.

"MY DAD, my real dad was a drug dealer. One of the ways I got into it. He was killed in 1982. Gunfight. I think it was in Vancouver actually. Out at the coast.

"I used to think about that, you know, 'I'm going to go down just like my dad. At least I got 'til forty-two to do it.' " Jimmy laughs. "That's exactly the road I was taking, exactly to a T. You see he had everything I wanted. He was a real handsome guy. Muscles. He had all the nice cars. Beautiful women. Money. And still lived dangerously.

"I remember my dad, maybe one of the two times I ever saw him. He played me this song and he said to me, 'You and me are two long grey sharks.'

"Two long grey sharks." Jimmy snorts. "I believed him.

"That's the only thing that man ever taught me.

"The first time I ever met my dad, he came down to Wetaskiwin and picked us up. Me and Missy. I liked him. You know, he was like, really really handsome. Like me." Jimmy laughs. "He had a nice suit on. You could see through the suit that he was really built. Really, really sharp-looking guy. And I forget what he said to me, something like, 'Hello son,' or something like that. And right then, you know, it was," he whistles, "pffff. It was the real thing.

"The home let us go with him. We ended up in Edmonton, I think it was the Holiday Inn. And he was letting me do everything. I'd drank beer before but he brought it right into the hotel room, you know. I could sit there and drink all I want.

"We got up the next morning and my dad said, 'Well, let's go to Calgary.' So we hopped in, my dad said he had a rented car. We ended up in Calgary at the Four Seasons Hotel. Really expensive rooms. Missy and me, we didn't have anything to do that day so he gave us ten bucks each. He said, 'Don't go down that street.' He was talking about 7th Avenue. I guess it's kinda like the skid row. So Mis and I, I think we went and seen a movie. We'd never been to Calgary before.

"And when Mis and me went back to the car to meet him, I was sitting there fucking around with the lights or something, waiting for him, pressing the brakes and the lights were coming on. Out of nowhere there were like four undercover detectives pointing guns at us. They thought I was him, because I look so much like him. They asked me my name and I said, 'Jimmy Mix.' And they said, 'Don't get smart.' I never experienced cops before. And I didn't know what the fuck to do.

"It turns out that he'd stolen this car. I guess what happened was he fucked up the front end in a parkade somewhere and somebody reported it and they found it.

"He tried to set me and Mis up. I think that's exactly what he did because the guy was on the lam probably most of his life, you know, and I don't think he really cared too much about who went down just so long as he was OK. I think he was across the street watching, sending us back to the car to see if anybody would pick us up. And then, like within minutes, the fucking cops. It was just incredible, man.

"You know, sometimes I think if my father were here right now I'd kick his face in. The bastard set us up. Wanted to know if he was being followed, so he set us up. The prick."

NOTHING IS SAID about the Famous Ancestor's Indian mother as her son is handed from Scot to Scot. One book says she died when he was a baby and that, motherless, "he grew up like a sagebrush – wild and free and tough." Others say she returned to her own people, the Black Elk tribe of the Bloods. In time, her only other son was shot in a whiskey-soaked dispute by a Blood brave named Good Young Man, who left the body for the dogs to eat. When the grieving mother rode up to retrieve her dead son's body, Good Young Man pulled her from her horse and murdered her, too.

Three months later the Famous Ancestor avenged his mother's and brother's deaths. Good Young Man was riding double with another brave on one tired horse; the Famous Ancestor gave chase on a fresh one. He shot Good Young Man in the back, shattering his spine. The second man he allowed to go free.

"I WAS ABOUT thirteen, still in the home, I went down to visit my real mom, she was in Ponoka then. Then I got a taste of the street. Pinball alleys. Tough kids. Leather coats and stuff. I said, 'Ah shit, if I can't be an Indian in the 1800s, I'm sure as fuck gonna be one here.'

"I seen those tough-looking guys. They looked great. They were free. They weren't bound by anything. They were just wild, you know. There was just a few rules you had to follow, just very few. And they were your choice.

"And I got to the orphanage and I looked around, basically said, 'Like where are these people going to take me where I haven't already been before?' I give 'em one of these" – he sticks up his middle finger – "and I left. I was thirteen.

"It was a little bit difficult on the street, trying to be a jock and play hockey, and be a drug dealer. So finally I just went completely over to the drug side of it. Booze. I was what they called a runner when I was thirteen. There was a guy in town who used to sell a lot of drugs; I was his main trafficker. I used to carry like two ounces of pot on me. I had a knife and I used it. And I'd sell all this stuff, take a risk for this guy. The stuff would have got me three years in a juvenile detention centre. But I just took the stuff and sold it. He gave me thirty bucks. He made two hundred.

"I met up with this other guy. His name was Stan. He'd gone out with my mom. And this guy took a really good liking to me. I'd go over to his place and he'd sit me down, feed me. And he'd talk to me. We'd sit around and drink rum sometimes. He basically looked after me for quite a long time. You know, he'd go to the bar and be too drunk to walk home and I'd be there on the steps waiting for him. Help him home. It was kinda neat.

"Then I think Social Services kept trying to drag me back into homes, group homes, trying to settle me down. I guess they thought I was some kind of, I guess like one of them machines broke down and they were going to try and fix it. I was a ward of the government and they didn't want this happening because it was too embarrassing." He shrugs. "I don't know why. It happens every day.

"So I ended up sleeping in hotels downtown, a lot of nights. I'd crawl in through the back, or I'd go in during the day. Sleep in the hallways. Other places. Just bummed around. Other people's places. Break into places. Lie. Cheat. Con.

"It was a good life. You know, when you're thirteen that's all there is, really. Especially now.

"I guess when I first got out on the street my mother was there ready to take me in. But that, it was just a fleeting kinda thing. It was just, 'Good to have you here, now we'll see you later.'

"She was drunk all the time. She was never around. With all different kinds of men all the time. What was I supposed to do, follow her around?

"She used to get beat up pretty bad sometimes. Ended up in

the hospital quite a number of times. I think most of it was drug abuse; she used to do a lot of pills. Still does. And they'd have to pump her stomach.

"She lives there now, on Hobbema. She is, ah, almost to the end. She does a lot of drugs. A pill-popper. She drinks quite heavy. She was doing good there for awhile. A number of years ago. I think now it's a lot of guilt because of the kids. She took off on us when we were really young and now she's trying to get us back, eh. Like we don't even look at her as mom anymore, you know, we even call her names. Just another fuck-up that we don't like.

"I almost wish, sometimes, I do wish a lot that she'd be dead and I could say I don't have a mother. 'Cause I don't like lying and telling people that I do.

"Even back when I was on the street I didn't care for her. But back then I didn't care for anybody. I didn't have a fucking care in the world. I think I realized at a very young age that you got to look out for Number One. That's it.

"I didn't want anything to do with anybody who couldn't help me get ahead. If I figured I could use that person to take another step up, I would. Anybody with that caring-and-sharing bullshit, I said, 'No way.' 'Cause I went through that for, God, for so many years in those fucking homes. I didn't want some guy to come up to me and say, 'It'll get better tomorrow. We love you very much. Why don't you stay with us?'

"That's what I mean by deceiving. Deceiving. Deceiving."

THE FAMOUS ANCESTOR killed his first man, a French Canadian, when he was twenty-three; the only white man he ever shot. He killed many Indians, in battle and otherwise. Once, alone on a buffalo hunt, at the click of a musket he leapt from the back of a horse and shot dead four of seven Crow who had conspired in their own tongue to kill him, not knowing he could speak their language. The surviving three ran away in fear.

"I WAS ON the street two years before I got arrested the first time. I should have been arrested a lot more times. I did a lot of things. I remember this guy in school, I was pretty popular in school then, I ran for boys' sports rep on the student council and I beat out this guy. He was calling me a jerk and everything after. And I'd been out of school for a couple of months, I was like fourteen, fifteen, and I seen this guy out on the street. I was a little bit high, a little bit hyperactive. He was with a bunch of girls, you know, a real good-looking guy. Always had girls around him. I went up to him, grabbed him by the hair and smoked him once, right in the beak. Just totalled his mouth. Broke his jaw. He lost a couple teeth, he had braces on. I really messed him up.

"I remember after I let his hair go, eh, he sort of slouched over. And all that came out, it was like a thick oil, blood, just blood just gushed out of his mouth. "And I looked at him and just laughed. Just laughed at him. Drove away.

"I was playing this arcade game the same night. It was Galaxian, I remember it really well. I was doing really good. I had 70,000 points on this thing. Hadn't lost a man. There was this tap on my shoulder. I said, 'Just wait a minute.' Another tap. So I told whoever it was to fuck off.

"And that was it. There was two great big RCMP officers. Down on the ground, handcuffs on. I didn't know what was going on. They threw me into the van and they told me I was under arrest for assault causing bodily harm.

"I had never felt like such a man as I did when I walked into that jail. I felt so good. You know, because I was one of those guys, those tough guys now. People were scared of me."

THE FAMOUS ANCESTOR was guiding two prospectors searching for gold when a war party of two hundred Sioux swooped down on them. The three men tried to outrun the Sioux, but the Indians' horses were fresher. Knowing they could not escape, the Famous Ancestor ordered the two prospectors to rein their horses around; they rode back through the astonished Sioux before the Indians had time to react. The three made it to a cabin. The Famous Ancestor realized the Sioux would simply wait until dark and burn them out. So, at nightfall, he wrapped himself in an Indian blanket and strolled into the Sioux camp. He cut loose three horses and sneaked them back to the cabin.

As the three men stole away, the story goes, the Famous Ancestor could not resist crying out with pride; a keening Blackfoot war whoop.

"THEY TOOK ME up to Edmonton. I'd never been close to a plane before. They threw me on this plane, handcuffs on, flew me down to Calgary to a detention centre. Same day. In twenty-four hours this happened. I beaned a guy and now I was in jail in Calgary. I tell you, what a life.

"And all through that time, all I could remember was, 'I'm going to get that fucker back. He's not going to get away with this.'

"About a month into remand they moved us up to this minimum-security holding place. I was there two days and I realized the door was open. I took off. What they call a 'go-boy.' It was back on the bus, man, back to Wetaskiwin. I was going to kill this guy.

"I had street-gang colours on. I looked pretty mean. I stormed into that high school, bashed in the door and said, 'I want you.' Man, I never seen anyone run so fast in my life. And all the older guys from school – this was high school, eh – they were scared of me. They said, 'Just leave it alone, man, we don't want any more trouble here.'

"So I went back to the arcade. That was really smart." He snorts. "I got busted there again.

"This time the cops didn't mess around. They grabbed me, handcuffed me. Treated me really rough in jail. Slapped me around. Got sentenced to three more months. And then they put me in a paddy wagon with some really heavy convicts. Fort

Saskatchewan types. Man, those handcuffs were tight. My wrist was bleeding, I still got the scar.

"I remember wanting so badly to run again. I didn't know where I was going to go, I just wanted to run.

"I didn't realize until I got older that my attitude had changed so much. By the time I was fifteen I was so cold I'd have killed anyone for a dollar. I didn't know that then.

"I think I realized that I was a lot tougher than people. That I had a look. My face, I could make it look almost psychotic. I scared people. I knew that. And it was comfortable. It was comfortable not telling anybody you loved them. It was more comfortable saying, 'I want to kill you.'

"The booze helped. The drugs helped.

"There was a time when I suppose I could control it. Like my emotions, you know, I could tell someone that I liked them. There came a turning point. It's like you have a cucumber, you stick in vinegar. Look at it the next day and it's still a cucumber. Leave it alone for awhile and it changes into a pickle, but you don't know when and how it changed.

"That's what happened to me."

JIMMY STARTS to move into my life. He helps decorate my Christmas tree. He tags along to a movie, *Henry V*, and declares it the best thing he's ever seen. On Saturday mornings he shows up where my friends and I meet for muffins. He drinks coffee and teases the women there, all in their thirties, all single. "You women are wild," he says, pop-eyed. He tells them he's never met anyone like them in his life. He shakes his curls at them, and grins a lot.

Afterward they tell me that he looks Italian. That he's a funny guy, easy to relate to. "It's a horrible thing to say," they say, "but he doesn't seem very Indian."

"WHEN I WAS fifteen, that was just the start. It got worse. I started living on the streets. Hanging out with street people. Ripping people off. Moving from place to place. Ending up in youth emergency shelters. Finally, I was out of control.

"I ended up in Toronto and, uh, I came into contact with this guy. He was homosexual. He was at the bus depot. I guess he liked little boys or something, and I knew what he was up to and I played into his game. When we got to his place, if it wasn't for the fact that I had seen a bottle of whiskey on his counter, I'd have killed the man. I would've stole his car and all his money.

"And, uh, afterward I made him give me a ride out to the highway, so I could hitchhike back to Alberta. I had no money. Just the clothes on my back. It was cold. I must have been hitchhiking out there for twelve hours.

"Finally this guy stops. Picks me up. Sympathetic guy. He was the type of white guy that you see out on the reserves – they accept you 'cause they like you. I knew he was like that. And the thought came to my head, 'I'm gonna rip this guy off. I need stuff. It's out of necessity.'

"He fed me, said that I could stay overnight at his place. He would give me some money and everything, and I could go on my way. And then I seen the whiskey bottle again. Poured it down.

"I went to bed and the next thing I remember is, I'm holding a knife to this guy's throat. I said, 'Give me your wallet.' And he, uh, he gave me his wallet.

"And then, something happened right then. I remember it so good. I was so sober. I wasn't drunk anymore. I was sober, and I was looking at this guy going, 'I hate white people. And you're first.'

"This guy was really scared. I mean, I've never seen anything so frightened in my life. And I enjoyed it.

"Then, somebody was looking out for me, because I did something really stupid. I stayed. I stayed for about fifteen minutes, just playing with this guy. Just saying, 'Whoa, look out buddy, don't move too fast, I just don't know who I am.' And I got up and got a beer out of the fridge. Turned my back on him. And he jumped on me. And this knife, it was probably about a foot long, he held it to my throat. I said, 'Go ahead.' "

Jimmy shakes his head. "Sixteen years old, I was doing this.

"He had me pinned down and he called the cops. It was the Ontario Provincial Police, they come and picked me up. And there was this lady cop. I thought it was so funny just seeing this lady cop, I was laughing. I almost just killed this guy and I'm laughing. It was just sick.

"And I looked at her, I was in handcuffs, I says, 'Hey bitch, what happens if I run?' She goes, 'I'll shoot you.' I said 'OK, I'm in the back of the car.' Wild sense of humour, eh.

"They put me in the big time, the big house. I was in there with men who had done hard time. That was the real McCoy. There was handcuffs, and shackles and guns. They told me straight out in jail, 'You try to climb the wall, we're going to shoot you in the back.' I wasn't laughing anymore. I got really cold. I just shut everything off.

"That was the first time I knew that I hated white guys. And that was the first time I knew white guys hated me.

"Got in a few fights. I was in with murderers, rapists, armed robbers. Just, you know, the glamorous part of society.

"I remember this one guy in jail. He was a child molester. Skinner. And he wanted to, he wanted to get it on with me. I fucking near killed that guy. I just," Jimmy shakes his head, "Wow. So they put me in this dingy little cell for three months. For my own protection mostly. It was just a single cell. I remember sitting in there and they had that really thick glass you can't see out of, but it gives in light. There was no light. The cell was about five-by-ten feet. It had a bed, toilet, sink. And that was it.

"I never seen the outside world for just months. They had an underground tunnel that would take you to court. High-top security, two guards, one with a shotgun, one holding you by the arm, cameras everywhere.

"I felt like I had just killed a hundred people or something."

THE FAMOUS ANCESTOR was ambushed by three Crow while he was out hunting with a cousin. The cousin was shot in the chest. The Crow, not realizing the Famous Ancestor could speak their language, plotted to trick him. In sign language they signalled they only wanted one scalp; his cousin would do. As he started to ride away, a rifle blast blew off his hat, more pork-pie than Stetson. Jumping from his mule, he shot dead the Crow who had hit his hat and then, one by one, the other two, who were too distracted to see him take aim, busy, as they were, stripping the body of his dead cousin.

"I GOT OUT of jail and took a train back to Alberta and went back on the street. I used to wear eye liner, black trench coat, earring, long hair. The eye liner gives it the psycho effect. People have to look at your eyes because they want to know what's on them.

"I don't want to say too much about the gangs. Just that they were there. A lot of it was highly illegal. I hung out wherever. Wherever I was needed, I'd be easy to find. And I'd be there. We all had special skills, I suppose. Mine, mine was scaring the shit out of people. I was good at it. I had the guts to jump up on a bar table and hold a gun to a guy's face. I really liked to be noticed. I think that was a big fault for me 'cause I always ended up in jail. Every time I showed my ugly face. I think somebody told me once, 'Ever considered wearing a mask?' No. Uh uh. I wanted them to see my eyes.

"Some of the things I did I could probably end up with a life sentence. My looks. My attitude. Everything.

"But I'm not like that; I'm a really nice guy. I just had a job to do, that's all. I think it was called survival, almost.

"How did I protect myself? Toward the end I lost it. But living in it, I bought friends. Paid them well. 'Watch my ass for awhile,' indirectly I told them that, 'because I'm going to get drunk. And if you mess with me, that guy is going to waste you. And if he messes with me, you waste that guy.'

"I don't know." He laughs. "When you got the money, you got a lot of friends. Eighteen, nineteen I was really popular because of the money. It was just highly unlikely that anybody would mess with me in that position. I was really dangerous then.

"I made it clear, too. I wasn't just your average normal rich guy that walked into a scuzzy bar." He laughs. "The high cost of low living.

"If I was to get back into it today, it'd be a whole different story. I wouldn't be just a punk off the street. I'd be a dangerous man. I know it all. You meet a thousand people that live the street life, underworld drugs, stuff like that. You pick something up, something off all of them. You want to get mean, you want to get ugly? You watch those guys. You see.

"A lot of times I really don't feel like being here. There's nothing really here that I want. The only thing that stops me from going back on the street – human dignity.

"There I'm just a monster. There I make it to the top, somebody kills me, there's a hundred and fifty thousand who'll take my place, easy. Only the faces change.

"I heard a saying once. Guy he told me, he says, 'Jimmy, only the good die young. You, you little shit, are going to live forever.' "

THE FAMOUS ANCESTOR had four wives. The first stayed behind when he moved from Montana up to Canada. He took two new wives to replace her, sisters who both died in the smallpox epidemic of 1870. And so he took a fourth. The women bore him many children, all but two of whom died young. One son he named Blue Gun, in honour of the blue-steel revolver he had stripped from one of the three Crow he'd shot dead, themselves busy stripping the body of his murdered cousin.

"WHEN I TURNED eighteen I got my oil money, my trust fund. The day I got it I bought a ticket to Hawaii. I got two grand wired down every second day or so. Spent it on drugs. Partying. Booze. Impressing women. I did a lot of tipping. Got really popular. Rode around in a limousine the whole time. I thought, 'Hell, I'm young. I'm rich. I might as well go have a good time.'

"My money lasted about a year. I was really, really flying. I was doing a lot of drugs and a lot of drinking. And I was travelling quite a bit. Never took Trixie along with me. Just went by myself. Went down to Kelowna a few times. Calgary. I had other girlfriends too, so she was kinda inconvenient.

"Trixie. Whew. That was the first, uh, real notice I ever took of anybody. I liked her. She had a nice ass. She had nice hair. She was sitting on the steps of this bar, trying to be a street kid. I told her, 'You'll never make it, you don't know how.' That freaked her out. Nobody had ever told her that before.

"She was still in school. I drew this picture, a really nice picture, it had mountains, nice sunset, rays coming up. I put on the bottom of it, 'Someone's watching you.' I gave it to my friend's girlfriend. I said, 'Give this to Trixie. Don't tell her who it's from.'

"I seen Trixie about two days later. I'd gone out with another girl and she'd given me all these hickeys. Trixie said something like, 'You don't fool me, Jimmy. Thanks for the picture.' Dragging your tongue all over the place for some girl, it's a little difficult not to notice.

"From that point on she really liked me, she hung out with me, bugged me, played with my hair. Then something happened. Just overnight. The drugs were gone, the booze was gone. The street was gone. There it was, it was just me and Trixie. House with a white picket fence and everything.

"Then she got pregnant. Six or seven months later, Trixie was out to here. I looked at her and said, 'I don't wanna be a daddy. I'm eighteen years old. I got forty grand in my bank account. I don't wanna be a daddy.'

"She started crying. It was just awful. I thought about it.

Finally we got back together. And she, we had Crystal.

"The night the baby was born, this is how cold I was, I went out with another girl. I got drunk. I said, 'Fuck it, I don't need it.'

"For about six months after that, I tried to get rid of her. But the longer I stayed, you know, the harder it was. If I'd have just took off at the beginning, I'd have been OK. But I just kept on procrastinating.

"The kid was getting bigger and was starting to play with my face, scratch me. I was starting to like it. Trixie got sick of my shit one day and just took off. Just said, 'I don't want to see your face no more.'

"By this time I was too attached to the kid.

"After Trixie left me I was bouncing off walls. I was getting in fights. I got in a fight with this guy Trixie was with in the bar. This guy just smoked me. I didn't hit him back. And then I went home.

"And this car pulls up in front of my place. I looked and I thought it was these guys from the bar, coming to finish me off.

"So I come out of the house, looking like a street punk. I had faded blue jeans on. Black leather jacket. And a gun. And I pointed it right at their heads and I said, 'You fucking move. . . . '

"It was the wrong people. It was the neighbours.

"It was just the look in their eyes. It was like, if you've never seen it, you wouldn't believe it. Their eyes were *this* wide. And they both knew they were going to die.

"They just looked at me and I realized who it was. What was I supposed to say? 'Sorry? Sorry for threatening your life, I gotta go now? Wrong guys, you know?'

"I just walked away with the gun. Ten minutes later, cops came. Guns out. One cop put his gun right here," Jimmy points to his temple, "and he said, 'If you move I'm going to kill you.' I'd been in trouble with this guy before; he was no stranger to who I was.

"I knew right then that I was quitting. There was no underworld stuff anymore. There was going to be no more guns. This time I had pretty well lost everything I had. I just told him, 'Do whatever the hell you want, just get it over with.'

"The guy that handcuffed me was the same guy that had handcuffed me before and threw me in jail. He gave me the opportunity to die. He put the handcuffs on one hand just so I could squeeze my hand out. And left the car door open. He stood up by the door and watched me. I remember I was sitting in the back seat of this cop car, looking at this guy. Slowly pulling my hand out. I got it out. This guy was just looking at me. For five minutes just staring at me. And I knew that if I got out, he'd shoot me.

"I put my hand back in. Squeezed the handcuff on tight.

"They let me out on my own recognizance. I walked into court a week later just fried. Burned right out. They read me the charges. I said, 'I'm representing myself.' The judge looked at me and said, 'Do you realize how serious these charges are, Jimmy?' I got a lawyer. He did really well for me. I ended up in remand up in Edmonton for two weeks. They put me on a year suspended sentence."

THE FAMOUS ANCESTOR had "a thirst a camel would envy," the books say. Whiskey was one favoured ameliorative. Fire water, a specialty of Fort Whoop-Up, was another. The recipe for fire water is given: one gallon wine; three gallons water; one quart whiskey; one pound chewing tobacco; a quart of molasses; a bottle of Jamaica ginger; and red peppers to taste.

When sufficiently boozed up, the books say, the Famous Ancestor liked to stand twenty-five paces from a friend, a fellow halfbreed, and "trim his moustache with bullets from his six-shooter." The friend returned the favour.

"I GOT OUT and I made a promise to myself that if I ever got involved with the street again, I'd shoot myself first. I couldn't go through it again. I just couldn't. I was nineteen years old and I just couldn't make it. No way.

"So I got a job. Real one. Honest money. I was working as a carpenter. It wasn't crime anymore, 'cause I knew I could make it there if I had to. I wanted to make it in the real world. And I tried about, God, fifty times. I always ended up in the hole. Drunk. Stoned. Messed right up. Started drinking more.

"Then I had my first experience with an alcohol withdrawal. A major one. I was in the back of this cab. It was like the most terrifying anxiety attack that you could ever have in your life. There it was, everything that I had ever done – whooomp. That was the first time I asked anyone for help. I said to this cab driver, 'I need help.' He says, 'Give me my money first.' 'Oh God,' I thought, 'when is this going to end.'

"So I came back to Hobbema. It hit me there again. The same anxiety attack. Day after day after day.

"They'd just given out a bunch of money, oil money. I took this money. A friend of mine had been beaten up. I came up to Edmonton. I was looking for a hit. This guy I met through the system up here gave me the phone number of a guy who would do it for a thousand bucks. I just lost it. I didn't believe I was doing it. I was following through again. I was going to pay somebody to get somebody.

"I remember all night I carried this phone number in my hand, with a quarter. I went to every scuzzy bar in town. I had a thousand dollars cash. In hundreds and fifties. I was thinking, 'I wonder if this guy would do me.'

"I didn't have the guts.

"Then I got so drunk that I was just terrified, I was screaming for help. The only thing I didn't have was a gun.

"Went back to Hobbema in a cab. Still had this, this number. I went to my sister's place. She said she had never seen anybody look like that before. For about half an hour this hot surge just went right through my body. It told me right then, 'If you don't fucking do something right now – pull the trigger.'

"And something happened. I asked for help again. And I got it.

"In two hours I was back in Edmonton. Detox centre. The

frigging ambulance broke a block away, so I had to walk the last block.

"I got in there and I looked at all these guys. All these bums. All these drunks. I said, 'Look at these fucking people, why are they still alive?' Then I got into the bathroom, took off my clothes, there was a big mirror and I looked at myself. I looked at the scars I had on my body from fights. I looked at the tattoos. I said, 'You piece of shit, you're no different than the rest.'

"I really hated myself. I started flashing back to jail. I started flashing back to my kid. And I started praying to God for all I was worth. I said, 'Hey if you're there, help me. Because if you're not, I'm fucked.'

"They forced me to go to these meetings. And, uh, this guy got up there and starting speaking. I looked at him, I said, 'What a loser, man. This guy's nothing.' He was talking about how good his life was today and all this crap. And then he told my story. To a T.

"And from that moment on I knew what I was looking for in life. The perfect woman I'd always dreamed about, you know, I'd be walking down the street and I'd come around the corner and there she would be, leaning up against a nice big Rolls Royce. I found out that person I had always been looking for was God.

"I was lying on the bed after this meeting. I was shaking, waiting for the bogeyman to come around the corner. DT's. I felt so scared. Felt so alone. I didn't want to be alone anymore. I was tired. Real tired.

"And then I started thinking about being an Indian. I started think about some of my crimes. About my daughter. I really flashed back to my childhood. And what it was like to be Native. And I didn't hate it anymore. And I said to myself that no matter what happened, I would not drink again. No matter what happened I was going to change my life."

ONE OF THE Famous Ancestor's four wives purchased a baby chamber pot. Later, to honor a white Colonel, the Famous

Ancestor served him water in the new cup. When told the intended use of the pot, the Famous Ancestor was astonished. White people, he said, were crazy. All that open prairie and they used a good clean cup like that for a kid to piss in.

"SO MUCH HAS happened in the two years since I sobered up, it would just take too long to explain. It's just the most incredible thing that has ever happened to me. I can't explain why. I don't ask why anymore. Things just started changing. It was phenomenal, some of the things that happened to me. I was actually helping people.

"I went back to Hobbema one time and I looked at all these Indian kids, all these Indian old people. I just knew they were a part of me. There was something in that culture that was a part of me. I could paint myself white, but I couldn't get away from it. The Sun Dances and the sweats. The sweet grass and the beads and the leather. It was just so natural.

"That had never been part of my life. But then I kept going, excuse the expression, the white way. I wanted to be that executive in a business. I wanted to be a lawyer. Architect. Because I knew, even though where I had been, I still had the capacity, the IQ, to be anything I wanted in my life.

"But I wanted it given to me. I told this one guy once, I said, 'Man, this world owes me, big time.' For the first time somebody agreed with me. He said, 'Ya it does, you just gotta work for it.'

"I got to thinking one day after about a year and a half, about where I came from and where I am today. That was the first time I was ever proud walking down the street, being an Indian. Going, 'Whoa, you don't even know who you are, man, but you're going to find out.' Being able to look people in the eye without going, 'Jeez, you're so superior to me.'

"I lay back sometimes and dream what it must have been like. Being a boy when there was none of this around. The laughter. Natives are funny. I like hanging out with them. My friends, even though there was booze and drugs, we were always laughing. We always had a good time.

"I like giving that to people, I like making them laugh. Because you know, life's really too short. It's really too short just to sit back and wish. I tell you, any asshole can go out there and make a million bucks, if he really wants to. I don't miss the money I had. I don't miss the girlfriends, or the cars, or anything. Of all the things I've lost, I miss my mind the most. Definitely."

JIMMY SPENDS MOST of the week before Christmas debating where he will spend it. He is thrilled by the fact he has invitations to two, no, three different places. He tells me he thinks he will just rent a car and drive from house to house; here, Calgary, the reserve. In the end he spends Christmas in Edmonton, at the home of a fellow AA member. Afterward the AA member's wife tells me Jimmy was a pain. He did nothing for a week but slump on the couch and ask to drive the Mercedes. Jimmy tells me he had a great time, even though he never got to drive the car. He doesn't make it out to the reserve until the day after New Year's and he says he feels guilty. They had gifts waiting for him and everything.

When he disappears he leaves behind all his presents – the mug and calculator the AA member's wife gave him, a gold earring his biker sister gave him, the present I gave him, too.

"NOT TOO MANY people make it out of Hobbema. Where would they go? The city? Nah. Not too many places an Indian wants to go in the city. Pretty scary out here when you come from there.

"Out there you know everything. You know who's lying, you know who's telling the truth. It's pretty easy to make your way around. It's pretty easy to stay away from the stuff that's not good for you, not healthy. Up here it's, I don't know, you don't have to look too far to see what I mean. You don't see too many Indians in offices out here.

"I hardly ever go back to Hobbema anymore. I'm not into it. It's a nightmare, you know. Only the faces change. It's the same shit over and over again. It's really depressing.

"I see a lot of families out on the reserve just wasting away, dying. It's all money. It's almost, it's almost white out there. Because people are stepping on people to get themselves ahead.

"I go out there to visit and I see these guys, grown men. Sitting in a trailer playing Nintendo. The big thing in their lives is to get to the highest level of Nintendo. Grown men who could do anything in the world, and all they care about is Nintendo levels. It fucking drives me crazy.

"You know what a relationship is in Hobbema? A relationship is, you meet somebody. You like them. You have a kid. You get married. You have another kid. Then you go to a party. And either you leave with some other woman or your wife leaves with some other guy. And that's it. It's the booze that does it. The drugs. It's sick, man.

"It's just really bad news. You know, where there's money, there's going to be some power struggles. Like I said, fire power, man, people ripping off other people at both ends, people get hurt. That's just not Indian.

"An Indian's in touch with the land. I always said – used to piss people off, too – 'all you white guys, you own all this stuff; all this land, we belong to it.'

"Then I look at me. I don't act like an Indian, I don't have a voice like an Indian, I barely speak my own language. And I've had to . . . Einstein says if mankind is to survive, we must develop a complete new change of attitude. Complete.

"I have to be very careful now. I'm very vulnerable. To get the full effect of my culture is almost impossible nowadays. Unless I'm on the reserve twenty-four hours a day. If I'm there twenty-four hours a day, I won't survive. It's just that simple.

"It's different out there, eh. There's a whole lot of stuff you never hear here in the city. Like the Montana Reserve out on Hobbema. It's probably one-quarter the size of Edmonton. And people die out there. Man, people are dying all the time. Like just recently there was this girl. Drove her car right off the bridge.

"They found her in the river, frozen to the car window, her face all pressed up against the glass like she was trying to get out. It was supposed to be pretty grim-looking when they found her because her eyes were still open. She died like that.

"Indians have a different attitude toward death, eh. They just take it for granted. Like it's natural. I mean, they have wakes and stuff but they treat it like it's just going into another room. I got the same attitude about it. Probably a hell of a lot better there than it is here.

"I often wonder like, why am I here. I lived a lifestyle that proved to me time and time again that you could be dead before you were twenty-five. Four of my friends proved that for me. One took a bottle and laid down and drank it on the railroad tracks. One shot himself in the head. They found him in a trailer not three yards away from the band office. Another one, I think he got murdered. The fourth guy, he was killed in an accident.

"The guy who took the bottle to the train track, he had it all, you know. He had the family. The girlfriend. The cars. Money. School. Christianity. And nobody knows why. Nobody seen it coming. I think he was twenty at the time. He wasn't on the street. He was one of the nice guys. Just hung around us. Maybe he was torn between the two worlds, I don't know.

"The other guy. Nice guy. Funny, just like me. Just a super guy to be around. His best friend found him. Most of him. On the wall. Blew his head off.

"It's a rough world and if you don't get tough you won't make it. When the drugs don't become a game. The booze doesn't become a game. And you're dependent. That's it. You're fucked. Period. You can go one of two ways, but you're gonna go.

"Death never used to bother me. It used to be like my best

friend. Death, it's really one of the most amazing weapons you can use on anybody. It works every time. I don't know what it is now. I've changed too much. Today I lose friends and it really bothers me now. It really bothers me to hear things about Hobbema and people I know. It's just a fucking waste of life."

"SEE, I TOLD you I was a cute kid." Jimmy hands me a photo of a small boy in front of a Christmas tree. Either the tree or the boy is tilting; the two stand at an odd forty-five degree angle to each other. The boy has curly hair and a sweet, tight grin. He is wearing a red velvet bow tie and red vest. The flash has turned the tree lights into sparking stars; a star shines from the middle of the boy's red chest, glinting from his vest button.

"Nah," Jimmy says. "You believed me? Suck-errr. That's not me. That's Paul. That's my cousin Joanne's kid."

"MY COUSIN, JOANNE. Before she was drinking, doing drugs, she was a really nice girl. She was working. She got married to this guy and they were probably one of the best couples you could ever see. They were always smiling, always happy, always together. He went to Wetaskiwin one day. He was at this place on the road, it's called Dead Man's Curve, and this truck hit him head-on and killed him. She really took that hard.

"I guess what I'm about to tell you probably took place within nine months. She never drank before, but she got into the drinking really hard and really fast. She started going around the bars, skid row, using up all the money they'd saved up for a house somewhere off the reserve. Neglected her kid.

"And then she met up with this other guy and she fell in love again. They started living together. They were doing a lot of drinking. This guy went out one night with his buddies. Guy lost control of the car; it went across the highway and smashed into another car. And that guy was killed also.

"That was two men, dead, in under eight months.

"Her little boy, I think he was about a year old, not even, and she went drinking down in Calgary somewhere. And she ended up in the hospital. Her face was all beat up. It was all swelled up, it was really, really deformed. I don't know if it was hemorrhaging of the brain or something like that, but she died.

"She, aah, probably got mugged. Probably got rolled by a bunch of drunks. Bunch of Indians down there. There wasn't too many details; she was probably raped and beat up. They were hoping she'd die where she lay there.

"There was really no inquiry about how she died, where she died, who beat her up. Now she's left her kid behind. And all that kid's got is a bunch of families that aren't going anywhere. That's sad. That really, really fucks me up. I hate that.

"I have this urge inside of me to go down to Calgary and take a look around. It scares me because it gives me an excuse to go back to the streets. I've been fighting that for a long while now.

"She was twenty, twenty-one. Same age as me."

THE BOOKS ASSESS the Famous Ancestor. They say his virtues far outweighed his vices. His flaws are listed: "a superstitious nature inherited from his Indian mother" and a "love for whiskey" which, combined with an undefined lung ailment, would kill him.

The books cite the following as "the humorous side" of the Famous Ancestor's Indian superstition. He was shot in the head by a friend duck hunting and fell to the ground. But he was not dead; the pellet from the gun had simply lodged in the lobe of his ear. He refused to have the pellet cut out, believing it was good medicine.

After that, whenever he was drunk, he liked to tell the story of his good medicine. One night, after a bout of drinking whiskey, he told the story of his good medicine one time too many for a NWMP officer. The officer leaned over, pretending to want to examine the scar. He flipped out his knife and sliced open the scout's ear, dislodging the pellet. The Famous Ancestor lamented this as a bad omen; his good medicine was gone.

Within months the Famous Ancestor was dead. He died after a long night of drinking, drowning in his own blood.

"TWO YEARS IN AA, man. I've just about driven myself insane. Trying to readjust. Trying to make it in the mainstream."

Jimmy takes a pen knife to a grey cloth belt. As he talks he rhythmically shreds the belt with his knife, growing angrier with each cut.

"It's really hard to change up here. You just like to run away. I've got nowhere to run. Where do you run to when you live most of your life in a foster home, the rest of it on the street? You grow up with people giving you away all the time. And then you finally want to straighten out. People tell you this is how you should be. I don't mind people telling me that; I just wish they'd fucking do it themselves.

"I've been struggling with this for so long I don't even know where I fucking fit in anymore. It sometimes feels so unnatural to be here. Because right now I feel like all I'm good for is being in the mob. I'm talking bullshit to a lot of people, telling them I'm feeling OK, I'm doing great. That's bullshit. I'm still on the street. I've been walking around Edmonton for two years clean and sober. And I've never had so many brilliant ideas about the street in my fucking life.

"This may, this may piss you off or something, but I've probably got about twenty-five different methods for getting back at white people for what they've created here. Just kinda turning the tables and sending it backward down their fucking throat. I'm not doing that, I guess I'm not doing that because they are white or because they are Indian. I am just doing it to people. Show them what it does to a person.

"What do I want to do?" He sniffs. "I don't think you want to know.

"You know how some things can really rip a person's heart out? Anything like that. Anything that would make a person feel like they are totally useless and helpless. Nowhere else to go. Nowhere else to run. In total control, me, somebody having total control over their life.

"Like what? Like wasting a family member." There is a long pause. "Sick, huh.

"You see I didn't, I didn't ask for what happened to me. I didn't ask to be put in that position – foster homes and shit. What pisses me off the most is they expect me to come out of this shining. Social Services, the government. They sit on their fucking chairs and they say, 'Well, it worked for him, we did it for him, we can do it for someone else.'

"Fuck that. I did this on my own.

"If I'da done it their way, I'd have probably hung myself. Sixteen, fifteen.

"I come here and I tell you all this, about what's happening to me. Fuck. I can't picture what it's like in your world. I automatically assume that you can't picture what mine was like. I come in here and I tell you about all these things, about how I survived it. People tell me I come out looking pretty good. And then deep down inside I think about all the people who don't look pretty good right now because of me walking all over them to get here. That's what it took me to get here.

"That's catching up with me.

"I think about my daughter. About Trixie. That fucking makes me ill. Jesus.

"Trixie, I, ah, slapped her around a couple of times. That's what's hard, you know. I type out a lot of these stories in here. The reason I can relate to them so much is because I'm the ugly guy that woman is talking about. I'm that asshole she's talking about.

"You know, I take a walk out on the street and I say hello to some old lady and give her a hand across the street. Last night there was a woman a buck short for cigarettes, so I give her a buck. I'm the guy who wants to go out with those little boys over there and play hockey with them all afternoon. And then I get by myself and I think, 'God, remember when you hit her?' That fucks me right up. Oh God.

"I mean, I just can't forgive myself. I'm not like that.

"I dream about that almost every fucking night. Trixie. I think about her every day. I've been celibate for two fucking years, man. I think about starting over again with someone new. And I can't. I have a real fear that I'm going to get mad someday and I'm just going to fucking smoke her. Once. And she's going to be just like Trixie – love me for what I was. Fucking bang. That's what I done. That's not very fucking funny. It scares me.

"Christ I wish. . . ."

And the interviews are over.

WHEN JIMMY IS gone and I am cleaning up the office, moving out myself, I take down one of the decorations he pinned to the wall. It is a greeting card. A cow opens a door to another cow, who holds up a book called *Cowintology*. The second cow says, "Listen – just take one of our brochures and see what we are all about. In the meantime, you may wish to ask yourself, 'Am I a happy cow?' "

The card is from a fellow AA member, to celebrate Jimmy's second birthday in the program. Inside it reads: "It's two years and much to be grateful for. Congratulations. Tell others of your joy and show that your life is full of an inner strength that has been given freely. We remain sincere, honest, ego-less and the rewards come flowing in for us to share with others. Use what you have and be good to yourself. Keep playing hockey, good striving for self-awareness, keep dreaming your dreams.

"God bless. Peace and strength."

THE LAST THING Jimmy tells me, before he disappears, is this. He was thirteen or fourteen. A punk. On the street. He saw a man, an old man, an old drunk stumbling down the road. And just for the hell of it, just for the pure, sheer hell of it, Jimmy ran up and kicked that old man in the head. Fucking bang, fucking right in the head. The man fell to the ground. And Jimmy ran and ran and ran.

He tells me this, slicing and slicing the belt with his knife, his voice full of anger. "You know I don't know to this day whether I killed that old man. I don't even know if I killed him."

Jimmy Mix (Canadian). Nowhere to run to. Nowhere to hide.

✪ GRACE

GRACE ROYER, MOTHER of Maggie, mother of Sarah and nine more, grandmother of Lisa, grandmother of Kicker, grandmother of Lester and seven more, great-grandmother of two, soon-to-be-three with the birth of Kicker's son – Crying Brian, Kicker will call him – Grace Royer is bent over on her hands and knees, scrubbing her bathroom floor. All that can be seen of her are the soles of her slippers and the seat of her flowered skirt. Nothing yet of her curly white hair and thick black brows, of the ropy scar circling her neck. Nothing of her crinkly eyes. Of her beauty. Of her short, stout dignity.

"Home Sweet Home" is embroidered on the deerskin shield fringed with feathers in her hallway. Kicker sits on her living room couch watching TV, his silent girlfriend locked under one arm. His face is a lopsided balloon. He was, he says, hit across the cheek by a cop with a nightstick. His offence: drunkenly lipping off the cop.

Maggie has come over to try to cajole Kicker into going to the hospital. While Maggie pleads, Grace abandons her scrubbing to entertain the white-woman stranger her daughter brought along. She leads the stranger into her sewing room, stacked with silky fabrics and ribbons and beads and feathers, to show her the Métis dance costume she's just made. White water birds – spiritual birds, she explains – are outlined in white beads on grey felt, trimmed with purple and fringed in white. The costume is beautiful.

She made it for a slim young man, she says, laughing as she demonstrates how it's put on, holding it up against her broad hips. "It's for a skinny guy. A real skinny guy.

"These crafts, no, I didn't learn them from my mom. My mom

did bead work, but she never took time to show me. I only started learning bead work in 1977, when I was fifty-four. I started learning because one of my daughters needed a powwow costume to dance in the opening ceremonies of the Commonwealth Games.

"I learned just by looking and going to Indian craft shops. And the powwow dresses, mostly I just get my ideas from the Natives who dance at powwows. So today, I have no problem doing bead work or anything anybody asks me to do. I just say, 'I'll try.' "

Grace sits straight-backed on the single bed in her sewing room, holding a blue silk ribbon shirt in one hand. In her slow, careful voice, she tells the stranger a story. She went down to provincial court earlier in the day for her grandson, Lester. She raised Lester herself after his father, her oldest son, was killed by a drunk driver. Lester is a rangy, handsome twenty-one-year-old now, in the Edmonton Remand Centre serving thirty days on a mischief charge. What kind of mischief he got into, she doesn't know.

Today, Lester was up on another mischief charge, this time accused of defacing shopping-mall property, of scrawling his name on a blank grey wall in red paint. Grace was waiting outside the courtroom for Lester's trial to begin when an elderly white woman sat down beside her. It turned out the woman owned one of the stores in the mall. She came, she told Grace, because she thought the cops were too hard on Lester. He wasn't the only one involved. Besides, the wall is going to be painted over. No one should go to jail over some red paint.

Grace and the white lady went into the courtroom. The crown prosecutor was there. The judge was there. Lester had no lawyer, so no defence lawyer was there. Lester wasn't there. The lady asked Grace, "Where's Lester?" Grace said, "He's in the remand centre."

So the lady went up to the crown prosecutor and said, "Did you know Lester is locked up in remand?" The prosecutor said, "No." And the lady said, "Well, you better phone over there right now and get him in here, otherwise he'll have another charge on his record."

"He would have, you know," Grace says. "If it hadn't been for that white lady, he would have had this other charge for failing to appear!"

"So we waited for an hour. And the crown prosecutor brought Lester in, and the judge said the case was dismissed."

Grace speaks gravely. "I was so happy. That was so nice what that lady did for Lester. That white lady must have a spot in her heart for Native kids. She didn't even know Lester. She didn't even know him."

MONTHS LATER, GRACE is living in a new apartment. She doesn't like it as much as the last one; that one had nice, clean white floors. But her landlord raised the rent and this apartment is cheaper. Three storeys above the intersection of a freeway and a six-lane roadway, it is also smaller and noisy, she says. But at least it's not damp.

Grace's daughter Sarah and her two sons are over visiting. The boys watch cartoons from the big orange couch while the white-woman stranger interviews their grandma in the kitchen. Baskets of tumbling, brightly colored plastic flowers fill an empty corner beside the stove. A brass plate etched with the Last Supper hangs above the table. A magnet stuck to the fridge reads: "Listen to your kids while they still know everything."

Two white doves flit around the living room, presents to Grace from Maggie. One coos persistently over the cartoon shoot-outs. Grace laughs when she's asked the doves' names, at the odd notion of investing so much sentiment in a pet. She says simply, "I never name my birds."

"I WAS BORN in 1923, born and raised at Saddle Lake Indian Reserve up north. In our family there was nine kids. Five brothers and four sisters. Two died before I was born. Two died after; a girl of whooping cough, a boy when he was just a baby. The girl died in my mother's arms. I still remember that.

"And when I was about eight or nine years old, my parents sent me to an Indian residential school at Blue Quills. The school was eighteen miles from the reserve. And there we had to live with the nuns and the priests. We spent our time there all through the year, except on holidays in June. We only had holidays for a month and a half every summer. We never had Easter break or Christmas break in our days. I find kids are very lucky to get Christmas break and Easter break nowadays.

"I was excited to go there. I thought it would be good. Nobody told me what it was going to be like. I thought the children there were happy."

Blue Quills Residential School,* 205 km northeast of Edmonton, was one of twenty Indian residential schools in Alberta in 1931, the year it opened and the year eight-year-old Grace was sent to live there, to be stripped, deloused, given a uniform and a number, and not allowed to leave again – except for forty-three days a year – until she was eighteen.

Ottawa, in 1894, gave Indian agents the power to compel the attendance of Indian children at residential schools, there to be "kept, cared for and educated." Blue Quills was owned by the federal government, administered by Oblate priests and staffed by Grey Nuns, Sisters of Charity, whose founder, now a saint, is said to have kept black and Indian slaves.

Despite pleas for two months off in the summer from the diverse bands whose children were forced to attend the school, the priests insisted forty-three days were sufficient. There were those who argued that even that was too long. A travelling nurse had discovered a thirteen-year-old student pregnant. An Indian man was charged. The man denied having intercourse with the girl. When Ottawa refused to pay for a defence lawyer, stating Indians only warranted lawyers when the charge was murder, the accused man agreed to marry the girl and charges were dropped.

To better civilize the children, to better Christianize them and to protect their morality from such incidents, some staff argued, the children should be completely isolated from all Indian influences. They should be kept out of their communities. They should be kept away from their families, at all times.

"I missed my family, because we hardly seen our families. They did come every once in awhile to visit us at the school. But that wasn't every week, just very occasionally, maybe once in two months, you know. But when we went for a holiday, well it was a privilege for us to be with our parents for a month and a half.

"The reserve, to me it was poor. We never had no such thing as welfare or family allowance during my childhood days. People lived from the land, catching fish and hunting and picking berries in the summer and putting up their gardens. A lot of them had cattle and horses. And then there was a lot of things for us to eat from the bush, you know, prairie chickens and ducks and geese. So people managed, well, all right with their food.

"And some men worked for Ukrainians off the reserve. But wages were very poor at the time. My father was working at thrashing for $2.50 a day. And fifty cents an acre for stooking. But we still managed all right for a living.

"My mother was a very good woman. I was very close to her. But my father, I wasn't close to my father. He didn't treat me like he did my other brothers and sisters. Just him pushing me to do the work, you know. He didn't allow me to sleep the way I wanted. Now that I'm older I get up a little bit later. But my father used to wake me up at four in the morning. Every morning.

"But that I don't regret, you know. I'm glad my father taught me how to get up early and how to work. 'Cause when you get older it's nothing for you to get up early and start working. If it wasn't for him, maybe I'd, maybe I'd be lazy.

"My father used to have cattle and he had chickens, horses. My brothers looked after the horses and my mother milked and I'd look after the chickens. As well as scrubbing clothes for my mother. Hauling water. Hung the clothes on willows – that was our clothesline. My brothers did all that, too. We all chipped in for work because we were told we had to do it.

"And then when we came home for our holiday from school, it

was the same thing. We had to work all the time.

"So I'm pretty well used to working. I can't sit around for nothing. Like Sundays, I try and keep it relaxed, but I find that I can't really keep up to it. I gotta find something to do all the time."

Indian parents were permitted to see their children at Blue Quills on weekends only. From Saddle Lake, by team, it took half a day to get to the school, and half a day to go back. Two shacks were moved from the reserve to the schoolyard for parents to camp in.

The school, an imposing brick monolith, was built according to federal regulations. Kitchen, laundry room, dining rooms, in the basement. Dorms on the second floor. On the first floor, a chapel, classrooms, and two parlours. One for Indian visitors, one for whites.

"Well, I did not enjoy the boarding school. I think we were really cheated out of our Indian culture, especially our language. We were punished for speaking our Cree language. We had to try and speak straight English. And for us children who didn't understand English, it was very hard and very unhappy for us.

"I had two older brothers at the school. My two younger sisters came in later but I had grown up by then, so I didn't stay too long with them. They kept the boys and the girls separate. Except in the dining room. The boys on one side of the hall and the girls on the other side. They really kept us so that we wouldn't be teasing the boys. It was really strict for us. The nuns didn't even allow us to talk to the boys. The only happiest time I think we had, was at Christmas. We had better food to eat and we did have a few days off from school during that time. But we had to stay right in school, right alone.

"At the Christmas concert we could talk to our brothers. But that was only for as long as the concert. After that, it was back to the same old thing. No talking to the boys."

GRACE'S FRIEND, DR. Anne Anderson, eighty-six, a Métis writer and holder of an honorary doctorate of laws for her work in teaching and preserving her mother tongue, Cree, on her three years at a Grey Nuns residential school:

"When I think of those nuns I could kick them in the shins. They make me so mad because they were so hard on the poor little Indian kids. Defenceless little kids. They were beaten, and the nuns would pull their ears; their ears got all infected. When I think of that I want to kick every nun I see.

"My mother was raised in a convent and yet she couldn't even write her name. Till her dying day she was so ashamed that she couldn't write her name. Those are the things that hurt me. They hurt me still, to this day.

"And you know, we were hungry all the time. And then, during Lent, you'd just have a piece of potato and a little bit of lard. Something cooked off a roast. And you'd cut up your potato into that and eat it.

"So, one Saturday us girls had to get our clothes ready for Sunday services. We had to shine our shoes for Sunday. We cleaned them off with lard. Some kind of oil or dripping. And when I smelled that cup of dripping to put on our shoes, it smelled like a roast of beef. It smelled so nice. And I started eating it like this, with my finger. And then, of course, everybody tasted it and then we ate it all. And we never did the shoes." Anne laughs.

"The nun, she always had a little stick. She hit me on the head with that stick for that. And then I had to do penance. Penance was something else. I had to kneel in a corner and hold my empty dinner plate over my head. Ooh, even after five minutes of that your arms just ached.

"Another time, the Indian agent came and visited us girls from the school. And he said, 'What do you do for fun here, girls? And one of us said, 'We pray.' 'And do you go to school?' I said, 'Yes. We all go to school, but we don't have teachers.'

"So, one day this Indian agent arrives with this great big box. Of course all the kids just went wild. The nuns said, 'Come back here, come back.' Nobody listened. We all stood around and he started to play this gramophone.

"The first thing I heard out of that gramophone was *The Over the Waves Waltz*. I told my little friend, 'Come on, Bessie, let's dance.' So we danced around and around and around. There was about twenty nuns all sitting there. And every time Bessie and I went by them, they took their aprons, these big aprons, and they hid their face. They'd go, 'Ahhh!' and they'd hide their face in their aprons.

"So me, you know, big mouth, I said to one of these sisters, 'Why do you always go "Ahhh" and hide your face? We're just dancing. My mom and dad dance and my brothers and sisters – we all dance.'

"And she answered, 'Because you rub stomachs.'

"Now, can you imagine? 'Because you rub stomachs,' she said. Evil-minded. Evil-minded woman.

"I started to hate the nuns then. Oh, I used to hate them. When one of my mom's sisters died away in the North, the family sent word that my little cousin Joe was in the convent with me. And they said, 'You try to talk to him 'cause they say he cries everyday.'

"The boys played in one yard and the girls played in another yard. They had this high board fence between us. Big planks, like where stock was kept in. And one day I heard this little crying, pitiful sound. And I went to the fence and I said, 'Is that you, Joe?' And he stopped crying and I knew then it was him. And I start talking to him. I said, 'Don't cry. My dad will go and see you on Sunday. You just wait.'

"One of the nuns saw me sitting by the fence talking. And she took a stick and she hit me on the head. She said, 'Shame, shame, shame!' And I was crying and I said, 'Shame for what?' And she hit me again. She said, 'You ought to be ashamed. You're trying to talk with the boys.'

"I got to hate the nuns from there, you know. I wanted to kick them every time I saw them.

"Then, too, my mother used to say, 'Be careful for men. There

44

are some men that fool around with girls. Don't let the young men touch your arms, don't let them touch you here, touch you there.'

"That was so new to me, I didn't know what my mom was talking about. But everything she told me not to do, I saw it at the convent, right away.

"Saturdays were a visiting day for the priest and he'd mingle around with the girls. I saw one time he was touching one girl between the legs, down here. I thought, 'Gee, even brothers and sisters aren't allowed to do that.' And then sometimes I would see this priest putting his hand under the breasts, you know.

"Some of the girls just stood, you know, while he did that. I don't know if they were in shock or what. They just stood."

THE DAILY SCHEDULE for children at Blue Quills Residential School, posted 1942. "Rising of the children at 6:00. All make the sign of the cross. All repeat 'Blessed be God.' Everyone must dress in silence. Morning prayer at 6:20. Immediately after prayer all must line up in silence and go to Chapel for Mass. Breakfast at 7:15. It is silent during that meal. Return to dorms 7:40 to make beds. At 7:50, housework for those appointed. Recreation at 8:10. School bell rings 8:45. Everyone stops play at once."

And so the ritual day began.

"Our food at the boarding school wasn't good." Grace looks around her sparkling kitchen. "The only best times we had to eat was Easter and Christmas. During the rest of the year, it was a very poor, poor food for us. And it was always the same thing we had to eat over and over, every day. Like stew for dinner as well as stew for supper. And then on Fridays we either had fish – it was a change – or beans. Just on Christmas or Easter, we had fruit. Younger kids didn't have tea to drink, just water. The older girls had the opportunity to have tea at their meals, you know, and milk.

"Then as soon as we were in grade four we went to school half a day, and we had to work half a day. When we worked we did mostly sewing. They taught us how to sew and patch and knit and sometimes embroidery work. And we would take turns working in the kitchen with the nuns. So I learned how to cook in there.

"In class we were taught by the nuns themselves. I guess they were not really qualified teachers either, you know. I learned how to read and write. But I only went up to grade six, you know, because I wasn't too smart.

"Anyway, I noticed they started educating Indians after the world war, you know. The Second World War. That's the only time I realized they started educating Indians. Before that they never had no, no interest in Indians, as far as educating. They had a little schooling and that was it.

"They finally let us out of school when we were eighteen years old. So from there on we never had the opportunity to be educated. I don't think they believed in educating Indians."

Blue Quills' monthly work rotation, for girls. First month: laundry, hauling snow for water, boiling it, hanging out clothes. Second month: kitchen duty, peeling potatoes, washing dishes. Third month: mending, sewing.

Later critics would say these "vocational" lessons prepared the children for exactly nothing. Except to work in a residential school.

"I, TO BEGIN with, I had my own language." Grace pours tea. "I couldn't speak English and I didn't understand. I gradually learned it from the other kids. And from going to school, I learned it.

"But I didn't feel right about those nuns when they were strict for our language. They put a stop to our language. I didn't feel right. But I made up my mind that I wasn't going to ever lose my own language.

"We were punished if we got caught speaking our language. They would, they strapped us. They gave us straps.

"They told us they did it because we were supposed to learn English quicker. I always think that was just because they couldn't use their patience with us to try and teach us how to speak English quicker. I know they could have been nicer about it, but they used their straps and all kinds of punishment towards us for speaking our language."

Grace ran away from the school, twice. "Yes, I tried. But when you got caught you really got a licking for that." Her father brought her back, ashamed. She was strapped. Nuns laid her on her bed, pulled off her clothing and strapped her.

Desertions from the school were common. The principal erected a wire fence around the playground to discourage runaways. Boys were punished by having their heads shaved. Some were made to go barefoot for fear they would run away again. Children were beaten.

One former student, interviewed by Diane Persson for her doctoral thesis on Blue Quills, remembers:

"I was about twelve or thirteen when I ran away. We got to our place about eleven thirty at night and my mother couldn't believe it. So they took us back the very next morning. The three of us were taken back that night and got a licking. I had welts all over. They had a big strap with little fringes and to top it off all the little girls were in their rightful places praying for me. I said, 'I'm going to run away again.' "

Another student:

"I remember one time this girl from Cold Lake did something real bad. We were called into the playroom about eight o'clock and then there was this big table in the middle. They covered her with this sheet and each of us big girls had to hold one of her hands and legs. She was strapped there naked. And by a priest too. My heart was just pounding and I was afraid I was going to collapse or faint. It was pitiful. I tried to hold her gently but I had to be careful, or I'd get strapped too."

As early as 1932, Indian parents were trying to get the principal, a priest, removed. The allegations – that two girls had been beaten with a rawhide strap and locked in an outside toilet during the cold winter; that the Sisters had "corrected some girls while they had menstruation." The charges were denied.

In 1939, Indian parents tried to have the school closed down. The allegation – that it had failed its duty to educate their children. School officials responded that criticism would not deter them, and that they only hoped the younger generation would be more appreciative of the sacrifices made for them.

The parents then tried to have the boys' disciplinarian fired. The allegations – that he hit a young boy in the face, and rubbed another small boy's face in his feces when he lost bowel control. The charges were investigated and deemed to be exaggerated. The disciplinarian was let go only when parents refused to send their children to the school as long as he remained there.

"They were really strict with us, you know," Grace says. "It made us feel unhappy. And they never took us anywhere. Just left us at the school all the time. Until another principal was placed. That happened after I had been there about five years. He was a priest also. But he was really surprised how poor the school was. Kids didn't have any games at all in their play rooms. It was very poorly organized by the first principal we had.

"The new principal started putting all kinds of games in playroom – checkers and playing cards and other games. And he finally started putting swings and, what do you call those that go up and down? Teeter-totters. He finally put those in the schoolyard. And a rink; he made a skating rink for the boys to play hockey.

"And he finally got us to go to movies in St. Paul, once a month. One truckload of boys and another truckload of girls. And it was a real treat for us because we've never seen movies before." She laughs.

"I think the first movie I saw was *Boys Town* with Mickey Rooney. And then the other movie was *Snow White and the Seven Dwarfs*. That was only once a month, you know. But we enjoyed it 'cause we've never seen anything like that before.

"The thing that gets me mad, when I think about my school days now, is those nuns. They made us do all the work, while they sat and looked at us and gossiped. They didn't live like real holy women either. They could gossip and feel lazy as they liked while we worked. They just pushed us to work.

"And what I didn't like about it was the religion too. And them not allowing us to speak our language.

"If they had known better, maybe they could have allowed us to speak our language one day at least. Once a week. That would have been a big privilege for us. But no. It was strictly no. And they really punished us with the straps if we got caught speaking Cree.

"The moment I got out of that school, I went straight back to speaking Cree.

"My mother was a strong Catholic, but I didn't like it. I was never strong on it. I wouldn't have kept up with it, if it wasn't for my mother's sake. As soon as I left that school, that was it with the Catholic church for me.

"I didn't like going to confession to a priest and kneeling down during the Mass. It was tiresome. Then having all those statues in front of me. I didn't like that either. I couldn't believe in it. Something always told me that it wasn't right for me.

"Today I have turned, I just turned my life to the Bible. I read it and I get a lot of experience of how to live from it. I just keep to myself and read my Bible. No religion is better than that."

Blue Quills remained a residential school until 1970, when protesting Indians demanded control be turned over to a Native board. Ottawa complied in 1971, making Blue Quills Canada's first Indian-run school.

SARAH, MOTHER OF Lisa, leaves her sons hooked to the cartoons and comes into Grace's kitchen to make them sandwiches. She is in first year Arts at U of A. She wants to get into science and is thinking of becoming a lab technician or a physiotherapist. She went to college last year for upgrading. There were a couple of times she thought she would quit. She felt very proud of herself when she graduated, she says, and she knew she was a strong person.

Her daughter, Lisa, sixteen, was the one who quit school last year. Sarah told her, "That's fine if you want to be on your own. But I am not going to support you. You can't just lie around the house here and do nothing."

"It was a hard time for her, but it was a hard time for me too," Sarah says. "I'd sit up crying wondering where she was. I was always afraid for her, that she would get pregnant, the way I did with her."

While Sarah smears peanut butter on bread, one of Grace's sons, last seen half-cut on Silk Tassel rye, playing cards at a house party, wanders through the front door. He joins the boys watching TV. Grace's youngest daughter, Pat, recovering from surgery for a ruptured gall bladder, limps into the kitchen in her velour housecoat. She is living with her mom till she gets married. She's engaged to a good man, Grace says. An evangelical Christian. Pat has that belief now too. Her fiancé has put the wedding off for awhile; he wants to save more money first. Because he is a Christian there will be no dancing at the wedding.

Pat in velour. Sarah in peanut butter. A hung-over son. Cartoon shoot-outs and grandsons and doves. Grace Royer in her kitchen, the centre, the safety to which her children and grandchildren and great-grandchildren return, again and again. Home. Home free.

"WHEN I LEFT school I went back to the reserve. And I went to work for Ukrainian people. Fifteen dollars was the biggest wages a woman could get in our days. I worked for twelve dollars a month.

She laughs. "Did I ever work for it! Oh, I worked. I used to get the cattle from the pasture every morning and milk them. Feed the pigs. Draw water from the well for the horse and cows, feed the chickens. I did some of their cleaning, like washing floors and tidying up the kitchen. And for the rest of the afternoon I'd weed the garden. And I baby-sat whenever they went away.

"Sometimes I used to feel sad that I had to work so hard. But then I used to just think, 'I guess I have to work. It's the only way I can help myself out. I can't really depend on nobody, so I have to do it.' Because we were so poor at home. We were a big family and it was hard for my dad to keep up with us. So I had to go out and work.

"Anyway, I only worked a few months for the Ukrainians. Then I met my husband and we got married.

"That was the worst part of my life, was married life. I don't really like to talk about it because I feel so bitter towards it. I never had a good married life." Her careful voice slows even more. "I hate talking about it.

"I met my husband during those, what you used to call, Treaty Days. I married him one month after I met him. My dad arranged for us to get married right away. I was just thinking I would go out like other girls, and I went out with him. My father went straight to the priest and arranged the marriage.

"He didn't even ask me. He just went one day and arranged it with the priest.

"There was no publication of the banns. No licence. No ring. I still don't have a wedding ring to this day. No wedding dress. It was a small wedding. My mother, she wept too. But she didn't say nothing. My father had already arranged it all.

"The old people, they were so scared of their daughters embarrassing them. Back then it was big talk, big talk on the reserve if a girl got pregnant. My father was afraid I would shame him, shame the family.

"I was nineteen when I got married. The funny part of it is, I wanted to get married. I thought I could be free, because I always thought my mother had such a free life. She went anywhere she liked and my father never complained about it. So I thought married life was a good life.

"My husband had nothing good in him anywhere. He didn't

work hard at all. The only thing he could do mostly was trapping and hunting. But at that time trappers were allowed to only trap in the spring, not like it is today. And hunting was allowed only in the fall because he was a Métis.

"And he was a miserable person. He was so strict with me that it was so very, very hard with my married life. As I grew older I thought he had no reason to keep an eye on me. It was no use. I was getting older. But he didn't take it that way. So I just had to stay; I just had to stay in the house all the time.

"And he was real mean. He was mean to everybody. Even down to animals. He used to slap his own father around, knock him over. He used to take the horses and take an axe at the blunt end and hit the horses across the nose with that axe. I tried to stop him from slapping his father, but for that I got slapped on the mouth, or in the face.

"No one could say anything to him. Never. He wouldn't hear it. He would just slap you or hit you if you tried to say anything to him. We were all deadly scared of him. All his kids were. They all grew up that way.

"His drinking, it wasn't too bad. He'd start out drinking, but he'd pass out before he got too far. He was only happy when he was out with his friends drinking. He'd leave us alone sometimes for one month, even two months. I think he had other women then. But I didn't care. I was just so glad to be rid of him. When I saw him coming back I would think to myself, 'Oh no. Here he comes back again.'

"He finally, he finally quit drinking. He was just as miserable, really, when he quit drinking. I suppose he was a dry alcoholic, you know.

"Me, I never had that chance to drink. Not with him anyway. Never had no chance to go anywhere. To have a good time, never. All I was allowed to do was stay and look after my kids and his parents. And I looked after his parents right till the day they died.

"His mother passed away first, and then seven years later his father passed away. And they would not have anything to do with the doctor, you know. They just wanted to be kept at home and looked after at home. I never had a decent rest.

"I don't know what happened to him in his life to make my husband so mean. I think he was just so spoiled from his parents. A lot of people who know him from childhood, they told me how he had his way all the time. Whatever he said, his parents had to do it. That was what spoiled his life. He was so deadly spoiled 'cause he was an only child.

"My husband wasn't a worker. He only worked when welfare got after him. He handled the money the way he liked, for himself only, not really for us. I had to get after him all the time 'cause he had no responsibility. I just couldn't stand it because he wasn't keeping up with the bills. I had to scream for him to pay them.

"When my kids were young I couldn't work. Not for wages, you know. It's only after we moved in Edmonton in 1965. Then I started working here and there, cleaning houses, you know.

"Too, I worked at a golf club every summer till 1974. Then my health started getting the best of me. I had to quit there. But I had, all my life during that time, I did nothing else but cleaning. I had no education for anything but cleaning and kitchen help. Dish washing with the machine and kitchen help.

"At the golf club I did meet a lady there, I think she was kind of prejudiced. I was the only Indian working there. She said she teased me, but it was more like an insult to me. I didn't like it. I finally, I got mad at her one day. And I just took my apron off and threw it at her feet and said, 'Take my job!'

"And they were so worried because they needed help, you know. So when they found out I was gonna walk out, the manager's wife come and talked to me. Got me back to work. After that, that lady sure did treat me different.

"Other cleaning jobs I've had here and there, well, it wasn't like that with prejudiced people 'cause, more or less, you're on your own when you're cleaning. That was the only place I did, well, I took a lot before I got mad at that lady. But I tried to be patient, you know, because I needed the money to support my family. I had eleven kids, you know. I really had to support the family by myself.

"The worst thing was, when I worked my husband used to keep half my pay cheque. Half. And I'd have to buy clothes and food for us from my half. He was getting richer and I was getting poorer and poorer.

"And then I had to lie to work. I never told Social Services I had a social insurance number. But we didn't have enough to eat. I had to lie. I had no choice.

"And I had no freedom. He wouldn't leave me alone for five minutes. And then he would yell at me and say I'd done this and that with all these different men. One time I got so mad at him I was screaming back to him, 'All these things you said I did with different men, I bet you did them all. When I was young I didn't care to know about that, because I was so happy when you were gone,' I told him.

"I wanted him to know that."

GRACE, SHORT, STOUT, dignified, marches into the office of the Landlord Tenant Advisory Board. She is wearing her good blue and white shirt for this encounter, and her soft white hair is carefully combed. Her ex-landlord, the one who hiked her rent, had the nerve to hold back her damage deposit. She is indignant. She kept that apartment spotless, cleaner than when she first moved in. He is alleging cigarette burns she knows weren't there, non-existent chips on the arborite. She always knew he was a crook. There is no darn way he is going to get away with this.

"I REMEMBER THE last time I was ever afraid of my husband. He was beating up on Sarah when she was just a little girl, beating up on her with his fists. She was screaming and hollering, 'Someone please help me. He's going to kill me.' We were all deadly scared of him.

"But suddenly I just couldn't take it no more. There he was, a grown man, beating up his little girl with his fists. I got so bold I grabbed a broomstick. I was not scared of him no more. I thought, 'I will hit him in the back of the neck with this.' He had his back to me, still beating on Sarah. I thought, 'When you hit someone in the back of the neck you can kill them.'

"Then I stopped myself for two seconds. I thought of my sister. My sister was out on bail at that time. She had killed her husband. And my husband was just like him. I thought to myself, 'If I kill my husband it will be bad on her, it will look bad for her.'

"So I turned around and I hit him in the face. He punched me back so hard I nearly passed out. But I got up and I saw a high heel in the middle of the floor – my daughter's high heel. And I started beating him right there in the back.

"One of my older daughters grabbed her brother and ran across the street barefoot to call the cops. This was in the middle of winter and she ran across the street in her bare feet.

"The cops came just as I was hitting him in the back with that high heel. One cop was so mean – he started yelling at me. I said, 'Do you think I'm going to let him murder that little girl?'

"They made my husband sit down at the table and they asked him what he was doing. He was such a good talker. He was so good with the cops they never even charged him.

"My husband threatened Sarah, under his breath. He said, 'Just wait till the cops are gone, you'll get it then.'

"My other son, my son who I lost, he came home then. We always felt so much safer when he was home. He came in and the cops told us all to go upstairs. We waited and waited. Sarah started crying, 'We are all going to get a licking.' I told her, 'Don't you cry. We're not going to get no licking.' I was so mad. I was not scared of my husband anymore. I was bold.

"The cops came upstairs and said Sarah should get out of there right away. I told her I would go with her. I had money stashed away my husband never knew about. We were going to go to Maggie's over in Londonderry.

"My son stood guard outside the door. He told me, he said,

'Mom, I'm not going to respect my father. Not tonight.'

"And I took the girls and we went to Maggie's.

"The cops called me the next day. They wanted me to take Sarah down to the family court and show her to them, all beat up. She had bumps all over her head, and bruises. But then my older son interfered. He begged me and begged me, 'Please don't do it, Mom. My father will go to jail. I don't want him to go to jail.'

"I said, 'Son, it's his time.' But he begged me and begged me. So in the end I didn't do it. I always felt terrible about that.

"But after that, my husband didn't scare me anymore."

"My sister went to jail for murdering her husband. She couldn't say it was self-defence because she shot him in the back. She spent three years in Kingston Penitentiary for that. She asked for Kingston because she thought she had to pay for what she had done. When she came back, though, she said she was so glad to be out of there.

"First off she got ten years. She got a new lawyer who appealed and she got five years. The people who knew her, they all signed a petition to say what she'd gone through with her husband. She used to land up in the hospital all the time, he would beat her so badly. He just beat her and beat her, so badly. And she was pregnant every year. When she shot him she was pregnant.

"Just like me, she had no freedom with that man. The one good thing in her life was that he was a good provider. Other than that, her life was terrible. And kids, he loved his kids. He never did anything to them.

"Their kids were young when she shot him. They started to turn against her for shooting their dad. But then they started to hear what she'd gone through and they started to turn back to her.

"I didn't have any freedom from my husband to go visit her so I didn't know what her life was like then. But she told me later it was all our mother's fault, the whole thing. Our mother made her marry that man.

"My sister is happy now. She had a common-law. He's passed

away now. But he was fair to her. He had an affair with an eighteen-year-old girl once. He drank, too, but he was different than the other one. And she's got a job now. She drives her own car. She is happy now."

PAT, SARAH, THE doves, continue to circle away from and back to Grace in her kitchen. "I think it was hard to be a parent after staying out on those residential schools," Grace says. "But my mother talked to me a lot when I was a girl. 'You will find out someday when you're a woman. You're gonna love your kids. And you don't want to do nothing wrong that would hurt them.' Plus, to begin with, my mother was a very good mother.

"And when I first had my child, Maggie, I know I loved her so much and I wanted to look after her. And I was really strong in ways. I guess that's the way I was brought up, you know. To be strong and have no self-pity on myself. As I got to stay longer with my husband and life was so miserable, I started getting that self-pity on myself then. But I still was strong.

"I stayed with him because I wanted to stay with my kids. He threatened he would take the kids if I left. And he threatened that I would never be free if I left. It was always threatening for me. I was so deadly scared of him that I just couldn't leave, until I finally had the guts.

"As I got older I just got braver and braver. I used to yell at him. And, you know, he got to be just like I was when he used to scream at me. Finally, I thought, 'I am getting old. You are getting old. We don't need nothing from each other anymore.' And I was thinking about my pension. I know if I stayed he'd take half of my pension.

"So I just couldn't put up with him any longer. I just had to leave. It was too hard for me. I had to get away from him so I could do things on my own, the way I wanted.

"I would have left him long ago but he told me if I left him he would come and find me and murder me. He could have done it too. That was the kind of man he was. But finally I thought, 'Well OK, if you find me and murder me, I don't care. I just don't care anymore.'

"I came to the city and I started living with Sarah. And I never gave my husband any chance to come near me. I just made up my mind, 'That's it. I'm not going back to you no matter what you do.'

"I didn't care what people said. Always for Indians there's big talk if a couple splits up. I thought, 'Let them talk.'

"To me, about my married life, I don't even feel guilty I left him. I don't ever feel guilty. I believe that a man has an obligation to respect his wife. But he didn't have that in his life.

"It took me forty-one years. I stayed with him till I was sixty years old. But now I am free. And I feel happier. I'm alone today, and I am free.

"I'm just starting to heal now. For a long time after I left my husband I wouldn't even talk to a man. I hated all men. Now when a man talks to me I can talk back to him a little bit.

"But he's getting his own medicine now. The daughter he lives with, she doesn't take nothing from him. Not that she beats him up like he used to do. But she makes him pay her rent and everything. I hear she's getting a new freezer now. So he's getting his own medicine back.

"He still phones me; he always knows my phone number wherever I move. Those girls give it to him. He phoned yesterday and talked to Sarah. Last summer he tried coming around again to see me. I told the girls I never wanted to see him again as long as I live.

"But the kids, they have forgiven him. They still love him. He's their father."

MAGGIE, ON HER father: "My dad, he's been making stuff for me. Like a flesher, that's a tool you need when you are tanning hides. And because of the fact he is very creative, I am very lucky that way. He is making games for me. And that is going to be a treasure for me to keep forever and ever, even if he's gone after. He is seventy-two now and he is not feeling well. But in that way he'll never die. I will still have him in that way."

"MAGGIE AND SARAH are the only two of my children who are sweet-tempered. One of my sons, Frank, he lost his leg on the subway tracks. He's a mean one. Just like his dad. Violent. I was telling his girlfriend to stand up for herself. She was waiting on him hand and foot when he lost his leg. And then he beat her up. He's even mean in jail; he had to spend five days in the hole for beating someone up in there. Just like his father.

"Most of my kids live in the city now. Except for one son. I hear he's working for the residential school at Blue Quills. He works nights. The old school is still up. They just use it for entertainments, like meetings, now.

"And Maggie's doing well. She's a social worker. And Sarah goes to university. Pat's working and my son is working part-time too. I am proud of them. My kids, I think they're pretty good at their lives.

"Only I think they're a little bit slow, because we were never free when we stayed with my husband. Nobody was free. They didn't get that chance to go out and work where they liked. They didn't get that chance to do what they liked. When they wanted some encouragement, my husband never gave it. He never encouraged his family for anything. The only thing he wanted us to do was stay put in the house and not go anywhere, while he went out himself.

"Like my oldest son, he joined the Little League ever since he was nine years old. And I didn't tell my husband about it. Each year I just paid my son's fees. My husband didn't know nothing about it until the manager started bothering us. The manager wanted Lucas and this Ukrainian boy to go to the States to train for a baseball league. And then the Ukrainian boy didn't want to go! I was so surprised about that boy, because usually white people are forward and it's Natives who are not very willing to go unless they're with somebody they know.

"So Lucas said, 'I'll go if Dick goes along with me.' But the boy just wouldn't go. And the manager kept asking us to encourage Lucas, and I did.

"But as soon as my husband was there to watch, he started putting Lucas down. And that just killed all feelings for baseball for Lucas. He just wouldn't play ball in front of his father after that.

"He never went to the States. It's sad. He could have made the big league today if he'd have went."

LISA, SIXTEEN, DAUGHTER of Sarah who is daughter of Grace, on her grandmother:

"My grandma. Oh ya. I used to live with her for awhile. She's a nice woman. She's gentle and she's warm-hearted. I love her. All my friends used to call her Kookum, all my friends in Dickinsfield when I still lived with my mom. They all just used to call her Grandma. Kookum."

"MY GRANDCHILDREN, THEY'D all stay here with me, if they could. They really love to stay around me. Kicker used to stay with me awhile ago. That's the one I feel so sorry for, is Kicker. He looks so pitiful all the time. I think when he stops drinking he feels very miserable. And he's such a nice person. He won't do nothing wrong when he's OK. It's when he gets down to drinking, that's the time he gets into trouble.

"But he's not a bad drinker, eh. He's real quiet when he's drinking. But he gets hurt when he's drinking. I think it's because he looks so pathetic.

"Kicker's always been the quiet one. He doesn't know how to speak up for himself. He gets so discouraged. So I took him down to the social worker the other day. His girlfriend is pregnant, and they want to live together. The social worker, she wants the girl and her mom to come down and talk to her. Her mom already wrote a note saying she would give her up to Kicker. But they want another note.

"I feel so sorry for that girl. Her parents, they drink. That girl is so shy. She wouldn't even talk to me. She's getting used to me now, eh. She even started washing the dishes the other day. Before that she was so afraid to move around. You know, she told me her mom never buys her anything. They drink and then they run out of food. That girl doesn't even know what size she is.

"I volunteer down there at that Native second-hand store. You volunteer there and then you can take things you need. I don't need anything for me. But I pick up things for that girl."

"MY GRANDSON, LESTER, I brought him up on my own. His dad, Lucas, was killed in a car accident. His mother is still alive. I don't know where she is though. She never seen Lester ever since she left him.

"She left him when he was five months old. She did come back for one year and looked after him. And then she left again.

"So, he's never seen his mother since the time she left him. But he remembers her, you know. He used to talk about her when he was small. I don't know if he would remember her now, if he saw her. She must look older now, quite a bit older.

"It hurts me to know Lester is in prison. But I really tried. I talk a lot to him. But I can't do nothing when he can't listen.

"Then the reason why he's always going to jail, too, is he pleads guilty all the time. He never tries to fight. Not like Kicker. My sister's son is like that too. Never tries to fight. I don't think he even stays out a month and he goes right back to jail. And that's the same way with Lester.

"When he was younger he always got into trouble with Kicker. They are cousins. They were close together ever since they were small little kids, hoboing together out on the streets. Most of their time they spent in the youth lock-up. And then they were, too, all over those boys' homes. And Lester still is going to jail.

"I had to sponsor Lester too, now, before he gets out of jail on the 25th. He said he was going to Poundmaker's Lodge, that Indian alcohol treatment place, to begin with. So that means he has to keep out of trouble. Poundmaker's, he was there before. He was in jail that time too. He wanted to get out early, so he signed himself in over there.

"Well, at least he says he wants to smarten up now, anyway. I don't know how true it is. I hope it's true.

"He's been working the kitchen in the prison. He's making money. He says he makes $210 a month. So he says he's used to making money. He wants to make money when he gets out."

Lester is later caught making moonshine out of potato peelings in the prison kitchen. He forfeits his early-release privileges and his stay at Poundmaker's, and sits in jail the full nine months of his sentence.

In the hole-in-the-wall Astoria Cafe, close to the landlord-tenant office, the art gallery, the law courts, Grace picks at a grilled cheese sandwich. "Lester, they found out he was making home brew and they threw him into the hole. And when he gets out of there he'll have to do the rest of his time. Till January. I was so upset when I heard that on Sunday.

"The hole – it used to be real bad. In the old jail. Lester told me one time he was in the hole for seven days. He said there was mice in there. And there was only one little window for him to look through and see the light. Other than that it was dark. And they just shoved his food through the door. Nothing to read in there except a Bible.

"I would go crazy in there. I guess some of them do too. They lose their minds in there.

"It makes me feel so sad. Sometimes, before I am going to bed, I just feel so sad for them. It makes me feel bad when Indian people have to go to prisons.

"Why they go to jail so much, I can't really say. Maybe it's some of the cops' fault, you know. Like, look what happened to Kicker's face. And they can't really prove anything because Kicker was alone while there were the two of them. It's really hard. I think that a lot of cops are prejudiced towards Indians. They just try to get them into deep trouble by putting them in jail.

"But I really admire the Natives that really help themselves forward to education, you know. It makes me feel happy when they put themselves where they want to be.

"I know some white people are prejudiced towards us right now. But there are a lot of good white people who love Indians. But the other way around too. You don't know that there's a lot of us Indian people who are prejudiced too. Against everything. Even the person who is trying to get ahead for himself and is a well-to-do person. They're really after that guy.

"Like, suppose Maggie went to work for Natives, somewhere on the reserve. And if they found out she's a well-educated woman, they'd be prejudiced against her. They would really try to put their foot down on her. Because she's smarter than them.

"So it doesn't really bother me if a white person is prejudiced towards me. I don't care because in my life I find Natives are very prejudiced themselves.

When Lester is released in January he finds a girlfriend who, Kicker says, is a witch, of the hexing kind. They get engaged and Kicker promises to be Lester's best man. Then both Lester and the witch overdose and end up in hospital, just shortly after Kicker overdoses himself, the same day his son is born. Lester is back in jail within the month. He asks Kicker to forge a bail cheque for him. Kicker acknowledges that to do so would be stupid, but says he would do anything for Lester. Lester is his brother.

"I REALLY MISSED my mother when I was in residential school. I missed her even more, especially when she passed away. She died when I was forty. It was so hard when my mother passed away. But I think when my son, Lucas, passed away, that was even harder. He was only twenty-five when he passed away. That was much harder for me than when I lost my mother.

"My son was hit and run over in Regina. And the guy took off that killed him. He was caught. My son went to Regina especially to go for training, how to drive those great big transport trucks. My son was a very hard-working boy. They needed men at the time to drive transport trucks into the States. He stayed a month and then he got killed.

"It feels so unnatural to have your child die first. It's very hard. That's one of the hardest things a mother can bear. I lost, I had lost two other little children. One was just about two years old and the other one was five months old, I think. One died of double pneumonia. One of pneumonia and the measles. But you know, I got over it in no time.

"But my oldest son, when he got killed, you know, it took me over a year to forget it. I couldn't really accept it. I still think about him. When I start thinking about him, it's just like it happened now. That is one of the hardest things a woman could bear.

"Lester, he was five when his father got killed. He was close to his dad. He was very close to his dad. After his father died, he used to talk about his mother all the time. He was telling me to try and get hold of his mother to come to the funeral.

"My husband, he used to be real mean to Lester too. But then when I got braver, then he couldn't do what he liked with him. By the time Lester started growing up to be about five and six years old, you know, he was so scared of his grandfather. I really got after my husband. He couldn't really do what he liked to Lester. He couldn't really do anything he liked to Lester anymore."

DRIVING GRACE DOWN 97 Street – the drag – back home from the landlord-tenant office. "You know, I never knew if my name was Grace or Faith," she says. "On my birth certificate it said Grace. But then Indian Affairs had me down as Faith. I finally thought, 'I have to do something for myself.' And when I went to get the pension, I told them my name was Grace. Grace."

"YEAH. LIFE HAS really changed for me since I left my husband. I even went to Winnipeg to do a movie. Did Maggie tell you?" Grace laughs. "I went and acted as a grandmother.

"I did that movie in 1985. When I first got a phone call I just couldn't believe it. I just first started laughing at the girl that phoned me. I said, 'You must have the wrong number. It can't be me.'

" 'No,' she says, 'You're the woman we're looking for.'

" 'Me? It can't be me.'

" 'No, I'm serious,' she said. Because I kept laughing. I couldn't believe it. 'I'm serious. You're the lady we're looking for.'

" 'I can't do it. I've never. . . . '

"And then she said, 'I want you to come down to the office.' They gave me a date to go.

"So they told me to go on the south side to this office. And I wasn't the only lady there. There was a bunch of Native women in there that were brought in to audition. Even my sister was there. So we went one by one in the room. And they took me to do the movie.

"And I just wanted to back out, because I'd never been in such things like that. I used to think that I don't feel fit for anything. So I told Maggie about it. 'Oh Mom, take it. Go for it!' And all my children when they found out about it, 'Go for it, Mom! We'll be proud of you.' " She laughs.

"So I did and I told the lady I'd try. So I fit in. And they took me to do the movie."

Grace, playing the movie's Kookum, tramps through knee-deep Manitoba snow carrying a dead rabbit in each hand. Her young granddaughter asks her, in Cree: "How come you are doing this? Don't the government give you enough money for food?"

Grace takes a knife to a rabbit's skin. "I don't take no government money. They don't give it away for nothing. You gotta pay for it somehow. A little piece of your heart maybe. Course, I got my pension cheque same as everybody else. Like that smarty-pants Trudeau."

Grace, in her colorful Edmonton kitchen above a freeway, the dove-that-has-no-name cooing in the living room, giggles as she asks me whether I saw her movie. "Them rabbits they gave me to skin," she says. "I didn't know they were tame rabbits. I couldn't scrape that hide off. Tame rabbits, their skin is real tough, eh. Not like the wild ones. Their skin is so loose. There was no way I could have skinned them rabbits." She laughs.

"And did you see me where I said, 'That smarty-pants Trudeau?' " She laughs and laughs. "I made that up myself."

"The movie people sent me to Winnipeg on an airplane. And I stayed at the Louis Riel Hotel. I was living like a queen. I couldn't believe it. Didn't even look like the lady that was hauling the wood from the bush anymore and doing all the dirty work. I had my own room in there with a TV and a kitchen. I couldn't believe it was me.

"It was supposed to be all my family in the movie. They were all my children and my grandchildren and my husband passed away. The scene where my husband is dead, we had to do that scene again and again. The man who played my dead husband, he was lying in the coffin all that time. And just, we were just hugging each other and we did that for half a day until they got the right movements they wanted. And that poor man was lying there, pretending his was dead, for that whole time." She laughs.

"The acting, it wasn't hard for me because I used to act a lot on the stage when I was in school. And the nuns used to like it because they told me I was a good actress. I could act real. So I just made up my mind. I had to act real.

"One of them guys come and ask me how many movies I did already. And I never done any others. So he asked me how I got into acting. I said, 'I never thought I'd be acting in a movie like this, but then I did act on the stage a lot when I was in school.' Then he says, 'Well, that's what paid off, eh. It paid off.'

"I met a lot of people. They were all so nice. All the actors and actresses were so nice to me. They weren't prejudiced at all. Course it was mostly Métis that acted in there. I met a few Cree Indians, but not too much. Mostly Chipewyan.

"I think once more I'd like to do a movie before I get a little too old. I think I would. If I had the chance I'd go for it again, 'cause I got more experience on it now. I would like to go and act like a grandmother again."

I tease her. "Did people want your autograph?"

She laughs at me. "I just had to hide away. If somebody said an autograph, I just slapped them."

THE MOVIE GRACE stars in ends in tragedy. Teenagers die. White cops lie about the deaths. In the closing scene Grace tries to comfort her granddaughter, who is grieving her dead friends.

"Don't take it so hard," Grace says, in Cree. "These things have happened to us before. That's why we all have to be brave and love one another, while we are together on this earth."

In her sparkling Edmonton kitchen above a freeway, Grace tells me this. Those words in the movie, those were her words, she says. She made them up herself.

"That was my way to say, 'Do unto others.' That was my way."

*Historical information on Blue Quills is from *Blue Quills: A Case Study of Indian Residential Schooling* by Diane Iona Persson, a thesis submitted to the Faculty of Graduate Studies and Research, Fall 1980, University of Alberta, in partial fulfilment of the requirements for the degree of Doctor of Philosophy.

✪ LISA

"SO. MY NAME is Lisa. I am sixteen. Seventeen, really, in two weeks. And I am a dancer. I want to be a dancer. I work full-time at McDonald's by the Cineplex here at the mall. I don't live at home, eh. I pay room and board to my ex-boyfriend's mother. It's kinda weird 'cause he lives there too. We argue a lot. It's kinda weird.

"I hate being sixteen. I can hardly wait for my birthday. My mom wants me to grow up so fast, eh. And I can't. Like I'm just sixteen. You're too old to do kid things and too young to be an adult. I really hate it.

"Hey, did you see those Halloween pumpkins on the main floor? Over by the escalators where you came in? Did you see that one from the dentist's office? They stuck real teeth in its mouth! Real human teeth they had like pulled out of somebody's mouth into the mouth of that pumpkin. It was gross, eh. Totally gr-oss.

"This tape recorder makes me nervous. Some people interviewed me and a couple of my friends at the Youth Emergency Shelter when I was living there, eh. And they were sticking this mike in my face and I didn't know what to say. I was so shy.

"You want a coffee? I need a coffee. And some smokes, I really need some smokes."

"SO. ANYWAY. OK. I was born on November 30, 1973, in Edmonton. In the Misericordia Hospital. The first thing I can remember about being a kid is – not much. I remember all the Christmases. I remember this one time when my dad and his wife – my dad was married – they wanted to spend Christmas with me, and my mom wouldn't let me. So they brought me a bunch of presents. I remember it was about fifty-seven presents. They used to spoil me rotten. And I remember this dolly that cried and peed her pants. I remember that from being a kid.

"I went and lived with them for awhile in Calgary. For about a year. And they gave me a cat and I named her Tiger, because it was orange and it had stripes, see. I didn't really like his wife at first, you know. And my mom said I couldn't go to the wedding, that I had to go school. So I couldn't go to their wedding.

"And I got a little sister. But I don't know who she is. Her name is Jennifer Dawn, um . . . I can't remember her last name. She's eleven or twelve. She lives in Australia. That's where my dad's wife is; she worked with the Army bases or something. She got moved out there.

"But I hope to meet my little sister one of these days. I always wanted a sister. My mom didn't want me to know I had one. See, she told my dad not to tell me. My dad didn't tell me till about a week ago. My mom thought it might hurt me, not knowing who she was. In a way it did hurt me because, you know, I didn't know who she was or what she was like or anything.

"I don't have any pictures of her. My dad seen her birth certificate and he seen a picture of her, but he doesn't know where she is or anything. One day I'll meet her. I want to find her.

"I get along really well with kids. Like I baby-sit all the time for my friends and my aunties and stuff. I really like kids. Old people too. Like when we used to live over in Dickinsfield? You know Dickinsfield Extended Care? I used to go and visit the old people there. Every once in awhile. I didn't tell my friends or nothing though. They'd think I was weird.

"One old lady, she used to give me suckers. Like she thought I was just a kid. She used to talk baby talk to me and everything too. But she was real sweet still. Really sweet.

"I always get along with kids. Except my two brothers. If we're not getting along my mother looks at me like I'm crazy or something.

"That's one of the things that is screwed up about my family, eh. Me and my two brothers, we all got different dads."

"MY DAD, HE'S a Métis. I thought he was here to stay for awhile. He was good for awhile. Then he went right back. Right back to where he was before.

"He lives in Edmonton. For now. He lives in real gross hotel rooms. Like the Cromdale. The hallways smell like piss. The elevators don't smell too healthy either, at all.

"He took me to see a movie last weekend, to see *Parenthood*? That's the first thing we ever did together was go see a movie. Go see *Parenthood*. I still got the ticket. It says, 'One Adult, One Youth.' It's in my wallet. I'm going to keep that ticket forever because that's the first thing we ever done together.

"And he's taking me out for my birthday. On Tuesday. It's my birthday in two weeks but he doesn't trust himself to show up. But he said he's going to take me out to dinner on Tuesday. See, he gets compensation. He fell off a building onto some steps, so he's getting compensation so he can afford to take me out for dinner.

"My dad – every time he'd see me, he'd try to make the best of it and I did too. But when him and my mom were arguing, it didn't help me much. I'd blame my mom for yelling at him; I always used to stick up for my dad. One night my mom said, 'Why do you stick up for him? He's never been here for you and I have.' And I just said, 'Well, because he's my dad and I never see him and I have to give him respect too.' It doesn't make sense, but it did at the time.

"He phoned me last night. He was drunk and calling me down and stuff. I ended up staying up half the night crying my eyes out. So I'm tired today. I don't want to go to work.

"See, my dad cares about only two things. His bottle and himself. He lies to me, you know. I don't deserve that. I never lie to him. He's drunk and I know he is. And he tries to deny it and I get really, really mad at him. Last night I just said, 'Shut up. Don't talk to me.' I said, 'If you're going to be lying to me, bullshitting to me,' I said, 'just don't even bother phoning me anymore.' I got real mad. I thought, 'I don't need to be treated like that. Why can't he be just honest with me?'

"The other week he phoned my work and he was drunk and he was trying to give me shit too. And I just didn't want to be at work if he was going to be doing that to me, you know? And coming there drunk. So now me and him don't get along like we used to. How I used to stick up for him and all that; now we just don't get along anymore. Once in awhile we do, but that's about it.

"I don't worry about my dad no more. I figure now that I've got a job and everything, I've got to worry about myself, not him. I used to worry about him, all the time every day I used to worry about him. I remember this one time I had been up in Edson dancing? And I came back and my mom was in the kitchen and she started crying and I thought for sure it was something about my dad. Then I started crying and I said, 'What is it?' And she goes, 'Kate died.' Kate was my mom's best friend in the whole world. She used to be in a wheelchair.

"And I thought, 'Oh thank goodness,' you know, 'it's not my dad.' I thought she was going to tell me my dad had died. And then I felt bad that I felt relieved, you know? I thought, I should feel bad because Kate died.

"I remember this one time. My dad was drinking Lysol and really gross stuff. What happened to my dad was, like he was alcoholic. So he had a seizure.

"I totally freaked. I didn't know what to do. You're supposed to lie them down, lie them on their side. But I didn't know what to do. I panicked. I just about lost it. I just took some water and splashed it on his face. And about an hour later he goes, 'Oh Lisa,' you know. And then the ambulance came and they took him away.

"I remember when I was in detox, there was this guy in there and he had the same thing, this alcoholic seizure. Every time I see somebody have a seizure, I just freak. I just tighten up.

"I just panicked."

72

"SCHOOL, SCHOOL WAS boring. I thought it was boring. All I did was go to school to meet my friends. And guys, mostly. I was fourteen, no I was thirteen when I started going out with guys. And I met this guy from Cold Lake but um, hey, this is kind of a neat story. We went out dancing in Los Angeles, California. We went there dancing because there was this big actor, his name is John Vernon and his daughter acted in *Pretty in Pink*. And he invited our dance group, the White Braid Society, to go down there because he was opening an Indian art gallery. And he paid for our rooms and our meals.

"And oh, it was just like, it was just like heaven sort of like. It was really nice. The rooms were really beautiful. I was staying on the eighth floor and you can see all the lights and everything. We went there dancing and I met this guy Dave? And he was down there and his dad's an Indian artist. And it was kind of neat because he's from Alberta and we met down in California.

"I really loved it out in California. We had somebody pick us up at the airport. It was just like in a movie. Like, you know you have guys come and carry your bags up to your room and everything? It was fun.

"Oh ya, and our dance group went to Norway. Norway was really amazing. We met black-people dancers. They were from Africa or something like that. And we met a prince. He wanted to marry one of our dancers. Not marry, but he wanted to take her out. He was a prince. I just couldn't believe it.

"And we danced at Expo '86, too, at Vancouver. At Expo I found a boyfriend too. He was from Fort Smith, up north. He had a really weird last name. His name was Toby Football. He didn't really know how to talk English either, so he was kind of stuck there. He was drumming with his band. He was good-looking.

"When we went to Expo, we had to stay where all the nurses stayed. It was nothing like Los Angeles. Los Angeles was perfect, eh. Everything you'd ever dream of, or imagine.

"I was three years old when I started dancing. I been dancing ever since. I never really actually asked my mom how I started dancing. I just know she and my Auntie Maggie used to take me. I used to dance with my cousin, Ian, Maggie's son. He used to be the best kid out of Maggie's family. Like he used to be in movies all the time, he used to go school and he used to dance. And then things started falling apart for him. It was kind of weird because after things stared falling apart for him, I started falling apart, you know?

"Now he's working with his dad out on the Métis settlement. He doesn't go to school anymore, or dance.

"I want to be a dancer. Jazz. Tap. Ballet. My mother, her name's Sarah, my mother says I can't be a dancer. But I tell her that's my goal, eh. She's always had her goals, to be a doctor or whatever. But I think, sure you can be a doctor and make a lot of money and everything. But what fun is it? You just stick needles in people and stuff. Get two weeks off. But if you're a dancer you can travel around the world. That's my dream. I want to take some lessons, then I want to teach other people what I know. I want to have my own studio someday.

"I could never take lessons before, I was too poor. But now I am working I can save up and take some classes.

"My mom doesn't approve of dancing anymore. She is a Christian now. She's going to remarry. This guy's an evangelical Christian too. I don't like him. Because of his past. I know you shouldn't judge somebody on his past, but he went out with my Aunty Pat and he really brought her down, eh. And now he's going to marry my mom. I just found out last night. My mother never tells me anything anymore."

"I WANT TO live in Mexico. That's where I want to live. I haven't ever been there. But a lot of people ask me if I'm Spanish. And I always have to say no. That's a really good compliment when people ask me, 'Are you Spanish?' I just love the Spanish people, I love their dances. I like the way the El Salvadoreans dance. When they have that festival in Edmonton, Heritage Days, we go there and I dance. And when I get off dancing I always go to the El Salvadoreans. The guys are gorgeous. Rock dances nowadays, you hardly ever see guys getting up there to dance. But El Salvadoreans, them guys are always asking everybody to dance.

"The only dance I ever took in school was social dancing. But they didn't do it very good. It's like, no offense or anything, but like the white-man sort of dancing. It was OK, I guess. Like all the guys had to dance, right, so I got a guy partner.

"With Métis dancing you have to be really good at keeping your upper body straight. And the hardest part, you know, is keeping your chest still. You know, your boobs. You are not supposed to stand there bouncing. Donna, this girl I dance with, she is really bad with hers, you know. I'm surprised she doesn't get a black eye.

"I didn't practise for that Métis dance competition you saw. I don't mean to sound like I'm bragging or anything, but when I used to go to dances with Maggie and my mom, I used to just sit there and watch other people. And one time when I was home by myself I put on a jigging tape and I tried it, right. And I turned around and Maggie and my mom were standing there watching me. I just kinda put my head down and I walked away and I didn't say anything. 'Is she *ever* good,' I heard them talking like that, right. 'Oh no,' I thought, 'they are going to take me to dances and they're going to make me go out there.' I was really scared of dancing in front of everybody.

"Then slowly I got into it. And the next thing I knew I'm in a group. The first time I did it I just about shit my pants. I thought, 'What if I forget the steps? What if I fall on my face?' But like, it was a breeze. I thought it was going to be really hard, but it wasn't.

"I haven't ever tried any other kind of dancing. I wanted to, so bad. Tap and jazz and ballet. Those three things I want to take up really badly. But it costs too much money. I want to meet Karen Kain so bad. She's a really good dancer. She's so beautiful when she's on stage. She's so tall. And skinny. And the legs. Sometimes I wish I had long legs, you know, just to be a ballet dancer.

"Every day I have to dance. Like even when I'm up in room, I just sit there and if I'm ironing or something, I just sit there and I dance."

"I JUST GOT rid of a boyfriend, Dean. Dean, there's not much to talk about him. When we were going out it was OK. We went out for about three weeks. And things kind of went too fast I guess. He was going to give me a ring though, like he bought a ring for me and I didn't want it.

"He thought I was pregnant, eh. When I went into the doctor's office he was almost across the border to Saskatchewan. Then when he found out I wasn't, he came back and expected me to take him back. I just told him, 'Forget it.'

"Dean isn't the first guy I slept with. The first guy I slept with was Tom, Tom Cardinal. I met him, OK remember where I was dancing over there at the legion? I met him there a year ago. The day before my sixteenth birthday I did it for the first time. It was kind of weird. I was scared. I told my mom about this when I was living with her. We used to be just like really, really best friends and when I needed a mom, she was there. She was kind of a best friend-mom sorta like.

"He turned out to be a real jerk. He used to hit me and all that. And I didn't really appreciate it, so I just left. I didn't want to be around him. And then he was bragging about how he screwed a virgin, I guess you'd say. Turned out to be a real ignorant prick. We went out about two weeks. I know that's rushing it, but I was young and stupid. I thought I was in love. But I wasn't.

"But I don't sleep around very much.

"Tom threw a cup at my head one time and it bounced off my head and it shattered against the wall. When I was walking down his hallway, he lived in an apartment, he was saying, 'No man's ever going to love you,' and all that. He goes, 'I'm the only one that'll ever love you.' And for awhile there I started to believe it. I didn't start going out with guys for a month and a half later because I thought something was wrong with me. But nothing was wrong with me. It was just him.

"I don't even know why I ever went out with him. He's got no front teeth. He got into a car accident and he knocked all his teeth out. But like, he's good-looking and he's got no front teeth and he's a singer, like he played thirteen different instruments. And he's a jigger, he can jig. He's got a lot of talents but he's a real asshole. In a way he reminded me of my dad, 'cause my dad can play a lot of instruments and my dad doesn't have no front teeth neither."

"AND LIKE I used to audition for movies. I was in a movie too. It's an Alberta film. I never seen it yet. And my cousin Ian was in a film and my grandma was in a film. I didn't see it. I turned on the TV about two weeks ago and it was on. All I heard her say was, 'All we have now is each other.' And I thought, 'Oh jeez, I should've watched that, I should've turned it on earlier.'

"The movie I was in, it was about my older brother, he was getting into trouble with the law and started doing drugs and all that. And my dad and mom were always pushing me out of the way, saying stuff like, 'Leave your brother alone, he's having a rough time right now.' It wasn't a big part. I just played his sister and I only came on once in awhile. The only things I had to do was sit around the table and eat and be at his birthday party.

"But it was fun. I was thirteen. They picked me up every day after school. I really liked it when I had to be out of school to be there."

"DO I FEEL strong on being Métis? No. Like I am proud of being Métis but I don't get into the culture, like Louis Riel and all that. I am proud of being Métis but I don't get into it like my mom and my uncle and everybody does.

"Most of my friends, now I could say most of them are Métis. But when I was in school most of them were white.

"It was hard to be Métis in school sometimes. A guy called me an 'f'ing squaw' and I turned around and I just belted him right in the face. He kinda flew back into the lockers and I grabbed him and I said, 'If you ever say that about me again, next time I'll do worse. I'll take you outside and I'll beat you up.'

"Like I had a few Native friends in there and they were always behind me when I picked on somebody like that. Like I didn't pick on him really; I just can't stand somebody calling me an effing squaw. That's mean. If they are joking around I can understand it. But this guy wasn't joking around. And he said that in front of everybody. So I kinda got pissed off about that."

"I USED TO hang around with punkers. But I kinda got bored with it because all they did was fight. Beat up other people, like teachers and that, and steal purses. Sticks and knives and switchblades and all that. I didn't really feel like taking their bullshit, so I just stopped hanging around with them. And I kinda went headbanger.

"Punkers are in posses. You know, gangs. Headbangers don't like punkers. My friends are headbangers. People who like heavy metal. And preps, preps don't count. They are just wimps. Totally wimps. Like we don't like their hairdos and we don't like the way they dress.

"We don't try to be better than anybody else. Like headbangers can be their own selves more. Punkers always have to put up a front. They have to put on this big ego. They have to be tough. But the only time they talk big is when they're all together. If one of them is alone they don't say nothing. It's kinda stupid.

"Like there's these two Adams brothers. Everybody knows them. They are in this posse. It's called Powerhouse Posse? And they've got this reputation of beating up girls. And if you screw with those two then you screw with the whole posse. They are pimps too. They steal cars and everything.

"Like I have friends who do that, but they don't have to be in a posse to do it. That's like I said, you don't have to dress a certain way, you don't have to be into certain things just to impress anybody. Headbangers can do whatever they want.

"I still see punkers, like my old friends and everybody. But I wouldn't want to hang around with them because all those girls know how to do is strut around and make themselves pretty for their boyfriends. I don't see the sense, why they get all prettied up to go see their boyfriends. Their boyfriends just beat them up. It's like they think it makes them look really good in front of the rest of the guys if they hit a girl. It's stupid.

"When I was a punker we'd pick on just anybody, you know. Just as long as my friends were there and they encouraged me to do it, I'd do it. My best friend, Denise, she'd beat the shit out of someone just because I didn't like them. That's how we were. We used to be little terrorists in our school.

"But I've grown out of that. Like now I only have to fight if I have to. Like if somebody comes up to me and they say, 'You want to go?' I just say, 'No. Why? I didn't do anything to you.'

"When I was in the gang I had an ego. I had a reputation, you know, like, 'That Lisa, you don't screw with her.' And I was kinda happy to have that ego because in grade six I always used to get pushed around by big kids and in junior high I was small. Smaller than I am now. And I was hanging around with Denise and everybody, and nobody even thought of touching me. So I thought, 'I am just going to build this ego up a little bit more.' So I would go around picking on people. Scare them a little bit. Like this one time I got really pissed off at this one chick, Ashley? She called me a bitch in front of everybody and like I didn't say anything to her. I go, 'Why are you being such a bitch?' And she goes, 'If anybody is being a bitch around here it's you.' And everybody just goes, 'Ooooh.'

"I just kinda turned my head and I looked at her. 'You wait till we get out of this class and I'll kick your ass.' So we went out into the hallway and I pushed her. And I said, 'Come on. You wanna fight, bitch?' And right when a teacher walked around a corner, I pushed her again. And Ashley, she started screaming at me, eh, like really screaming at me.

"So I grabbed her and I pushed her up against the locker. And I said, 'You think you're tough just because the teacher is here now? Let's go. Right now.'

"So she threw her books down and she came at me. And she grabbed me by the hair, right. And I thought, 'She's a dirty fighter.' So I pulled her, she was on my lap and I was on my knees, right. And I couldn't get at her. So I kept on punching her in the stomach and she wouldn't let go of my hair.

"So I came around and I grabbed her by the front of the hair and I pulled her off me and I let her go. And she hit her head on the cement, right. You could hear this big bang.

"I got scared. So I took off.

"I guess she got hurt when her head hit the concrete. She had to go to the Medicentre across the street from our school 'cause she got a big goose egg on her head, eh.

"So when I got home my mom goes, 'You know, that girl could have been really hurt.' And I said, 'Good for her. That's what she gets for calling me a bitch in front of everybody.' "

"Like I don't know. I think most of that has to do with the way you have to be around your friends. And I guess if I hadn't started hanging around with Denise and them, I would be at home right now going to school.

"Because I kind of blame it on my friends because they were the ones doing most of the drugs and all that. And that's why kids are the way they are nowadays, is because of their friends. Most of them don't live at home. They are on the streets, wondering when they are going to get their next meal, or where they are going to get it from."

"GO BACK HOME? No. I can't. Because right now I like my freedom too much. And if I ever moved back I know my mom'd treat me like a kid again, you know? I can't ever see myself moving back in with her. I've tried it about eight or nine times now. It didn't work. I was always moving in and out. So I'm just not going to move back in ever again. We fight a lot, eh. Once in a blue moon she'll push me and I'll push her back and all that. But she beat me up, one time, real bad. You know how little things bug you and then they just build up and build up? And then she needs an excuse why she was hitting me. She said I was fifteen minutes late and she was going to beat me up for that.

"But I hit her back, you know. Like I pushed her really hard to get her off me, right, because she was just giving it to me, eh. And I was screaming and everything. Like, 'Get off me, get off me!'

"Like she slapped me in front of my boyfriend and all my friends. 'Get the fuck home right now,' and she'd slap me up the side of the head, right? And all my friends were standing there and I thought, 'She's not getting away with this, I ain't gonna let her do this to me.' So I turned around and I said, 'Fuck you,' really loud. And I was crying and I took off.

"And I went to my grandma's to pick up my bag and I sat around at my grandma's, right. And my mother came in and she told me to get the fuck home. So I had to go home. And when I got there she beat the shit out of me. So. That was the first time she ever beat me up real bad.

"When she beat me up she used her fists, not on my face but on my arms. And she'd slap me all over, on my legs and everything. I got red marks from her hands and all that. But that was about it.

"But I made her feel bad. I really rubbed it in. I took a mirror and I smashed it around my eyes, trying to make a bruise, you know, just to make her feel real bad.

"And two days after that we got into an argument and I took her last ten dollars and I took all my clothes and I was gone. I ran away. That was the second time I ran away.

"That was when I was fourteen, fourteen or fifteen. I was staying at friends. Staying everywhere. Here and there. And every once in awhile I'd get caught by my mom and one of my relatives, right. So I'd have to go back.

"Now we talk, me and my mom, but not like we used to. We argue more now. But I'm proud of her, eh. I'm really proud of her. I can't believe she made it there, to university, you know, after putting up with all my bullshit. Taking off. Moving out. I'm really proud of her.

"My mom, she's sober now. She got back to doing drugs but she didn't know it. Like, you know when you're taking Valiums to help you sleep? She got hooked on those. And on those antidepressants, she got hooked on those. But she didn't know she was hooked on them. 'Cause the doctor was giving them to her because she's having a rough time with me and her family and my dad and everything, and my brothers' dad. So. She didn't do it on purpose or anything.

"She went to detox for a week. Me, my mom and my dad all ended up in detox. Not at the same time. Separate times. First it was my dad, then my mom, then my dad, my dad, dad, dad, and then it was me. So. We were all in there. Next it will be my brothers.

"My brothers don't do drugs. My little brother, don't tell anybody this, my little brother smokes cigarettes. But I told him, 'I don't want you to ever do drugs or booze.' Like they don't know I do drugs. They know I drink, right, because my mom had to come and pick me up a couple times. I just warned my brother, I grabbed him like this, 'If you ever do drugs I'll kick your ass.' I'm really protective of them.

"I won't let them know I do drugs because if they see me they'll think, 'Well Lisa does, why can't we?' I know that for a fact because I used to do that. I thought, well my cousin, Kicker, and all those guys do drugs. I can do it 'cause they've handled it, they didn't die. So I tried it out. More and more and more.

"I've talked to my Auntie Maggie about this stuff. I've talked to Maggie about a lot of things. Like me and Maggie used to be really close, until I started quitting dancing and being my own boss sort of. But every time I'm depressed, she talks to me. She always asks me what's wrong. My mom or nobody was there for me, she always was. Her and this guy I met at the Youth Emergency Shelter when I was staying there, Terry. Her and Terry, those are my two favorite people in the world.

"Maggie gave my mom heck for not coming to my dance competition at the legion. She did. You know, the next day my mom was apologizing, 'Oh Lisa, I'm so sorry I didn't make it.'

"Like, 'It's OK. This is just once.' "

"I HALF-FINISHED grade nine. I quit school last year because everything just started slowly falling apart. Like I started drinking and doing drugs. My mom didn't trust me and I was arguing with her, arguing with my dad, my brothers. The whole family didn't like me anymore because I quit school. That's when my mom kicked me out.

"Nobody was too surprised when I quit school. Because they seen me, you know, skipping school a lot and doing more drugs and more booze. So they knew it was coming. Hash, pot, oil. And for awhile there I was getting into pills, Valiums, Halcions, all that.

"I ended up in the hospital because I did too much pills. The ambulance picked me up from my friend's that night, when I took all those pills, took me out on the stretcher 'cause I was really doped up and I didn't know what I was doing. My friends were trying to slap me and all that. And I was laid out on the floor. My best friend, Karen, she was crying. She said when I looked at her my eyes were rolling and all she could see was the white and she was getting scared. They threw water on me, they tried everything. So they just called the ambulance. They come and picked me up and I went to the hospital.

"And my mom was there. She asked me where I got the pills from and I was really really high from these pills, right. And I told her that I wasn't going to tell her. I said, 'I ain't going to say anything,' 'cause I didn't want to get my friends in trouble, right. And she goes, 'I didn't come down here for you to pull this bullshit on me.' She started getting abusive. I just said, 'Well leave,' I said,

'You always told me to leave. Now I'm telling you, leave.'

"And I was puking because they gave me this black charcoal stuff. Oh, it's really gross. They gave me two bottles of that to puke up all those pills. And I was just puking my guts out and she's giving me shit and all the doctors are standing around watching her give me shit. And I told her, I just said, 'Leave. If you don't want to be here you don't have to be. I wasn't the one who called you, you know.'

"The next day I went back to the Youth Emergency Shelter, 'cause I was living there then. And my eyes were really awful, they were puffy from crying. And two days after that I started drinking and I was trying to take pills again. I just thought, 'No I better not.'

"And the next day I was really depressed and I thought I better do something about this, this was getting out of hand. So the shelter suggested I go to detox. And I kind of wanted to go too. I didn't tell my family or anything, or my mom either. I just went. I stayed there a week, no five, six days.

"And everything after that slowed down a lot. Now I got a job, I'm out on my own, paying rent, you know. So everything turned out to be OK. For awhile there everything was falling apart. I tried suicide and that. But now I'm OK.

"See, I tried to slash my wrists and take pills. But nobody knew I took those pills, right, until about an hour after. Like I was laid out on the floor, that pill bottle was in the bathroom and I was kind of out. I think they were Halcions, I'm not sure.

"That time, when I took the Halcions, I was living at my friend, Shari's. I was trying to find a place to live, trying to find a job, do all that at the same time. It just wasn't working.

"But I'm OK now. Now I'm over at my friend's, my ex-boyfriend's mom's place. Like I said, he lives there too. We're arguing all the time. Like, so it's kind of awkward."

"I JUST DO drugs once in awhile now. Not like I used to. And I never do pills anymore, I don't do pills. Never. Cause the last time,

I OD'd. Drugs I'll do if I'm going out once in awhile. I'll have a couple of hoots. But I don't do it like I used to.

"And when I drink, I drink to have fun now. I don't drink to get drunk and forget about my problems. I drink to have fun.

"Now I have way different friends. Instead of friends that go to school, I have friends that work and make money and all that. I got tired of sitting there watching them make all this money while I was going to school, eh. So I thought, I better get out there and get a job. So I went out and got a job and now I have money and I'm not left out.

"This job I have now, I've worked there, it's been about a month now. My first job I ever had was at Minit Car Wash. The second one was Bubbles Car Wash. Then I started getting into food jobs. I worked at Fuddruckers for awhile. And there's another one, I can't remember. I don't keep jobs for very long, you know. I just start and then I quit and then I start again. They're boring. Like they are too easy, and once you get the hang of it you get bored with it. Oh ya, and I worked at Kentucky Fried Chicken.

"At the car wash, you get burned out easy. And you use your arms a lot, like my arms got really hard from wiping everything down and being fast about it. That's one thing I liked, I got my arms strong. But they went solid, you know, like rock.

"It was OK there. People were nice. Your hands get really wrecked though. Like in the winter, because of the wind, and you are always sticking your hands in hot water and that roughens your skin. And your skin starts to peel. But it's not too bad. They don't pay too much, $4.10 an hour. It's not a job you want to be at for the rest of your life. It's not that kind of job.

"I pay $120 for room and board. With the rest of my money I go out and have a good time. But like I can't buy nice clothes I've always wanted. Or expensive jewelry and stuff like that. I have enough to get me by. I just buy a few tapes here and there. Just go and blow the rest on video games and taking out my friends.

"So now I work on cash at the McDonald's at the mall here. It's OK. It's pretty easy but you have to, like if something goes wrong, if you have personal problems you can't let that get in the way with your job. You always, always have to be happy there. I find that kind of hard when you're pissed off or something, or there's something like I said with my dad, you know, when he's bothering me. It's hard to be happy when something like that is going on. But I have to be really happy when I am there.

"I need another coffee. You want a refill? I'll go get us a couple of refills."

"THE YOUTH EMERGENCY Shelter. Ya, I stayed there that one time I ran away. It was OK for the first two weeks. Like nobody bothers you, nobody invites you to parties and all that. Which is good, 'cause you want time to adjust to a place like that, right. So for the first week I wouldn't talk to anybody. I was scared. And two weeks later I got invited to a party. So I said ya because by then I knew everybody in there.

"I always thought that place was bad, like the kids and everything. But once I got to know the kids it was OK because those kids care about what happens to the other kids, you know? Like they stick together and they don't let any adults piss around with their heads. They're really good to talk to, like the kids are open and honest. They're not what adults make them out to be. They make them out to be crazy. It's not like that at all.

"The adults that work there, they don't ever give the kids the benefit of the doubt. If the cops come there and say, 'It's this person that broke into this place,' they just say, 'OK. Take him.'

"But there's this one guy who volunteers there, he's unbelievable. Terry Story. He's the best friend you could ever have. He's the best dad you could ever have. He's always talking to kids, you know. If you needed money he'd give it to you, and those youth workers and volunteers aren't supposed to give you money. He was just like Superman.

"I still see him. We go for coffee once in awhile. He said I was like, you know how a teacher has a pet? He said I was one of those, like I was his favorite and everything. Oh, I just loved that guy. He was right on.

"Anyway, if you came back to the shelter drunk or high, you'd have to try and hide it, you know. If they knew about it, then you'd have to sleep in the smoking room on a thin mat, like *that* thin, and one blanket. And they were very itchy blankets, eh, and no pillows. And you'd have to be up by six and out by seven and you couldn't come back until five o'clock in the afternoon. So that was kind of our punishment.

"You have to sleep in dorms, right, like the guys are separated from the girls. And you'd have to make your bed every night and you'd have to take the sheets off every morning and throw them downstairs for them to be washed because of scabies and all that. When you first come in they give you this special shampoo for your hair and your parts and all that. Some of those kids that stay there are from the street, so you have to keep them pretty clean.

"And when you're first staying there and you're staying in the dorms, they give you lockers to put all your stuff in. And you either have to be working or going to school. And when you're working full-time or going to school, you get put in 'Start.' That means you get your own room and they give you a closet. Like you have to lock your closet so no one goes in there.

"I was there for a long time but I didn't make it to 'Start' because it was hard for me to look for a job while all those kids are drinking and doing drugs and they want me to go party with them. I almost made it to 'Start' twice but I just kept on screwing it up for myself. But I didn't really care because I didn't really mind having a locker as a bedroom, right.

"It's a good place if you don't have a place to stay, but I'm not saying you should go there just for the fun of it. Because that place screwed me up bad, like really bad. Because the kids there, all they do is drugs. There were a lot of drugs.

"When I tried to suicide, that was when I was staying there. That was the time I was fighting with my mom and nothing was going right for me. I couldn't find a job. And I couldn't find a boyfriend. I wanted a boyfriend. And, I don't know, just a lot of things were falling apart. That's when I thought, I don't want to go through this pain all my life. So I just tried it.

"I did make my wrists bleed but not bad. They were bleeding but they weren't like gushing out or anything, like you see in the movies. But they were bleeding a little bit.

"I used, you know, those things that doctors cut open, they cut people open with? Scalpels? I took that from the hospital one time when I was there for my migraine headache. And I took it back to the shelter and hid it under the ceiling tile in the bathroom. 'Cause like they went through your bags every night to see if you had any razors in there, because kids do pretty stupid things in there, eh.

"And then that one night everybody was downstairs and I snuck up the back and I went up there. I was crying and all that. I just took my wrist and I kept on, you know, kinda cutting. And then I just kinda sat there. And then somebody walked in and they seen me and I just threw that scalpel across the room.

"I took off outside and I went and sat in the ravine for a long time. For about five hours I sat in the ravine, just sat there thinking. This was dark out and the ravine isn't the best place to be at night, right. But I just sat there.

"I came back and everybody was concerned about me. No no, it was my friend who walked in on me, right. And I told her that if she told anybody I'd beat her up, so she didn't tell anybody. And I patched my wrists up and I wore long shirts so nobody could see. But Terry was wrestling with me and he seen. And I just looked at him and I didn't say anything. He said, 'Well, what are these?' I didn't say anything. I just walked away and I went to the store. And when I came out of the store he was standing there waiting for me. And then he started talking to me and he gave me money to go look for a job the next day, twenty-five bucks I think it was he gave me to go look for a job, get some cigarettes for myself.

"And he said he wasn't going to ask me why I did it because he knew, right, why I did it. Because everything was falling apart."

"SEE, I ENDED up at the shelter 'cause my mom kicked me out. It was more or less like me leaving and her kicking me out. She tried kicking me out and I said, 'No, you're not kicking me out, I'm leaving.' So it was more or less like that. It's between kicking and me leaving.

"At first I usually went and stayed at a relative's, but this time I went and stayed at the shelter because I was sick of my mom's family and I was sick of my own family. So I just left.

"That's about it. That's how I started going out on my own. I was always in and out of places. Like I was always staying here and there. Nobody knew where to get a hold of me.

"This is the longest that I've ever stayed at a place and had a job. It's for a month and a half now. So I'm proud of myself. Once I get into dancing, it'll be even better. It will be even better. I will be really in my highest glory, then."

✹ JANE

JANE ASH POITRAS, artist, on paper. Her resumé, printed on the inner flap of an invitation to a New Work exhibit, is dense with detail and accomplishment. Bachelor of Science in Microbiology, U of A, 1977. Summer printmaking program, Yale, 1982. Bachelor of Fine Arts in Printmaking, U of A, 1983. Master of Fine Arts, Columbia University, New York, 1985. Selected exhibitions: Los Angeles, Tokyo, Paris, New York, Brazil, Spain, Ottawa. Selected collections: McMichael collection in Kleinburg, Yale University, Canadian Museum of Civilization.

In the body of the resumé a quote from Jane herself, in italics: "Essence of art is the timelessness of its aesthetic beauty."

And a quote from NOW magazine, Toronto's self-styled news and entertainment voice. Jane, smiling like an imp under her straw Panama hat, in her In-Wear T-shirt and beaded earring, was a NOW cover story in 1989. "Sweeping images blend Bugs Bunny and sweetgrass spirit," the headline read. The quoted passage: "Rich colours and tight compositions come together in utopian landscapes and collages that layer artifacts of mainstream pop culture and Cree history to embrace the whole contemporary Native experience.

"The impact is stunning, and in the past four years Poitras has become one of Canada's hottest artists."

Jane Ash Poitras, one of Canada's hottest artists, on paper. The cover of the New Work invitation is a reproduction of her 54" by 60" oil painting, *Mythology Shield*. The painting is red, yellow, blue, purple, grey, pink, green, orange. Crude figures are scrawled over the surface in white and black paint, or scratched into the impasto. There is an owl, an eagle or a dove rising in a spray of red and orange, a chick, or a child, tumbling below. A deer. A buffalo. Indeterminate beasts. A star. Tepees. Rows of circles that are shields, or warriors. A brave on horseback. A fish. Multiple crosses. Arrows. And above a red sun striped white, the floating, hollow-eyed face of the shaman.

ONE OF CANADA'S hottest artists, in person, at her Edmonton studio, nursing her baby son, Eli. Her son Joshua, a year older than Eli, cannot resist taking advantage of his mother's relative immobility to stick his hand between the bleached jaws of the buffalo skull on the table.

"Buffalo spirit doesn't like that," Jane cautions. "He bites. Don't do that, Joshie."

"Ee put dat in dere. Ee bide it?" Josh looks up at his mother.

"No, we don't want to break him. This is very valuable sculpture. See his horns and his eyes? And there's his nose and mouth."

"Yaee. Ee dat. Bide de hand."

"Josh and I have this real understanding. I always treat him like I would an adult. I show him some respect. I don't talk down or up. And I always stick up for him."

"Look at ee's feeth! Look at ee's feeth!" Joshua's long squeal swells into a howl. "Me broke it. I brok-ken, Mommy."

Jane detaches Eli and catches the skull before it falls. "No," she says calmly. "No, no, no, Joshie. The buffalo's going to cry. Big tears are going to come out. Don't make the buffalo spirit cry."

A crisis averted. Josh, unchastened, starts to unwrap a roll of toilet paper he's retrieved from the women's washroom out in the hall. He trails the roll through the foyer, into and out of his mother's airy studio, under and through the legs of his daddy's computer; a blonde, tousled, latter-day Hansel intent on marking his way home.

Jane, satisfied Joshie is content, flips back her long hair and slings Eli over her shoulder. "Let's see. Where should I start?"

"I HAVE BLOCKED a lot of it out, eh. I know one thing. Like, I was born up in Fort Chipewyan in 1951. And when Mrs. Runck got me – this was in 1957 – I looked really neglected. You know, really thin. And I had this broken nose and this rupture. And I had pimples all over me or something. Who knows. It was probably scabies.

"She took me to all these doctors and they couldn't figure out how to get rid of this skin thing. Finally, this one doctor put me on this table and shone a big light on me.

"And Mrs. Runck asked, 'Does that light help get rid of these pimples?' Apparently he was a psychiatrist. And he said, 'No. We're hypnotizing her and we're talking them away.'

"I don't remember any of that. I don't even remember what my real mother looked like, and apparently I was with her. My Indian memories are all blocked out. My memory only starts when I was with Grandma; I called Mrs. Runck my grandma. And I was already six-going-on-seven by then.

"I can't even remember when I used to live with Grandma's daughter. She was the lady who took me in first. What happened was, this lady had three boys and she wanted a little girl. Plus the family had money problems. So one of her solutions was to take a kid from the welfare, and get paid this hundred dollars a month.

"But it didn't work out. There was so many problems at the start with me that it wasn't worth her time. And there was the money thing; she already had all these other kids, and her husband didn't want another mouth to feed.

"So her mother came by her place. The story starts out, Grandma had no intention of picking me up. I mean, she was sixty-five years old. But she said, 'I came by to visit my daughter and you were sitting outside the fence on this little curb with this little grungy bag and this torn-up dirty dress on, waiting for the welfare car to pick you up.'

"And so Grandma went into the house and asked, 'How come Janey's out there sitting on the curb?'

" 'Well, she's out there because I can't keep her and I'm gonna send her back from wherever she came.'

"And so Grandma said, 'You can't do that to that poor little girl.' And she came out the gate and she just put out her hand and said, 'Why don't you come home with me?' And I guess I left with her. And we walked all the way home. She was the type of woman, she'd walk all over town to save a nickel. I remember walking all over town with her after that for seventeen years.

"I'm still living in that same home. I ended up buying it. I guess it's almost like having her spirit there. Like, how some people manicure a grave, I manicure her house for her." Jane laughs. "Maybe I think she's gonna come back someday or something.

"Anyway, after Grandma picked me up at her daughter's, in about two weeks one of her sons popped in, unexpected. And she says, 'I have something to show you.' It was like she'd picked up a cat; it was really funny. I guess she had me hidden. She brought me out of this closet and she said, 'Look what I found – this little girl. And I want to keep her.'

"And her son said, 'Well, where did you get her from?' I guess I was really shy, really scared. I wouldn't talk or anything.

" 'Well, she was sitting out on the curb with this little dress on. And this is all she has.'

"And he said, 'Well, Mother, you can't just pick these kids up off the street. They belong to somebody.' He thought I was Oriental 'cause I looked like a typical Oriental kid. He said, 'We better phone the authorities.' He was very businesslike.

"Here the child welfare had no idea I was with her. They said, 'The police brought Janey to us. She was left at the baby-sitter's and we don't know where she lives or where her mother is. There's not very much information on her. Nothing but her birth certificate.'

"So, the child welfare came out to Grandma's place and looked over the situation. And they said to this sixty-five-year-old lady, 'You can baby-sit Jane until her real mother comes back or her people come back. Because someone is gonna eventually show up looking for her.'

"So, a year passed and no one showed up. The social worker came by again and she said, 'Well, Janey looks pretty happy here.' And they just left me there."

Jane transfers the cooing Eli to his carriage. She stands up, thin, coughing, racked by some bug she says is eating her up, and rhythmically pushes the baby back and forth.

"I can remember when I first got there, I knew I didn't like it. I kept saying to Grandma, 'When are they coming to get me?' I'd wait and I'd wait on the back porch. And then after awhile I stopped waiting. I guess I just accepted the fact I was there to stay. And I guess I made the best of it.

"The first year she had me, I know Grandma tried to send me to kindergarten, and I took speech therapy and I was in the hospital for a rupture, and I was seeing that psychiatrist for the pimples or whatever they were. And this guy must have realized I had some really negative memories, so I guess he did something. Because I remember where my memories really start. They start when I had to try to pass these goofy exams to get into grade one.

"I remember sitting at this desk at Sacred Heart school and the teacher was saying, 'Circle this, circle that.' I didn't even know what the hell 'circle' meant. Needless to say, I flunked the exam. But then afterward they showed me my mistakes. So I associated the word with the picture, and I figured it all out.

"They said, 'She can't go to grade one because she can't speak and she's retarded. She got all her things wrong on her grade-one entrance exam.' And it was just simple things, like, 'Circle the ball, circle the doll, circle the wagon.' But if you have a really upsetting background, you don't know what those things are.

"So they said, 'Put her in Winnifred Stewart,' this school for mentally retarded kids.

"Well, Grandma just wouldn't buy that. She said, 'No way this little girl is retarded.' So she took me to a different school. They gave me the same exam again. This time, one hundred per cent. 'Wow! This kid is brilliant!'

"I guess that kept me out of Winnifred Stewart. But it didn't get me quite into grade one." Jane laughs. "They just weren't ready to buy it, so they left me out a year.

"See, Cree was my first language. That's probably why they thought I was retarded, because I didn't know a word of English and they thought I was speaking gibberish. They had this big thing about, how could I be six years old and not know how to speak the language. So when I was saying 'wa wa,' they thought I was saying water. I was saying egg in Cree. That was my favorite thing, was egg sandwiches." She laughs. "I always wanted an egg sandwich. I never did get one."

JOSHUA HAS BEEN scouring the studio for his mother's paintbrushes, collecting them from every rim and jar and box he can find. He carries them to Jane now in both hands, proudly, like a bouquet. "Here, Mom," he says, the brushes waving and dipping in his grasp. "Here, Mom."

"Anyway, when I was a kid I ended up becoming Grandma's best friend because she started telling me all her troubles with her family. Once I learned the language and I saw the way she lived, I could see the good heart in her. So I was always there to use whatever logic a child has to comfort her. But in the process I ended up being a psychologist to an adult.

"Later on I saw all the kids up in Fort Chip just running wild in the village having fun. They were all fat, sassy, and happy. That's the way you're supposed to be when you're a kid. You're not supposed to be worried about a sixty-five-year-old lady, worried about how to be a diplomat in her family, caring for her.

"If I had to do it all over again, she could have adopted some blonde-haired, blue-eyed kid and I would have liked to have gone up to the reserve. Although I was really good to her, I suffered for it. But now I'm being blessed in life. So maybe because of the suffering I did earlier, I am being blessed now.

"See, when Grandma first got me she was really poor. Welfare gave her a little money for me, and she used that just to survive herself. She rented out the house, all the little rooms to all these funny little people. And I used to sleep on a blanket on the floor beside her. And I grew up to be really thin, because if we had soup on Monday, we had the same soup Friday. And she'd cut the mold out of the bread. Seventeen cents, I remember, was for fresh bread, thirteen cents was for day-old bread, and after that you got it free. We'd go get it free.

"I didn't want to eat a lot of times, so there would be more food for her. And when I got a little older, I started stealing groceries for her so she could eat a better. . . . She never knew. If she'd known, she would have rolled over in her grave. She probably is rolling over in her grave right now, because she was really Catholic." Jane laughs. "I was brought up a good Catholic.

"From all that kneeling in church I have the biggest, knobbiest knees in the world. I got the ugliest knees for a girl." She smiles. "And that's where I got them from, kneeling for hours in those hard churches.

"I got a lot of good things out of it, too, but that's the one thing I hated about being with her. She was such a fanatic. Her whole life was church tea parties and bazaars, going to church every morning, saying the rosary every night. Her husband passed away when she was forty-five, so she'd already been living alone for twenty years by the time she got me. She wasn't all of a sudden going to change her lifestyle just because this kid showed up.

"She used to make me get up at seven every morning and go to church. Even when it was forty below. And then we wouldn't be able to get home in time to get a good breakfast before school. And when I got home from school, we'd have to go to church again at five thirty and I couldn't see Woody Woodpecker.

"And sometimes I'd get to bed really late because the ladies would go to their novenas, their devotions. I'd be all tired the next morning. And then I'd have to get up to go to church again.

"This went on for pretty well my whole childhood. It was like my whole life was about going to church. I was always the only kid around all these old ladies. So I really felt out of place. I wasn't all that happy, that's for sure.

"But now I think, it kept Grandma happy and she had some company. I guess I don't mind too much, because she was a really good lady. So, I had to kneel a few extra times and go to church a few extra times. So what.

"Maybe I was selected by the spirits. They wanted me to go through that because they had other intentions for me when I got older. I had one medicine man tell me that. He says, 'Well, you're a holy woman, so that's why these things happened to you.' I asked him what a holy woman was. And he says, 'You're a teacher, you're a philosopher, aren't you, Jane?'

"And now I'm giving a lot of lectures on spirituality, and art. I'm used as a role model. I give talks to Indian kids on how they should do their education. And not just Indian kids, other people too.

"So I guess that came from being raised with her. 'Cause she was a real holy woman. She had all these philosophies ingrained in her – really universal philosophies. To be meek and humble and kind, and be happy for your accomplishments, but also don't flaunt it in front of people.

"She would continually stem that into me. So I had these strong beliefs, and I've always stood by them.

"And she was good to me. She gave me the love I needed. And she did really love me. I know that for a fact, she did really love me."

AT AGE TEN Jane believed she could fly. She stood on top of a laundromat in the rain, holding up her open umbrella, staring thirty feet down. It took another, much younger, child to convince her not to jump.

JOSH HAS CRAWLED into the mouth of a folding chair that looks ready to snap shut and swallow him up. "Josh, you better get out of there. If that chair closes you're going to end up in half." Josh immediately demands medical aid. "You carry me, Mommy. Take me dock-tor, Mom!" He is successfully extricated, without medical intervention. He turns happily to pulling paper out of a waste basket.

"Grandma's grandchildren were the same age as me, so that's where the real problem started. Actually, it was just the one family who were really hard on me. Grandma was really hooked on me, so she always stuck up for me like I was one of her real daughters. But they looked at me as a foreigner.

"Evidence of it was, Grandma went into the hospital for an adhesion and they thought she was gonna die. And one day they came and said, 'Oh, Grandma is dead.' Just told me like that. And they had my suitcase packed, and they said, 'You have to go back to the welfare office downtown to find out what they'll do with you.' They were trying to weed me out any way they could.

"I just was stunned. I think I was fourteen years old. I phoned her son right away because I knew he'd tell me the real story. Well, then all hell broke out. He brought me up to the hospital and showed me Grandma was alive. And he said to Grandma, 'They tried to put Janey in the welfare office while you're here in bed.'

"That put a real knife in. That put a real slice in that family.

"So then, Jesus, it was in the sixties, and I'm in high school and everybody grows pot. Some friends give me some seeds and I don't know what the hell they are. So I got two pot plants growing on the window sill. And Grandma looked after those plants for a whole year. She thought it was so wonderful that I was into horticulture, 'cause she was quite a horticulturist herself. And she never thought in a million years someone could go to jail for growing a plant. Well, neither did I.

"So, you wouldn't believe it. Her stupid grandchildren come in and they have a few too many beers and then one of them says – this one who was on my case my whole life – she says, 'This is marijuana. This is illegal. You're a big dope pusher, Janey.'

"So what I did was, oh, it was so stupid. I took the plant over to my friend's place and I said, 'Here, take this for awhile because these guys at home are getting all upset with it. And I don't want to throw it out. Grandma's heart would be broken.' And I didn't in a million years think that, while I was transporting this plant, this granddaughter would phone the morality squad. I couldn't believe it. The morality squad. It was like, 'Let's put this kid away. Let's really get rid of her.'

"I was stupid though, too. I'm coming back home and I just had my stocking feet on and this little thin dress, and this old man and old lady drive up in this beat-up old car. And they say, 'Could we ask you some directions?' And I said, 'Oh, are you lost?' And they said, 'Yeah. Are you Jane?' I said, 'Yeah. How did you know that?'

"And they just grabbed me and handcuffed me and threw me into the car. 'What other kind of drugs do you take? Where is that plant? If you don't show us that plant, you're gonna get in a lot of trouble, young lady.'

"Oh, what a fool I was. I believed them. If I never took them to the plant, they never would have busted me, and they could have interrogated me and whipped me and chased me all night long.

"So they took me downtown and threw me in jail and they mugged me and handcuffed me and totally humiliated me. It was just terrible.

"I came home the next day 'cause they let me home. And my poor grandmother didn't even know what had happened to me. She was just, she was in bed almost dead. She thought they killed me or something. She never spoke to those grandchildren again, right to the day she died. We saw them at her funeral, but they wouldn't even show their faces to me. It cut another real knife into that family.

"And then when she went for Christmas dinner with her other family, I was never invited. I wasn't allowed cause I was the . . . you know. That used to hurt me a lot. But she had to go to save some kind of family. And I'd say, 'Yeah, go, it's OK.' And what I'd do was, I'd walk around looking at all the kids having Christmas dinner and know that I was not allowed because of the color of my skin.

"Anyway, that's the kind of pain she had to go through. They always did these little piddling mean things to her concerning me. It was hard on me, too, but I felt her pain. Even though I hated to go to church, I put up with the church B.S. because it made her happy.

"And she wasn't making me go to church all the time to be mean to me, no way. She just didn't realize that, jeez, I was just a little kid. And little kids like to go to the circus and to the zoo, go to the mountains, go camping. I never got to go out like all the other little kids did. And I didn't have a mom or dad. I didn't know what a mom or dad was.

"And Grandma would always tell me the social workers were going to come take me away. So I was always scared. One time, when I was about six, this cousin came over I'd never seen before. I thought something really bad was going to happen. But the cousin just brought out a Humpty Dumpty book, and read it to me.

"No one had ever read a book to me. Even my grandmother never did that because she was German and she had a hard time reading. There was no nursery rhymes in our house, no music, no toys. Anyway, I was so shocked that this cousin read this book to me, and I was so happy at the same time. But I was so, like, 'How could you do this for me? What did I do to deserve this kind of generosity?' Some simple little thing like that.

"I read books to them all the time now." She gestures to the sleeping Eli and to Josh, now cheerfully shredding paper in the corner. "It was really important for me to have them happy. Clint, that's their father, and I really back each other up when it comes to positive raising of children 'cause we never want our kids to be sad. I would never in a million years want what happened to me to happen to any kid."

JOSHUA HAS DECIDED. He wants to go home. "Mommy, dee go home!" He hands his mother his coat. Jane laughs. "He's exactly his mother's son. Clint went and bought him a new winter coat and Josh absolutely hates it. The two of them were just so hilarious fighting about it. Finally I just put this old one on him, and we put five layers of sweaters on underneath. His new coat would be really warm, but it isn't stylish. And Josh is already just like his mother. It has to be stylish."

"WHEN I WAS a kid, I was always wondering, who did I look like? I went all my life wondering how come I chew the skin around my nails, how come I like to sleep in my clothes. I really wondered, was I an alien? Was I a human person? Because I had no family, no physical family. Here I am stuck in this foster family amongst all these German people and they're fighting like cats and dogs. And I got this kind, little elderly white lady looking after me, but I knew I didn't belong to her.

"You see, here is this brown mouse. You're looking around and all the other mice are white. You do see the odd brown mouse, but they're on skid row, and everyone is saying, 'Those mice over there, they're drunks.' And you're thinking, 'Oh shit. I'm one of those mice.' So you're brought up with this tremendous guilt. Being so ashamed.

"I mean, I wasn't brought up to be proud I was Indian. I was actually told to not say I was Indian because if I did, I would have an even harder time. So you lie. My grandmother, I can still see her saying, 'You tell them you have a little bit of French blood and that's what gives you your dark colouring, but don't you tell them you've got much Indian blood. If they ask you, say you have just a drop in you and that makes you strong.'

"And I said, 'Well, what would you do if I was full-blood Indian?' But she never even entertained the thought. Later on in years when I did tell her how much Indian I was, it really upset her. She kinda felt, 'Oh my God. I've been raising this Indian all my life and here I believed she was French.'

"Still today it exists, this weird European attitude about minorities. Like, when I took Joshua to the Yugoslavian baby-sitter and the First Ministers' Conference was on TV, this guy said to me, 'Look at you people, you can talk! You sound so intelligent!' He was so excited, because he believed we all live in tepees and we're all running around clubbing each other. There's this really funny misconception of what we're like. And I think she had that attitude too.

"So she would lie to herself because she loved me. The only aspect she didn't like was that I was dark and I had brown hair. She loved me, but she didn't love the idea I was Indian.

"And the social workers primed her. They told her they didn't know my mother, and that I could have been Italian, French. They knew what she wanted to hear. It was like, 'Let's not tell people these kids are Indian because, if we do, they are never going to be fostered out and we're going to be stuck with all these Indians in orphanages.'

"But when someone would say, 'What nationality are you?' I knew. I had this feeling, this gut feeling I was Indian. But I'd been taught Indian is dirty. So I grew up always looking in the mirror, totally misplaced, this urban Indian who tells everyone I'm white.

"And Grandma used to make me do these strange things – and it wasn't 'cause she was being mean, it was to make things not so hard on me. She'd try to make me as white as possible. She'd scrub me. She tried to make me wash my skin white. And when the summer came and I got a little suntan, boy, I really got scrubbed then. She'd take me out of the sun and she'd try to curl my hair and put white powder on my face and do all these stupid things to make me as white as possible.

"So I grew up lying. Always telling people what I thought they wanted to hear. And I grew up being ashamed. I never knew really why. But I'd look in the mirror and I'd be mad at myself because I didn't have blonde hair and blue eyes. And if people said, 'What do you want to do when you grow up?' I'd think, 'I want to be really white.' I just hated, I hated looking the way I did. "After I graduated from high school, I had doctors remove the hump on my nose, so I wouldn't look so Indian."

THE PHONE RINGS. Jane refers the caller to another number. "*Canadian Art*. Who wants to talk to *Canadian Art* magazine. Not me.

"Anyway, one thing I learned from living with Grandma – because she had a couple of people in her family who were millionaires and we'd visit them – I did see the difference between classes. I got to see the better side of life really early. And I realized, 'Wow, this is first class. So how do you get there?'

"And all I could hear was, 'So-and-so is a doctor, so-and-so is a lawyer.' I realized, at a very young age, the way to live good is to get a good education. So I decided I was going to university and become a doctor. I wanted her to be proud of me.

"And, too, the only release I had as a child was school. I made the most out of school. I guess the teachers recognized me for my talents and for my mind. So they spent a lot of time on me. And I did really well.

"I started painting right from when I was in grade one. I had this infatuation with art. I can remember the greatest thing at the old lady's house was she had all these ball-point pens and these indelible pens. And art every Friday, that's what kept me in school. You could draw all Friday. I lived from Friday to Friday.

"I loved to do art, but I never thought in my life I would be making a living off it. I thought you had to be a genius to go into the fine arts program at university." She laughs. "So I thought I'd do something simple like go be a doctor.

"And then, when I was about fifteen, Grandma sold her farm. She kept the oil royalty, so she landed into all this big money. And then all the renters went away, and we had food like it was Christmas every day. It was really weird. But I was so used to living in poverty that I still thought we were poor. I really didn't think she was that well off.

"But here, when she died, here she is with a quarter-of-a-million dollars tucked away in hydroelectric in Manitoba. Christ Almighty. And I'm sitting there and my pants are almost falling off me and I'm going, 'Huh? What?' And I thought about all the groceries I stole for her and all the clothes I stole for her and everything I did just to please that old lady because I thought everybody in the world was mean to her.

"And she never gave me one cent towards my university. Because that wasn't her policy. I was supposed to get married and have a husband support me. I wasn't supposed to be educated.

"And here at that time she did have the money. She could have supported me."

THE CALLER RINGS again. "Ash Enterprises. Ya, this is the president." It is Clint. He works as an administrator with the Métis Association, and has just spent the day defending the association in a controversy over financial records. "I hear you're a big movie star now; your picture is on TV and the whole bit! Tonight? No, I cancelled everybody out, cause I feel kinda shitty. Can you come back to the studio and do some more work? We got to get this place whipped into shape 'cause we got that big reading next week. And this is major. Not really, we don't. You'd be surprised at our itinerary; it's just incredible."

After she hangs up Jane explains she'll be hosting readings by Native writers at her studio. And, on top of the bug tormenting her, she's come down with what she calls "this goofy arthritis thing."

"It's a genetic thing. All the people up north, they all get it. It hit me really bad this year." She laughs. "If it hits any worse I might just move to Palm Springs like everybody else.

"Anyway, I was dyslexic, so I never read anything. I didn't know the trick about putting the book in the mirror. I only found that out when I went to Yale and they said, 'Come and do this psychology test and we'll pay you ten dollars an hour.' And it was really funny because I didn't know, no one knew, I was dyslexic and here I was supposed to be the norm. They were doing these tests and everything was going haywire. And they said, 'Just wait a minute. Are you dyslexic, Jane?'

"Oh, God, what a relief. I said, 'Jesus Christ, that's what's been my problem all my life.' I used to walk around with this big burden on my shoulders thinking I was retarded because I could be so smart in certain things and yet so dumb in others. I mean, here I was twenty-five years old, two university degrees under my belt, and still I had to struggle to get over those problems.

"That's why I went into science. In science you don't have to read that much. You just have to listen really well and have a good memory, and then do multiple choice. I mean organic chemistry. What is it? There's no reading. There's triangles and Cs and Hs and equals. Just symbols. It is just visual. You show anybody who doesn't normally look at a science book and doesn't know algebra, and it looks backwards to them anyway. So for me it was just wonderful.

"So it was only natural for me to think I would make a great scientist or a great doctor. I would have probably made a wonderful doctor. But that's a whole part of my life that only I'll know about, why I'm not a doctor. That all has to do with being a woman and having to deal with my womanhood, and men. I don't want to get into that. That was probably the most tragic part of my life." She is silent for a minute.

"And then being a printmaker; it was so natural because everything is backwards or reverse anyway. That was wonderful; they thought I was a genius on a print plate.

"But all my life I couldn't figure out what the hell was wrong with me. In school I'd get one hundred per cent in math and if I didn't study for the spelling tests, I would barely make it through. When I was in grade two, at night when everybody else would watch TV, I'd sit down with Grandma and we'd go through these spelling exercises. I used to hate it. I used to go to school and I'd have everything written up my arm and on my fingers and nails. I would go home the night before I had to read something out loud and ask my girlfriends down the block, 'What's this?' And they would read this thing to me and I would memorize it. So the next day when I was asked to read, I'd just fake it.

"And so I had this burden, even when I got to university. I thought they were going to find out I had this mental deficiency and that, because of it, they were going to throw me out.

"Now Joshua will drag me into the bathroom and he'll say, 'Mommy, look at my poop!' And I'll go, 'Oh, big one! Good boy, good boy.' " She laughs. "I want my kids to feel good about themselves. I went through a lot of being condemned, so I'm sure as hell not gonna condemn anyone.

"Like her grandchildren. They called me retard. 'You can't spell and you can't read and you're retarded.' We'd have things in church where you had to go up and read, and I'd get all the words wrong. Obviously I couldn't fool them all the time. And so they would just assume, 'Well, you're retarded. You're stupid. You're Indian, and what do you expect from an Indian.' "

"ANYWAY, WHAT FINALLY started making me feel good about myself was my academic achievements. I mean, high school, everyone can pass high school. But when I cut it my first year of university, I realized, 'Jeez, here I am this stupid Indian and here I am in Chem 250 and it's really hard and this Chinese guy over there and the East Indian guy next to the blond kid, they're all getting eighty per cent and I'm getting eighty per cent.' I mean, I was sitting in a class with four hundred students, and I'm in the top ten per cent. You feel pretty damn fucking good about yourself then. You don't care what colour you are.

"But I still didn't have the knowledge or the guts to tell people I was Indian. So I just let people go on believing. With this straight hair and bangs I made just the perfect Japanese little girl. And I just sank into their culture for awhile.

"And then I sank into the Chinese culture for awhile, too, really heavy. I was going to go into med school, so I really got in heavy with the Chinese guys. And they just loved me. They just accepted me. They didn't care; they just assumed that I was Chinese. This guy Simon, my Chinese boyfriend, he was gonna marry me. He's a doctor now and he was deadly in love with me." She laughs. "Actually, I would have done OK; I should have married him.

"But that was when I really started to get happy at university, because I started to click into a social circle. Before that I didn't get accepted by any of the groups. There were other Indian students and they had their social clubs and that, but I was never gonna admit to being Indian. So I really lucked out when the boys from Hong Kong accepted me. I wasn't so much a loner.

"I was a terrible loner for my first two years of university. I was so terrified someone might realize I was Indian. See, I had this stupid belief – and here I was this eighteen-year-old girl – I believed that if they ever did find out I was Indian, they would kick me out. That's how I was brainwashed.

"I was a shyster though. I got all mixed up with the wrong group after that. I got into alcohol. I just went from being this really respectable pre-med Oriental girl to being a really. . . . I just snapped one day and I just went really wild. I woke up one day twenty years old, and I spent the next seven years in pure hell.

"I don't wish what I went through on anyone. I don't know why I went through it. I don't know what the reason is." She pauses. "Got mixed up with the wrong boys."

She will say nothing more. Other people, who knew Jane then, tell stories of her wild days. Of Jane, drunk, hanging by her knees from the railing of her apartment balcony, ten storeys above the street. Believing she could fly.

CLINT WALKS INTO the studio, a burly, bearded man with the fair hair and blue eyes Jane, when she was ten years old, swore to marry. Clint is the one, this time, to rescue Joshua from the omnivorous folding chair. Joshua informs his father he wants to GO HOME.

"Grandma saw Joshie for five months before she died. And she was crazy for him. Here I was this dark little Indian girl and I got darker and darker every year. And then when I popped out this blond-haired child, she said, 'Wow, you did something right!' 'Cause in her day it was a blessing to have a fair child. And if it had curly hair, too, that was more of a blessing. And if it was a boy, wow!

"So she would joke for hours. 'Was God ever good to you. He gave you this one with golden hair, curly hair, a boy, a strong boy with blue eyes and white, white skin.' Joshie is almost like an albino Indian. Just a gorgeous little fellow. And so she got a real kick out of it.

"When I was in that German family, I almost hated myself because I didn't have blonde hair and blue eyes. And I said to myself that when I got older I was gonna marry a man with them, because then the kids would have at least some chance of it. It doesn't matter now, because that's so silly. But that's kinda the sad part about it. If I was a kid brought up around Indians, I wouldn't have had that wanting to have blonde hair and blue eyes.

"Anyway, everything changed when I was about twenty-eight. I was working as a microbiologist at Burns Meats and teaching it at the university. I took an evening drawing class and I met Nora Yellowknee. And she saw right through me right away. She said, 'Come on, Jane. Cut this bullshit. You're not Japanese. You're not Chinese. You probably got some god-damn band within fifty miles of Edmonton. And if you phone up Indian Affairs, I'll bet they could trace it right away and tell you where you belong. And you could meet all your people. And the government will pay for your university.'

"So I thought, 'Well, OK, if you can get benefits by being an Indian, why not be an Indian for awhile.' So I phoned up Indian Affairs. And within minutes they told me exactly where I was born. They even told me I had a treaty number and that I had all these people. I was just so shocked.

"They thought my mother was still alive. They told me to

phone up the Bureau of Vital Statistics and see if they had a death certificate on her. And sure enough, they had one. She died October 12, 1957, at the Aberhart Hospital, the same day she went in. She collapsed on the street and died from tuberculosis.

"When I held her death certificate in my hand, it was really strange. I read the information over and over and over again. The colour of the eyes. The height and weight. How she died. It said pulmonary tuberculosis for four years. Just to try to get a grasp of what she was really like.

"So I went to find the doctor at the Aberhart. He told me, 'Oh yeah, we knew your mom. But she never told us she had two little girls out on the street.' See, I have a sister. Her name's Marlene or, no, Marjorie. And her nickname is Skedoodles.

"I don't know if she's alive or not.

"And then when I finally went up North, of course I met my mother's sister and her brothers and her aunts and uncles. They all said she was really neat. They had these little pictures of her. In those days you stand five million miles away from the camera, so all you can see is this little, tiny faded person. But she looked really pretty. She just looked like this fat little Indian chick.

"I never did know who my dad was. There's different stories. I guess in those days the Indian girls would, you know, a nice man, you would go to bed. So there's a few different stories of who my father is. So on the form they just say, 'Dad not sure.' There's just no way to prove it. Maybe she didn't know either.

"She should be alive today. But one of her old beaus told me she was just so full of anxiety. Instead of getting bed rest like she should have, she never stayed in hospital more than a couple of days. Instead she'd go to Johnson Creek, she'd go to Fort St. John, chasing after these different men. And that's what killed her in the end. She just would not rest. Not until the day she died.

"I guess when her father died up at Fort McMurray, my mom was pregnant with me. And she was so ashamed of being pregnant and unmarried that she wasn't gonna show herself at his funeral.

She just hid by the creek. The same guilt I had about being Native, she had about being pregnant.

"She was so ashamed she tried to chase the proper man to make a family, to get married and raise us girls. And so she was always leaving us off here and there, chasing these men. And she wouldn't tell the sitters when she was coming back and she'd come back two months later. She was just a lost soul.

"And someone told me she used to get beaten up, too, by some of the guys she'd go out with. I know one picture I saw, she looked pretty bruised. So having tuberculosis and us two girls, and not being married and all these relationships, things didn't work out for the best.

"See, her mom and dad died from TB. So she didn't have her parents' values and beliefs to come back on. And you need that. When she was twenty, I'm sure she needed her mom too. But her mom was dead. So that's probably what drove her out of Fort Chip.

"Anyway, after I found out who my people were, the next step was to go back up home to Fort Chip. It was the first time I had been home in over twenty years. I got off the plane, a small plane, and all my relatives were there, people I'd never seen in my life. All the old people and the aunts and uncles and the young kids. It was the best day. It was like the day I came home from the hospital with Joshua. I'll never forget it.

"Everybody was really ecstatic to see me. But they also were really shocked. Like, 'My God, how did this ever happen?' They knew my mom had died. But they didn't really know what happened to us kids, eh. They didn't even know I was alive. But they just accepted me right off the bat. I was just a lost child. That was my Indian name anyway, Kiwachu Wachis. That's what I was – orphan child.

"So I spent two weeks in Fort Chip just eating this wonderful, really thick, really greasy duck soup and meeting everyone on a real intimate basis. And I'd go gambling with them and I really got to feel their life. It felt like I'd been there all my life. Like I never left the place.

"It was a really big relief to see relatives, to figure out why your hands are this way, why your nose is that way, to see yourself in other people. 'Cause you grow up never seeing yourself in anybody. It was such a relief to realize you're not some Martian off another planet. To actually feel roots.

"That was a really good time, too, 'cause then I could come back and say, 'This is where I'm from. This is who I am. So watch your ass because I got people behind me. You can't throw me in jail and you can't stamp on me. You can't knife me in the back.'

"You see, I grew up with no one to fight my battles. So that family could do anything they wanted to me. They could phone the police and try to put me in jail and do all the stupid things they did. They could rape me all they wanted. Who's going to believe me? I didn't have a father, an uncle or a chief.

"I got myself into some tight situations where one of those grandchildren's husbands would give me a ride home from baby-sitting and then try to paw me and do all kinds of things to me. And then they'd threaten me if I ever tried to say anything.

"I had a lot of fighting them off. They'd come have beer parties at Grandma's house and I'd be coming out of the can, or they'd come upstairs into my room. And I knew what was coming. So I ran or screamed or wiggled myself out of situations. I had to really watch over my shoulder.

"If I was their cousin, if I was really blood, they wouldn't have done that to me. If I was white. But they looked at me as Indian trash. 'Oh, she's just Indian trash.'"

JANE ASH POITRAS. The "Ash" is the mystery name, she says. The secret name. No one will ever know from where that name came.

CLINT HAS TAKEN Joshua, old spring coat, five sweaters and all, out for a walk. The studio is strangely silent. "So my mother died and instead of us kids being transported back up to Fort Chip where there would have been grandparents and aunts and uncles to look after us, instead of being put where we belonged, we were separated by social welfare. They just conveniently. . . . Well, Mrs. Runck said she'd baby-sit me, so that problem was taken care of. They could just close the file on that one.

"Social Services should have just made a few phone calls and found out where I really belonged. And then phoned Fort Chip and said, 'Look, we have one of these kids. We've done some checking and her mother is dead. Any aunts and uncles want to take her?'

"And then what would have happened is, I would have been taken right into the community, grown up with lots of other kids, lots of community support and lots of meat. There wouldn't have been any of this being anemic all my life. 'Cause that's one thing we got meat up there, and fish. Those Indians up there, they're not fat just because they're breathing it in. People say things like, 'Why are Native people so smart and why do they have this witty sense of humor?' When you think about it, it's their high-protein diet. It feeds the body, it feeds the brain.

"There's just hundreds of us out here who should have been repatriated. I've met a couple of them and they've really been struggling with their identity, to be proud to be Indian. That was a really big thing for me to finally admit and to be proud of it, to finally find out for myself that we're not all a bunch of drunks on 96th Street and even the drunks on 96th Street aren't so bad. They're pretty neat people actually. And there's just as many drunks in any other culture.

"See, what happened in the fifties, with the population boom and all our parents dying of TB, instead of social welfare trying to find out where these all damn Indian kids came from, they just left us in the city. If they had just put us back into our communities, with our own people, there wouldn't be half the problems there are today. Half the problems are because of these displaced urban Indians.

"Wayne, I grew up with Wayne. He is a full-blown Sioux Indian and still today he denies it. He's in Vancouver and he lives like a millionaire and he got a master's degree in Business Administration. He did grow up with his parents. His mother was Indian, but she was also taught about this dirty Indian thing. So she denied her roots and told her husband she was East Indian. And then when her husband found out she was Sioux, he divorced her 'cause he was so horrified.

"Her husband met her in Thompson, Manitoba. What else can you meet in Thompson, Manitoba, but Indians? So I don't know how he ever believed that story anyway.

"But Wayne totally denied everything. And we went through high school together. So he actually reinforced that whole, 'Let's not tell anybody we're Indians.' It was sorta standard rule.

"The funny thing was, after I found out I was Indian, I found out I kinda already knew what it was to be Indian. Grandma Runck used to love to cook baking powder biscuits. Exactly the same recipe as the bannock my Great Aunt Eliza had up in Fort Chip. So I'd been eating bannock all my life. And my grandma would make duck soup. The same thing in Fort Chip. And she always cooked the meat to death, and it was just the way the Indians liked it up North.

"That's what I found was really neat, was the fact that she cooked just like a traditional Indian woman. She grew up on the bald prairie on a dirty, dusty farm. And she cooked the prairie way.

"And I found out that lots of the philosophies she had, they had up in Fort Chip too. The Native people are very, very Catholic. So they all knew the same songs I did. All my cousins, we could talk to each other because we were all brought up in Catholic schools and we all had the same stories.

"And Grandma, she was a teenager in Germany in the 1800s. I was a teenager in 1967 in the midst of Canada and hippies and drugs and all that craziness. But she would tell me about stories about the old times, horse and buggy and all that. And her elders lived just like the Indians lived on the prairies before everything became automated. So I got all the old stories, the same stories I would have gotten from my real elders.

"So in a way, it was funny. I grew up Indian."

"BUT FINDING OUT about my people, that gave me the room to do the art degree. I was already working in microbiology and teaching it. And I didn't like what I was doing. Then, when I really realized about my roots and my people, somehow I had more confidence to do art. Maybe that was the white attitude, to become the doctor or the lawyer or the microbiologist. And once I knew I was an Indian, I could do what the hell I wanted to 'cause I didn't have to live up to anybody's expectations. I could just go ahead and do what I damn-well pleased.

"So when I went to art school, I didn't have to lie to anybody. I just went right in there and I said, 'I'm Jane Ash. I'm a crazy Indian, eh.' I ran into some of my microbiology friends that I'd lied to for so many years and they'd say, 'You always told us you were Japanese from L.A. How come now you're Indian?' I just looked at them and I said, 'Oh, I was that too. You can have a little Japanese blood in you, you can have a little bit of Indian. I just left out the Indian part until it was safe.'" She laughs. "Or I'd say something stupid like that.

"The more traditional Native spirituality, that was the part I really got ecstatic about. Going to the powwows, I was so excited I was hopping around like a chicken on a floor for days after. And I guess that is when I started to live my childhood. That's when I started to have the fun of a child.

"Yeah. And then I started doing paintings and doing things about the spiritual side, about the sweat lodges – then I started to be really happy. Then I knew who I was.

"Grandma saw some of my art before she died, but she never understood it. She didn't understand how you could make a living at it. She still had the idea that you had to be a teacher or a nurse or a dishwasher and that artists starved. When I told her I was teaching at the university, or lecturing a little bit here and there, she could relate to that. And she thought, 'Oh, good, I don't have to worry about Jane. At least she won't end up on the streets starving.' Basically she just didn't want anyone starving.

"She got to meet some of my family in Fort Chip just before she died. She was very scared that I was replacing them with her. But I reassured her she was always Number One in my life. I didn't come up and say, 'Oh well, they're so much better. Oh, I should have been repatriated. Oh, I hated church.' That would have hurt her too much. I can say it now 'cause she's dead. She's probably in heaven saying, 'Well, I guess next life I'll know better. I won't make Janey kneel so much.'

"She had good intentions. But when I go back to Chip and I see all those kids running around – wow, they love life. I think I'd be just as good an artist as I am today if I'd been repatriated. Maybe I'd be happier. I don't know. Maybe I'd be an artist up there and all the curators would have to run up there to see me, and I wouldn't have to suffer with all the headaches. There is a real tension being in the city."

She turns to Clint, back now with Joshie, and asks whether he thinks she would have been a better artist had she grown up in Fort Chip. "I don't think your recognition and acknowledgement and success would have been as great," Clint says. "You may have been successful, but it would have taken a different form. I don't think you would have pursued your education as vigorously and to this high a level. And I don't think your work would be as sophisticated and as complex as it is, and have such a range of references. Because your travelling and your education and all those things in an urban setting contributed a great deal to what's in your paintings."

"Yeah, but then look at me inside," Jane says. "All the shit I had to go through and the pain I had to go through to get here. Does everyone have to suffer that much pain to get to this point?"

"Everyone suffers pain, Jane."

"That much?"

"Not everyone, certainly not. But what I'm saying is what's

happened to you is part of what you are. And, as an artist, it is reflected in your work."

JANE'S BLACKBOARD COLLAGES are dark – newspaper articles, old photographs of Indian children, painted ABC's, Cree symbols, Catholic prayers, Cree prayers, the scrawled face of the shaman. Across one collage, propped against the sunny west wall of her studio, Jane has painted the words: "And Jesus said, 'If you receive a little child in my name, then you receive me.' "

"INDIAN AFFAIRS ASKED us to do this one show and they wanted to have just Indian women in it. And I said, 'That's just further ghetto-izing Indian art. And double ghetto-izing it.'

"I made my name as an artist just as an artist, regardless of whether I was woman, Indian or whatever. I used to go under 'Jan' as an artist, 'cause I didn't even want to have a sex to it. 'Cause I had this feeling women were still getting the short shrift.

"Sometimes I'd even tell people I was male. I just did it for the fun of it. They put it on my driver's license, and I got away with it. It was the days when I had no boobs and I put my hair in a hat and I could look asexual. And I found out when I went to credit departments and applied for credit cards and said I was a male, I got totally different treatment. I even told one guy I'd had a sex-change operation." She laughs.

"Life is like that. You can do anything in life. I can have a mental sex change. Be a man one day and female the next." She laughs again.

"I guess, some people who know I'm Indian, they hold me in higher respect. They treat me with honor. And there's others who, for example one of my advisors at the U of A, she saw me for the first time in years. And she looked at me and said, 'Jeez, we haven't heard anything of you. Are you OK? What are you doing with yourself? Are you still painting?'

" 'Yeah,' I said, 'I'm doing the odd little painting.' And Tom, this guy who knows my whole history, he's standing beside me and after she left he just looked at me and he scratched his head. 'Jesus Christ, don't they know what this girl has accomplished since she left their school? I'm gonna go back and tell them.'

"And I said, 'No, don't. I love it when I see them on the street and they just think I'm nothing.' You lose your power if you let everyone see your guns.

"Some people just have this weird attitude. Like this guy at the Provincial Museum asked me, 'How did you get to university? How did you get there?' And I said, 'The bus.' " Jane laughs.

"It's like, in science we had all these Oriental guys going into pre-med. So everyone who had slanted eyes, we automatically thought they were geniuses. We stereotype all the time. So some people stereotype Indians as smart and spiritual, cultural. Other people stereotype us as dumb and drunk. Other people stereotype us as romantic. And other people stereotype us as unsophisticated and needing to have everything given to us.

"So what you do is, you figure out how you are being stereotyped. And then you just have a gas with it. I just let them believe whatever their stereotype is, and then you get back in at them through the art. The artist can get revenge, you know. Because I am an artist I can put in my triptych the face of the shaman, and it will get on the cover of school books and it will get hung in the National Gallery.

"And justice is done, right. Printmakers at the University of Alberta would love to have a solo show at the Edmonton Art Gallery. I don't think one of them has had a solo there yet. I've been ostracized from all their group shows, even though I had prints I would have loved to have shown with them. And lo and behold, now look who's having the first real nice show at the Edmonton Art Gallery. That was justice done. The spirits move in strange ways."

JANE IS FEATURED in an Edmonton Art Gallery *Exhibitions* magazine article accompanying her show Sweat Lodge Prints, thirteen dark etchings based on her spiritual cleansing in a sweat lodge out in the bush at age thirty-two. The article describes the sacred ritual; the lodge of arched willow branches and skins, the heated rocks, the humidity, rattles, drums, pipes, prayers.

"Participants sometimes have visions," the article says, a sign of the spirits' blessing, a sign of healing.

"Jane Ash Poitras saw a pale, blue flame," it says, "an archetypal image, she is told, that symbolizes purity and goodness."

"YOU KNOW, I was never angry about what happened to me. I guess it's like Grandma used to say, no one has it all. It would have been nice to have Grandma and at the same time grow up Indian. But I couldn't have both. I mean, having her and being able to share her spirituality and her philosophies which haven't hurt at all. Just look around, she must have instilled something in me.

"But when I found out about my people, I felt so relieved inside. I was really ecstatic. I think if I had never found out, I probably would be dead now. 'Cause once I found out who I was, it was just a big load off my mind. I just . . . I wasn't very happy in my childhood.

"I was really lonely. We were both lonely, Grandma and I, a lonely little girl and lonely old lady. I think I only stopped feeling lonely when I had my first child. That is one of the major high points in my life.

"Now, actually, I'd probably die for a bit of loneliness. To get a few minutes to myself is really precious. When you have kids, Mommy's everything. When Joshie comes home, he just runs to me, and he'll cling to me for the first hour." She laughs. "After that he'll cling to me every five minutes.

"I guess I never really felt like I had a childhood. But I'm having my childhood now. I think the spirits worked it that way. Most people have to go to work and punch the clock. I get paid to paste paper and do pictures and play art. Art was the most enjoyable thing when I was a child. And now I get all this space and it's all paid for by the art.

"And now I have my own little kids, my own little playmates. I don't have any brothers and sisters, but I've got just as good. I've got little Josh and little Eli. And I get to have them for the next twenty years."

JOSH, EVER INSISTENT. "Mommy, dee go home!"

Jane concedes. "OK, we'll go home." Coughing, she starts to pack up the gurgling Eli. She folds him into his snowsuit and zips up one leg. She stops then, and laughs.

"Those damn egg sandwiches. That's the one thing I remember about being with my real mom, back before Grandma got me. I remember my mother would take an egg and she would just soft boil it, and then she'd bust the yolk and put it between two big pieces of white bread. And it was the most delicious thing in the world.

"Grandma never did that. And I used to just love that."

I ask: "So, do you make it for yourself now?"

"Actually I don't. I don't." Jane seems surprised by her answer. "I don't know somehow . . . I don't know why. Maybe it's denial; maybe I don't think I deserve it now.

"Maybe that was my mom's special thing. Maybe it's just something that had to be made for me by my mom."

And, so saying, Jane Ash Poitras turns back to her baby son, Eli, and encloses him completely in his soft blue suit.

✪ CASEY

THE KISS IS slow. Wet. Rolling. Lots of jaw and tongue. Rene's girlfriends, all in heavy-metal mall hair and skinny jeans, cigarettes dangling from their hands like extra fingers, circle them, giggling. Casey pries Rene from his mouth – two moist suckers plopping apart. "Bye," he says. "Call me." Pushes back his New York Mets baseball cap and bangs his open fist on a locker door. Smiles at me, all white teeth and Paul McCartney eyes.

"Girls. I swear they *are* my life."

Casey Lewitson, fourteen, headed home from school.

"Hey, today's Thursday, isn't it."

"Yeah, today is Thursday."

"Right on, man. Party tomorrow at Dave's. Dave is my best friend. Known him for a few weeks. Since we went partying. That's when I met my girlfriend, eh, Rene. Oooh man, we went and got drunk that night. Got just wasted on a twenty-six of Silent Sam. We had such a good time. It was the best time I've ever had in my life – even though we did get a little bit worked over. Dave, he had the boots put to him. Man, it was funny.

"Ever since then, I'm going to Dave's house, seeing him and phoning girls. Not even our girlfriends. I just phone them 'cause, you know, they want to get talked to.

"I swear they're my life, man. I'm always phoning them, they're always phoning me. I go to Yellowhead Youth Centre yesterday, that group-home place, eh, just to go get my jacket from this chick. These girls go, 'Can we have your phone number?' It was like, 'Chill, man.' I was pretty cool. So I give a couple of them my phone number. I say, 'But don't be phoning every five minutes, 'cause I got other girls waiting on the list.'" He shows off his teeth.

A week later, Casey Lewitson has a new girlfriend and an old problem: he can't decide which babe to keep and which to dump. He had to ditch his last girlfriend, the one before Rene, because she was seeing some other guy. He got a few girls in the school to slap her out; he never beats up girls himself. This latest girlfriend lives in a shelter for teenage prostitutes. "But she ain't no hooker," he assures me. "I would never go out with no hooker, man; it would give me a bad rep.

"Besides, I would never go out with no girl with no bugs."

HOME IS A sixty-day receiving home in a small bedroom community outside Edmonton, a green split-level with detached two-car garage and a swim-blue pool. Red and yellow Christmas lights blink from two tall cedars flanking the front door. The living room is furnished in mossy green plush. Christmas presents swamp the couch, the floor, the dining room table. Five Pekinese buzz the back door when Casey and I walk in, two-and-a-half pairs of frantic bedroom slippers yipping at our ankles. The slippers sniff at us anxiously, then swerve en masse to strafe the kitchen table. The table is laden with a steaming ham, whipped potatoes, corn, salad, and three different pies – blueberry, cherry, pumpkin. Casey's "mom" is expecting us for dinner.

Mom is Marjorie Gaboury, a large woman with a rolling limp from a car accident that killed two of her friends and did its best to kill her, but marked her instead with an unshakeable faith in God. She follows the Pekinese to the door and pumps my hand warmly, distracted. Two of the boys, other foster kids, are still waiting to be picked up from school in Edmonton; her son must have forgotten and now she has to go into town to fetch them. But I will stay for dinner? I look too skinny; I could use some fattening up. She shrugs herself into her wooly winter coat. "Don't be shy. Dig right in."

"My mom, our mom right now, I don't know, I think she overspends on us," Casey tells me. "She leaves us for three days, she buys us over a hundred dollars worth of silver. Just, you know, for the hell of it. She bought me a silver eagle and, uh, the rest crosses. She spends, like, thousands of dollars at Christmas, and, like, she doesn't think we have enough. Like, we're her life, eh, 'cause, like, she don't have a husband or anything. Kids are her life.

"It's the best place I've ever been. Like, I was only there for two days already, and I was already calling her mom. Any kid that goes in there, like, she'd treat them just like her own son.

"She's cool. Yeah. Don't take no shit, either."

I have been issued a warning third-, fourth-, maybe twelfth-hand about Marjorie Gaboury. Hints that she cannot be believed nor trusted that she has sexually abused foster children in her care. The rumour-spreader says she herself cannot believe this. Marjorie is a troublemaker as far as Social Services is concerned; she encourages her foster kids to speak up, complain, even talk to the press about what happens to them in government care. That, the spreader said, probably explains the evil rumour, the nasty little warning.

I find it hard to believe the rumours about Marjorie Gaboury, this big, smiling woman in her brown fuzzy coat. I do not believe them. Casey calls her mom. When some other kids called her a fucking bitch, Casey loyally trashed their bikes. If she buys one of her own kids skis, they all get skis; she believes in treating them all the same.

Still, I find myself wondering. It is as though one has an obligation to wonder.

CASEY: "I DON'T have no status. I'm just Métis. I'd rather be black."

Me: "Why?"

Casey: " 'Cause blacks have jerry curls. That's the thing that's in right now. That's what I want."

Me: "Your hair is curly."

Casey: "No, no no no. I want it to look like that. Like little springs, springy like that. That's what I want man. To be black."

"I bug people 'cause they're Native. I go, 'You chug. You stupid wagon burner.' They go, 'What're you talking 'bout? Look at yourself.' I go, 'I know man, but I'm cool.' Like, I walk in here and I go, 'Look at the bunch of Indians, man. They're all drinking their Lysol.' And they go, 'What are you, man? Stupid Indian.'

"I hang around with a lot of Natives, though. You get used to them, you know. But any white boy that says anything, I go, 'Well yellow's OK, brown's OK, black's OK, green's OK, even gold's OK, so shut your mother-fucking face.' We all stand up and the guys go, 'OK, man, chill.' It's like brothers, man, like blacks, like they help each other out. We help each other out.

"The whites, they're all kind of spaced out. They are! Whites are really spaced, man. Say this guy is getting beaten up, eh. Whites just look, man. If that was an Indian, or black man, or a spic, every guy'd get off his ass, man, go right for it.

"But like, I don't want to be . . . I don't want to know nothing about no Indian background shit. I'm brought up in a white society, eh. I'm not brought up in Hobbema or drinking Lysol or shit like that. I was brought up not bad, not great, I suppose. Just OK."

TWO OF THE five teenagers living in this green split-level are Marjorie's own children. She tells me they, too, are Métis; her ex-husband was an Indian. Her son, whose red '69 Cougar is the pride of his life, is a nice kid who wears a Fuck-you tattoo on his biceps. He tells me high school years are the best years of your life, so he's taking his time. Of the three foster children, Casey is the veteran. This is the first time in government care for the other two, both apprehended because their parents beat them up. One, a pale boy with frizzy red hair, the most abused, has been with Marjorie for nine months. He shares a bedroom with Casey and has taped a collage of busty, tire-calendar babes and leathered-up heavy-metal chicks over his dresser. On the other side of the room, where Casey sleeps, are three framed magazine drawings of unicorns. Casey, it is clear, has not bothered to mark his territory.

According to Social Services regulations, Casey should be in this receiving home on a temporary basis – only until a more permanent placement is found. The regulations, out of practical necessity, are ignored. There is no more permanent place for him.

Casey has already lived with Marjorie for a month and a half. He will stay there for another three months, until his next court date and sentencing. He is up on charges for a "five-finger discount" after helping himself to some gold rope chains.

"I'm charged with possession of stolen property and theft over, and a mischief, but I think they're gonna drop that. They have me caught with theft for the one rope chain, right. 'Cause I had it in my hand. But the other is my own rope chain, right. I stuffed it in my ginch so that they wouldn't think I stole it, eh. The cop told me to strip, and he sees my rope chain there and, fuck, he takes it. He says he's charging me with possession but they don't have me on possession. Just because it's the same style of chain doesn't mean shit all."

Marjorie's eighteen-year-old daughter, Julie, tells a story about how one of the foster kids stole her car, a brand-new Omni, and ripped off all her money. Later Marjorie says it has been good for her kids to share their home with foster children, and asks Julie to tell me some of the lessons she's learned from the experience.

Julie says: "Keep your purse with you at all times. Keep your money in your bra, and sleep on it."

CASEY AND I drink coffee in a grimy Chinese restaurant across the street from his "Second-Chance" school. The coffee tastes like swill. He says it's better at lunch; if it's no good, kids make sure it's free. I ask him to tell me whatever he wants about his life. He starts by trying to list all the places he has lived.

"You end up where you end up, more or less by chance. See,

they take you to crisis after you've AWOLed, to the Social Services crisis unit downtown. And then they put you in this little room and they have to find placements. I got my choices. I go, 'Are they all out of town?' They go, 'Yeah. Can't find you any other place.' I say, 'OK, well, I'll go to this place.' And that's how I ended up where I am now. Just by luck I guess.

"Before Marjorie's, I was at Tower Road group home. It's real burnt. Stupid. And I decided to leave so I went AWOL. Went for a little bit of a party, vacation, whatever you want to call it. AWOLed for a month. I went to Calgary for two weeks. Partied it up there. Wore cowboy boots and hat. I had a good time, man."

His "man" comes out in three syllables. "Ma-a-an."

"And then, uh, I got bored out there so I came back. It was like, 'See, well, I'm a little bit hungry here. I don't know what day it is, you know, feeling a bit tired.' So I thought, 'What the hell else, Social Services wants me back,' he shrugs, " 'so I'll go back.' "

"And before Tower Road," there is a long pause, "Yellowhead. Yellowhead Youth Centre. It's all in a big complex and they have a Social Services secure unit there and a receiving unit. A loony bin. Recreation.

"Yellowhead, it's real burnt. I AWOLed from there, too. It's easy to get out. You're not locked in there except when you're in secure treatment. You get stuck in secure treatment if you are suicidal, high-risk AWOL, damage to other people or to yourself. Stuff like that.

"I was on a recognizance order – it's an order you keep the peace, good behavior. I said, 'Screw this man, I'm getting outta here.' I went through my window. A locked window. I took the whole window apart, took every piece off it. You know there's this black stuff around it, little black sticky stuff, keeps the window in there? Well, it was during the summer and it was on the south side so I went in there and took a pen and picked it all out. I pulled the whole pane out, poked my head out. AWOLed from there too.

"Before that I was in YDC. I always get put in YDC. I've been put in YDC, Youth Detention Centre, twice, three times. It's a lock-up, right. That's where I was before Yellowhead.

"The first time I was in YDC, uh, let's see, I went in for breach of recognizance." He shakes his head. "No, the first time it was break and enter, and I got another recognizance order. I broke that so I was back in for another three months. I went to court and I got off on," he laughs, proud of his luck, "on twelve-months' probation. It was just last year.

"The break-and-enter wasn't my first charge, eh. My first charge, I had attempted assault with a deadly weapon. Twelve years old. And it wasn't true, man. They found me guilty, eh. But I got off. Since it was my first offence they said, uh, I'm absolute discharge.

"They said I supposedly tried hitting this staff member with a metal bar about *that* long, about two-feet long, and it's solid, solid iron. But I was just sitting there tapping it on the ground, swinging it around when she was trying to give me all her little lecture, eh. 'You're being bad,' and all this shit. 'Ah, fuck you.' "

He smiles at me, a handsome kid who smiles often and often for no reason. His smiles never reach his eyes. The eyes are dark and flat, their only expression a fractured anxiety.

"Before Yellowhead . . . I'm working backwards here. Maybe I'll start at the beginning. 'Cause otherwise I'm going to get confused."

"I WAS BORN in Edmonton. Charles Camsell General Hospital. February 20, 1976. So. And I lived with my parents. Six months, no, three or six months later, Social Services came and apprehended me from my parents. And I went to a foster home, to a foster home, to a foster home, you know, and so on down the line.

"And then I stayed at this one place, man, and that's where I started getting into trouble. I used to like bugging teachers, you know doing little petty acts like chucking rocks at windows or stuff, you know. So they kept on moving me out.

"The first group home I went to is, uh, Children's Treatment

Centre. CTC. When I went there, I was around seven or eight. Like, before that, I'd just been moving and moving, eh.

"I mostly just remember one place. They were pretty cool 'cept they gave me up 'cause they moved to Ontario. I said, 'Fine man.' I was only, like, six, seven. I really didn't know what the hell was going on. So they moved me away. That's when I went to that CTC." He sucks back the dregs of his coffee. "They had some retard kid in their house, so I didn't like it very much anyway."

"And, uh, I lived at CTC for a couple of years and then, like, they go, 'To get out of here you have to be good' and all this, you know, like all their little psychiatric shit. So I straightened out my act a little bit and got out of there into a home which was foster home for future adoption, eh. So OK, I thought that was cool.

"And then we moved and I met some new guys. I started getting in shit. Stealing all their alcohol and being a real bad-ass kid. I'm bad. Well, I'm not bad, my actions are. That's what they all tell me. They told me to go see, well, they take me to psychiatrists and these psychiatrists, they expect to change you and shit like this. And it's like, 'Get these drugs away from me,' and shit like this, 'so I can lead my own life.'

"Anyway, this foster home for adoption kicked me out 'cause I was a runaway and shit like that. I went back to the CTC for a couple more years.

"And, uh, I used to get in shit there too. And then I guess this teacher, he felt sorry for me 'cause I lived in a group home and shit like this, so he took me in. And the same kind of shit happened. They were saying I stole all their stuff and shit like this. And I'm not going to mention no names because, like, they might read this book.

"I didn't do it. I told them all I took was the smokes. That was it. And they were saying I tried raping their daughters and shit like this. There was this inspector and everyone on this. And they were saying I stole a bunch of their jewelry and shit like this. I go, 'Yeah, yeah whatever.'

"They kicked me out and I went to another group home. Stayed there for awhile, you know, got things back together. Then, uh, 'Sick of this place man, I gotta leave,' so I left.

"Waited till I was discharged, went back to Social Services, found me a new place just down the road. And, uh, it was good there, even though they didn't give me a lot of money or anything, eh. Let me stay out, do whatever I wanted for awhile. I wasn't going to school at the time. I'd come home late at night really drunk or stoned. They'd, oh, 'Go downstairs to your room' or whatever, eh. And then they kicked me out 'cause I had a fight with their nineteen-year-old son. They said, 'You're outta here.' OK. 'Fine. I don't want to be here anyway.'

"That's when I started getting in a lot of shit. I used to hang out with some guys from Dickinsfield area and we used to go looking for people just for fights and looking to steal bikes. So then I got charged with a bike. Four months probation.

"After that I went to Opal Smith's house. She's a receiving home. Sixty days. I had a good time there. She understands, eh. She sits you down and talks it out with you. And to keep the relationship there, you kind of write letters, you know, personal letters every night. How was your day and shit like that.

"And then I met this guy on the way to school and he goes, 'You want to get stoned, man?' I say, 'It's cool, man.' So we got baked, really fried, eh. And, uh, you know, 'We need some more of this, right. Let's think of somewhere to get some money.' And he goes, 'I know this good house, eh.' So we go to this house and take this hockey stick and bust the window. We go in and take all their liquor and shit like that, rings, VCR, stuff like that, eh. Clothes. And then I guess the guy who lived there dropped his wallet or something and I found it.

"I come home really fried, eh. This kind of English guy I shared a room with, eh, I start talking to him. I go, 'Hey man, do you want to go out for supper tonight?' He goes, 'With what money?' And I pull out this wad of money and he goes, 'Holy shit. Where did you get that?'

" 'Oh, from a couple of friends.'

"And I guess Opal overheard us talking. She phoned the police, eh. And, uh, I had a hard time cause I had built a relationship there, eh.

"I got put in the YDC then for awhile. She got me out on recognizance order in court, eh. I went back, I breached it.

"They put me back in the YDC for a couple of months and I got back out, breached, breached another recognizance order, got put back in there.

"And then they thought I was loony or something so they put me in Alberta Hospital. And, uh, Dr. Brand gave his little report to court. He says I showed no remorse. I go, 'Why the hell should I show you some remorse.' " He smiles.

"I got off with twelve months probation. Then I took a fling and I left for a couple days and shit. And I partied, got caught. And that's how I ended up here."

MARJORIE STARTED OUT as a full-time foster mother for one of her daughter's friends whose parents starved him. When he moved into Marjorie's home, he was 5'9" tall and eighty pounds. He used to steal food from the kitchen and hoard it under his bed at night. He was afraid that when he woke up the next morning, there would be nothing there.

She says a lot of the kids are like that. If there is food around, they eat until it's gone. They believe that if they don't get it now, they will never have another chance.

She says she has seen lots of kids like Casey who outstay the Social Services' regulations and are taken out of her home, and then run back to her, running away from their new placements in forty-below weather, walking miles, sometimes, back to her from the city. And then she has to phone Social Services to come pick them up again.

She starts to cry, small, gulping sobs. Her wide shoulders heave. She says Social Services tells her she shouldn't be running a foster home because what she provides is not real life. When kids run back to her, she says, Social Services tells her to explain to them they can't look back. That her home was only temporary. Just "a way station on their road to a bigger and better life."

"HOW IS YOUR social worker, Casey? Do you like her?
"She's OK. I think my other one was best."
"Do they change the social workers a lot?"
"They change 'em, you know. I had Alice for a year. I've had Joyce ever since September. I had about four or five in my life. I'm going to keep counting them. I've been too many places, you know. Too many things have happened. I just think that if I'm gonna be in so many places, man, why should I take everything so seriously, man? When you live in so many places, you don't really care. You just think it's like, I'm here and that's it. I'm here to be living here, to have a roof over my head, to have food. That's it, man. The rest of the time, fuck it. That's it. That's all I think, man. It's in my head."
"How many places have you been in? Have you ever counted?"
"Twenty-three, twenty-four. Round it off to about twenty-five, thirty.
"I don't care no more. I used to get pissed off at Social Services. Now I say, 'Screw this, man, why get pissed off?' I got my friends, and now it's, like, I've got a mother, Marjorie, who cares. I got a brother again. It's cool, man. It's cool.
"I think my life's OK right now. My whole life has been the shits in the past before. I take it, every new place is a new start. You can't really, like, just total total total forget about it. You put it in the back of your mind. It's still there, but you're never gonna see these people again anyway, so what's the use.
"Except for the mom I'm living with now. I don't think I will, like, stop contacting her when I leave. Or like Opal, you know, I haven't stopped contacting her.
"Opal right now, she won't let me over there because she's got

good-looking girls over there. She goes, 'I don't trust you to keep your dick in your pants.' Like, 'Right, man.'" And he rolls his eyes.

THE LAST FOSTER kid Marjorie Gaboury had was Eric, sixteen. Eric was taken from her home to live with a youth worker, who eventually kicked him out. Eric called a reporter and told her, drunkenly, that he had been on the streets for three weeks, that his social worker refused to find him a placement and had suggested, instead, that he go to the Youth Emergency Shelter.

"A shelter isn't a home," Eric was quoted as saying. "I wouldn't want to live there. I need a real place to live."

He has been a government ward for twelve years. In that time, he said, he's been in forty different homes and institutions. He admitted he was no angel; he is in the Northside Bloods, one of Edmonton's posses, street gangs.

"You name it, I've done it," he said. "Right now, I'm just waiting for the day. Maybe I'll straighten out in time, but if something bad happens, like jail, then that's my life, and it's blown."

The newspaper story prompted angry letters from Social Services spokesmen, who said rules of confidentiality prevented them from telling their side. They questioned whose interests were served by the story: the child whose past may come back to haunt him, or the paper's. The then-Social Services Minister Connie Osterman, questioned on the incident, said kids in foster care are sometimes left to fend for themselves after the department has "tried everything" to help them.

A month after the newspaper articles ran, Eric was in jail.

"ERIC, HE'S WILD, man. He's, I don't know, too streetwise for me." Casey yawns. "You know, tough, and macho attitude. 'Nothing hurts me,' and shit like this, eh. We all know, we all know he wants to come home, eh. He wants to come home for Christmas and shit. We know that, but he doesn't want to admit he's soft. Soft, soft underneath."

"And how about you? Are you soft underneath?"

"Well, I show it more often than a lot of people I know, eh. Shit, it's like being with my parents, man. It's been too long so it's just like, why in the hell should I care about them? 'You left me, man, it's OK.' My brother said he'd kill our parents if he ever saw them." Casey laughs.

"Yeah, I know who my brother and my sister are. She's older than me, fifteen. He's seventeen. I see him sometimes. When I need help. There's another two of them that are lost. We don't know where the hell they are. They were living with my grandmother, but I don't even know who that is. I don't even know who my parents are.

"But I have a brother who lives by himself. I found out he was my brother through social workers and stuff. I have a sister that lives in a foster family out in Leduc. I don't know, I don't think she wants to see me or anything. Her family says I'm, uh, what do they say, I'm not a good influence." He shrugs. "I'm like, 'Yeah, OK.'"

Casey parties with Dave on Friday night, on Saturday night. Sunday night he goes with his brother to a pool hall over by the Molson Brewery. "Quite a classy place for a pool hall," Casey says.

For some reason Casey cannot or will not explain, his brother abandons him there. Casey follows his brother home. He rings his doorbell. His brother pretends he isn't in. Casey walks back to the pool hall and spends the night there, sitting up in a chair, watching TV.

When I ask him why his brother did this to him, Casey says his brother figures he is a bad influence. I ask him how his brother figures that. He says his brother must have gotten it somehow from social workers, and from everybody else.

DRIVING CASEY HOME from school, he asks me to take a detour to Dave's place. Dave's place is a grey concrete walk-up trimmed in blond brick and brown wood, just across the subway tracks from a car wash and trailer park.

"Dave lives in the same apartments that I lived in when I was born. I just noticed that yesterday."

"Why are we going here?"

"I gotta pick up a tape. OK, you gotta hang a left on 142 Street."

"So how do you know this is where you were born?"

"I saw my birth certificate once." He yawns. "It has the address."

THROUGHOUT DINNER MARJORIE'S phone rings constantly. Casey lunges for the receiver every time. It is order night for Marjorie's home-cosmetic business and she warns Casey to stay off the phone. He waits until she's out in the backyard taking the five Pekinese for a whizz. Then he calls his girlfriend. He tells her he's not going to let her drink this weekend. She gets too sick. He asks her what she is going to buy him this weekend. He asks her to come over to do his dishes for him. If she does, he says, he will pay her ten bucks.

"SCHOOL IS DEADLY. It's awesome. If it wasn't for this school, I wouldn't have met my girlfriend. Seriously. And like, you work at your own pace. I don't think I could ever go to a normal high school 'cause they push you, man. In this school it's like, 'Go ahead. You're here for yourself, so we're just here to watch over you and help you out a bit.'

"The other school, it's like, 'Work! Work!' 'Cause I've gone, I went to a lot of schools. I think the best school was St. Mary's, up there on the north side of the city. Really straightened me out a bit. It was like a bunch of priests that told me what to do and they kick your ass. They have the right to kick my ass when I'm there, eh. So I said, 'I'm not screwing around here.'

"So you wish more people kicked your ass?"

"No. I like the way I am now. I'd like to live where I am right now. Forever. Cause she won't give me, she won't give me shit if

134

I'm drunk. She says she'd rather I was drunk than stoned but . . . sometimes it happens. You know, somebody pulls out this joint, you're already drunk. 'Well fuck man, let's go smoke this joint.' And you go smoke.

"That's what we did yesterday. Yesterday at lunch we, uh, went and had a couple of joints and stuff like that, eh. And then we got really baked in school. Well, Tuesday we were baked in school. I come in and I got kicked out of school for a day 'cause I almost punched John, the teacher, in the head. He goes to escort me out of classroom, 'cause I wouldn't do what he told me. I go, 'Fuck you, man.' I took a swing at him. Then he goes, 'OK, then just sit down and work.' I go to him, I just said to everyone, 'Did you see that? How scared he is of me now?' " And Casey laughs.

"MY FAVORITE SPORT is playing soccer. That's what I want to be. Professional soccer player. But if I don't, they're always saying if you don't go to school, then you don't get a scholarship. I go, 'I'll inherit money. I'll make it. I have a straight life. I'll inherit it.' And they go, 'Where you gonna inherit your money?' And I go, 'My brother's will.' " He smiles. "I'll sell his ghetto blaster.

"I want to go to Europe. You make money there, man, money. You know how soft Canadian soccer is? You don't make money in that. You make about five hundred bucks a game, that's it. In twelve games.

"So, well, I plan on finishing school sometime. Then just, you know. See if Social Services will pay for my schooling, college, or stuff like that, eh. And go to university and get a scholarship for Europe or something, soccer. But I want to be an MD or something. I want to do something that makes me look rich. Like wear a lot of gold, wear all Adidas, Pumas, you know, all the rich clothes.

"I love gold. If I could own a jewelry store, I'd just wear every gold chain. Especially them rope chains. Gold makes you look rich. Silver makes you look a little bit more businesslike, you know, you gotta wear them with nice shirts and stuff like that.

"Why do I want to be rich? Because you're rich, you get the girls.

"Girls are my life. I swear they are."

I DRIVE CASEY to his probation office on the upper floor of a north-end shopping mall. He has to check in once every two weeks for twelve months on the theft-over and possession convictions for the stolen gold, the VCRs, the clothing. He tells me his probation officer is a bitch.

There are two other kids in the waiting room, one a skinny guy with a red bandanna tied over the knee of his jeans and fake handcuffs dangling from the hem of his jacket. He and Casey shoot the shit; it turns out they went out with the same girl for awhile. Casey asks the other, a hulking guy in a football jacket, whether there are any posses in his high school.

"Ya," the hulk says. "We got 'em. But we don't like 'em, eh. They don't do anything and if they did the football players would pound them out."

Gangs are really cool, Casey says. He asks me if I've seen the movie *Colors*. He says his jacket, his red, white and blue Adidas jacket, is the colours of one of the gangs in the city.

He advises me that you have to be careful on the weekends. "You can't wear your Adidas or your Pumas stuff, eh, because you'll get rolled for it by other posses.

"I used to be in a gang. I am right now. Youth posse. Have you heard about them? That's what I'm in. Eric, he's a Northside Blood, eh. Him and his Abbotsfield boys, eh, are real tough.

"I am trying to think of a name for my posse. I was thinking of a better one like, like Hard White Posse or something. Macho Man Posse or something like that.

"What does my posse do? Go rush people. See, you shoulda seen, there was this single guy walking down the street with a nice Adidas. I walk over there, 'So Holmes man, that's a nice Adidas you

136

have there.' He's like, 'Yeah, so?' I go, 'I want your Adidas.' He goes, 'No man.' I go, 'I want your fucking Adidas, man.' He's like, 'No no no.'

"And I go, I start shaking him, eh. And then some guy, one of the guys they go down on their hands and knees behind him. I push him and he just falls, eh.

"You get down, you beat him up. Work his face over, eh. Take his Adidas.

"I think trouble just finds me, I guess. I think trouble finds me, that's the way I look at it. Trouble finds me. Sometimes I go looking for it, but I think trouble finds me a lot of the time."

MARJORIE'S PREDICTION FOR Casey is that he will move through the round of foster homes and youth detention centers until he is eighteen, whereupon the system will boot him out – or he will end up in prison. She says Casey will be quite resigned to being in prison. If that is what life deals him, that is what he will take.

"I NEVER COMMIT B and E's with more than one person 'cept for one that we just did recently. The cops don't even know it's us. Fourteen hundred dollars in cash from the Social Services place. It was pretty funny.

"I made sure I was straight, because I knew the money was in there somewhere. The front window was already busted. There was a little hole in there. You could put your arm in and unlock the door. And it has a sign, 'Please walk right in.' So we walked right in, tore the place apart.

"I was sitting there prying apart this filing cabinet. You know those ones where you open it up and fold out and the files are hanging? Those kind there. We ripped the thing off, there's files in there, we ripped the next thing off, there's files in there. The last one was a real hard bitch on the bottom, a real bitch to get open.

So we took a screwdriver, eh, poked a bunch of holes in it until there was a big hole in it about *this* big.

"Pssh. You use your brains, man. You don't know how much brains you got until something like that happens, eh. Until you're in a fine mess.

"Then I see this money box, eh. I noticed it first, so I took it. I heard it jingle, jingle. Yeah! I opened it up, took all the change, looked in the bottom. Rolls of twenties, man, and tens and ones. So we just took all those and we screwed off.

"I had a good night, man. We slept in The Westin. We had a good night that night. There was three of us. We split fourteen hundred dollars evenly. Put two hundred dollars into pool. Billiards hall up by 23rd and 105th. I made a hundred bucks out of it, so we only lost a hundred bucks.

"I was making big bets there, man. I was laying down fifty bucks at a time.

"I'm a real bad-ass kid. I've always been that way."

"Are you proud of that?"

"Sometimes when I do a good scam. I was proud of that one scam at the Social Services' office. Really proud of it."

"Do you ever feel bad about doing it?"

"No. I don't know the person. Like, I don't know anybody, man."

"Would it make any difference if you did?"

"Yeah, a little bit."

"Do other kids respect you because you are a bad-ass kid?"

"Some of them. Some of them are real shitting scared of me, man. I'm scared of Eric, man. He's nutso. I just think I'm bad though. I do too many bad things. I go out on the weekend just to get drunk, and stoned. And I think, 'Well, well, we run out of money, man, we'll just do a scam.' Like, that's the way I think. Definitely. Maybe that's why they sent me to Alberta Hospital. I'm a money-aholic, man. I'm addicted."

"LIFE IS A joke. Well, it is. Well, it's not really a joke, it's just, life isn't for work, it's to have fun. That's the way I look at it. You don't work, man, you just party. And when it gets down to real business, like money business, it's time to work. You know, it's sorta fucked, really screwed up. But it is kind of a joke to me. It's like, you know, take life calmly. Let's go, let's do this.

"I have fun with life. Yeah. I like screwing up people's brains. I do, man. I like screwing up psychiatrists' minds, that's the best. They are easy to screw up. They are, man. Psychiatrists are dumb. They're dumb. 'Cause they use all this scientific shit on you, and you don't even know what the hell they're talking about. You're sitting there, they're sitting there talking. 'Oh, you're an emotionally disturbed kid.'

" 'Kay whatever, man, whatever you say. Like, fuck you, man. I don't have to listen to this shit.'

"I don't feel like I'm an emotionally disturbed kid. No, I'm just, I'm a normal person, man. I'm a normal everyday person that wants to have fun with his life, not no stingy old asshole. Money is, money is like a hole in my pocket. Just whenever I get it, it just goes."

IN GROUP HOMES the workers don't care if kids come in wearing something new, Marjorie says. Don't care if they're wearing gold chains down to their yin yang. Whereas if Casey comes in wearing something new, she wants to know where he got it. Did he steal it? If he stole it, she makes him take it back.

She has been to court with Casey three times. He is supposed to be seeing a psychologist. He refuses to go. She doesn't make him go.

"So they sent you to Alberta Hospital for awhile?"
"Two, three weeks."
"And what was this thing you were in?"
"Assessment."
"And how come they sent you out there?"

"They thought I was crazy, man. I thought, 'Well it will help me get out of jail.' "

"What did you do that they sent you there?"

"I don't know." He laughs. "I didn't do nothing. Being locked up makes you want to be suicidal, man. It does. I went and tied myself up." He laughs again. "It was pretty funny. They wanted to stick this needle in me and I wanted to freak. I said, 'No, you're not sticking no needle in me, man.' I was just freaking out on 'em, eh. They were gonna put me, they roll you up in a sheet, right. Poke a needle in your ass and you fall asleep for twenty-four hours. But they didn't. I just calmed down."

"So you threatened to kill yourself? That's why they. . . . "

"No, I wasn't gonna kill myself. I was just joking. I like life too much. Life's too fun to kill yourself."

MARJORIE'S DAUGHTER, JULIE, and her boyfriend, Brian, sit down to eat. The boyfriend wears a black ponytail, spiked-up bangs, black spider-stomper boots, black ripped sweater. He's so cool he's beyond speech. Julie's hair is dyed jet black and permed into coils. She wears a black sweatshirt, black pointy boots, a black jacket, and powdered white skin. She is friendly and voluble.

Brian is from Chicago. He and she have been pen pals since they were twelve. They fell in love a year ago when he came to visit for the first time. He's here again because he's having trouble with his old man. His father beats him up, Julie says. Beats him up all the time.

Julie and Brian are wiped out. They and some friends just spent six hours with the Ouija board. It was wild, she says. "You should have seen all the spirits that we got. We tried to get Elvis, eh, but the spirits told us he wasn't in." She laughs. "But they told us he is dead. He is, like, def-in-ite-ly dead.

"Then one of the people there, she had this friend, eh, who got killed when she was nine. Got run over on her bicycle. So we asked if we could speak to the girl who got killed. And like, this friend of ours, she was really, really freaked out because the Ouija board repeated back the same words that were the last words she spoke to her friend. The exact same words. Everybody freaked right out."

"I bet ya she cheated," the frizzy-haired foster kid says.

"Nah, she didn't cheat, her hands weren't even on the board. It was just me. I wasn't even pushing. I just was resting there, my fingers steady on the plastic heart, the steel needle in centre pointing the way." She demonstrates, her forefingers and thumbs joined together, moving through the air. "A." Slide. Halt. Wait. Slide, slide, slide. "C." Pause. "C."

"I was not pushing."

Casey stands splay-legged in the middle of the kitchen floor, his New York Mets baseball cap pushed back on his curls. He doesn't give a shit about baseball he told me; he wears the hat because New York is the home of rappers. Blacks. He has been running up and down the stairs, torn between the computer game in the basement where he is the high scorer – the champion killer of endless eel-like creatures and the occasional Frankenstein – and this conversation.

He breaks in. "Next time ask for my dad, eh. Darcy James Lewitson. Darcy James Lewitson."

Then he laughs. It is typical of his laugh, hesitant, unconvincing. When he laughs he checks out the faces around the table for clues. Is this funny? Is this what it means to be funny? His eyes are flat. He laughs and his eyes are constant – huge, dark, and expressionless.

"I figure he's dead. I figure my dad's with the spirits. I figure he must be dead."

Julie ignores him and turns to her mother. "It freaks me out, you know. Like, it seems to me the spirits were telling us that they are lonely. That it's dark in there and they can't see anything and they can't talk to anybody else. Like, I have this vision of all these souls lined up in shoe boxes. It was really sad. It's really sad."

She asks her mom, can she phone her aunt in California? Her aunt is an ordained minister of a spiritualist church in Montreal and does exorcisms on houses. Her aunt could tell her about the spirits, Julie says, whether they are lined up in shoe boxes, and whether they are sad.

Marjorie explains she believes the spirits of suicides are the only ones who get caught in limbo. This is a belief her sister, the California spiritualist, shares, she says.

Casey interrupts, loud, impatient, wearing his nervous smile. "No, I mean it, man." He laughs again. "See what he has to say, man." Ma-a-an. "I want to know what my dad has to say."

"IF YOU HAD something different, what would it be?"

"About my life?"

"Yeah."

"I would have been born by better parents, you know, like not no alcoholics."

"Is that why they took you away from your parents, 'cause they were alcoholics?"

"I guess so. But there was five of us." He yawns. "I guess my parents were real boozers. So."

And then he laughs. "I don't really give a shit. To say the least."

DRIVING CASEY HOME from school he asks if I think Social Services has an insurance policy on him. A life insurance policy. He wants to know because he's wondering how much money he'd get if he chopped off part of a finger. He figures that if he chops off just part, the insurance company will consider it loss of his whole finger, and he'll get a big pile of money for it.

Later, while I am standing at the kitchen counter carving the ham Marjorie has set out for dinner, Casey walks up beside me. He watches for a moment, silent, as thick slices of running, pink meat fall onto the platter. Then, like lightning, he sticks his finger under the knife's descending blade.

And he laughs. Flat. Dark. Expressionless. Casey laughs.

✿ JOKES

THE JOKER IS a woman. She is beautiful, with strummed hair and pulpy lips, and her face is on TV. She tells the joke to other reporters – print, TV and radio, male and female. It is one of several she tells, some dirty, some not. She is on a roll.

The other reporters, the regulars at Edmonton's city hall, are grateful she is there and rolling; the mayor is late for their scrum and they are bored, edgy, sick of each other and each other's stories. She is a distraction, a curiosity, like a pretty aunt or stranger who arrives from out of town carrying exotic handbags and chocolate bars, smelling like mystery and another life, to break the tedium of a hot afternoon.

It has been a long, dry summer. The city-hall regulars are cranky. The only story their papers and stations have been interested in for weeks is cats. The Edmonton cat debate – prompted by a north-end alderman who received a complaint about kitty defecation in a sand box – drags on and on. The people are polarized; cat lovers want their felines free, the anti-cat faction says keep them on chains.

The mayor, who is anti-cat, tries to steer clear of the raging controversy. The Board of Health is called in. A pro-cat activist is threatened by rabid anti-catists, and he moves his family out of the city. The item attracts national attention. CBC does a feature.

Later the mayor, at a reception held to honor his civic contribution will say, privately: "Why do you want to write a book about Indians? Nobody gives a shit about Indians."

The media room is cramped, smoky. The pretty joker perches on the coffee table and performs. When she finishes the joke she laughs, clapping her hands daintily on her knees.

The joke she tells goes:
"What's the definition of confusion?"
"Father's Day on the reserve."

THE JOKER IS an editor, white, male, and overweight. He is only in town for a few days; he is in between jobs and on his way to the coast. He shows up at a Christmas party. He drinks several beers. He calls Indian women "smoked meat." It is late in the evening; the band is into its third rendition of Blue Suede Shoes and nobody seems to care.

The jokes the editor tells go:
"What did the Indian say the first time he saw pizza?"
"Who puked on my bannock."
"What do you call an Indian with an IQ of one hundred?"
"A tribe."
"Little Running Bear is talking to a friend. 'My mother saw a small bear running by the window the moment of my birth,' he says. 'What did your mother see, Two Dogs Shitting?' "

THE JOKER IS a newspaper reporter, Métis, female, with Tina Turner cheekbones. She tells the joke to another reporter, white, female, in the middle of the newsroom.

The newsroom is trashy. Printouts, press releases, lunch bags are piled in grey drifts throughout the room. Squashed ketchup packets and the salty residue of cafeteria lunches are abandoned on computer terminals; the islands in between are stacked high with old clippings and empty Styrofoam cups.

Later the Métis reporter will fill out a sexual-harassment survey, and tell the white reporter a story. One day one of their bosses, a man, white, drunk, came up to her and said: "So. Tell me. Is it true Indian women have no pubic hair?"

The Métis reporter, on her way to buy french fries with grrey-vee, as the Scandinavian cook who works in the paper's dingy kitchen calls it, and the white reporter, coming from the can, cross paths. The cop radio sputters. The photo-assignment editor's radio sputters. Telephones ring.

The joker stops. She raises her hand and points a finger at the white reporter. She says, "Hey. I got a joke for you."

The joke she tells goes:

"What do you get when you cross an octopus with an Indian woman?"

"I don't know either, but it sure as hell can play bingo."

THE JOKER IS Ricky, Treaty, male. Ricky is sitting on a green velvet couch in his cousin's living room on the Enoch Reserve the same day he is released from the Edmonton Maximum Institution. He has just served five years. Six months in the Max, four and a half years in Drumheller. Drumheller was better, Ricky says. There he did carpentry. In the Max there's nothing to do.

The TV is on. A blond woman on *The Days of Our Lives* wants her son back. She can see it in his eyes, she says. Nothing will stop her. A man in a suit shakes her by the shoulders. "Listen to you," he says, disgusted. "Just listen to you."

Ricky has a silver stud in his left ear. The front of his hair is cut like an accountant's; the back twists away in a skinny braid. His face is freckled and he wears glasses with silver aviator frames. His cousin, who has her own five kids living with her, plus a woman with two kids who was kicked out of her reserve house, plus a guy named Sky with nowhere else to go, has said Ricky can stay if he wants. The cousin has just wallpapered the feature wall in her living room black; she plans to do the same to the wood-panelled wall in the kitchen. Ricky nods his approval. He watches the soap. One foot jigs.

Ricky hardly got any sleep last night, he says, his last night in jail. "Cleaned up my house and then I just sat there, man. Just sat there. Waiting. Waiting to go." He laughs.

"There's a fat guy nicknamed Chug-a-Lug in that prison. Chug-a-Lug, he holds aerobic classes for the guys. He told all the guys he was pregnant." Ricky grins. "Then he told them he had an abortion."

"Ya Chug-a-Lug, she's got a nice shape," the cousin says. "A nice womanly shape. Nice fat thighs."

The cousin is painting her nails pink; she is getting ready to go to a prison Round Dance. She says her guy in there, Danny, has found another woman. A thirty-four-year-old. A counsellor with Native Counselling Services. "I'm the best thing that ever happened to that guy," the cousin says. "I guess he's just not ready for something good." She laughs. "At least I've still got my chief. He's not so good-looking, but he's pretty good to me, eh."

The cousin shakes her hands in the air to dry her nails. A heavy silver chain clinks on her wrist. She has tattoos hand-pinned in blue ink on every finger. Her left hand, from index to baby finger, reads LOVE. Her right hand reads HATE. As she shakes her nails dry, LOVE and HATE flicker around her face. She says, "Last time I was in visiting him, eh, there was these two making out right there behind the piano. Right in the middle of the visiting room."

The cousin used to be a drinker. She used to want to kill herself. But she's sober now. She laughs a lot, and takes good care of her kids. Her father lives on the reserve too. He used to travel with the Royal American Shows, running the Ferris wheel and the Zipper. No one says much about her mother.

The cousin tells a story about another guy just out of the Max. "He's fun-nee too, eh. Like Chug-a-Lug. I was driving him downtown through the drag and we drove by one of them hook-ees. He flings his hair over his shoulder" – the cousin waves one pink-tipped hand over her shoulder – "like so and he says, 'I gotta chase that girl away. She's doing business on my corner.' "

Everybody laughs. The cousin screws on the nail-polish cap, holding her fingers out straight so her enamel won't smear. She asks Ricky whether Chug-a-Lug still swallows spoons and knives. Ricky says, "Ya. Ya, I think so. He does it all the time inside. Trying to do himself in."

Ricky remembers Chug-a-Lug from the street when he was a kid. "My mom used to sell him junk," he says. Ricky hangs his hands, joined at the wrist, between his knees. Ricky says his sister, two years older than him, died last year from cranking junk. Twenty-eight she was, he says. Maybe twenty-nine.

"The prison wouldn't let me out for her funeral. They told me I was a security risk. Here I am in a medium-security prison and they tell me I'm a security risk. Suspected of trafficking. Even though I don't have a single drug beef on my record.

"I used to crank too, eh. You know what I mean by cranking? Started about, oh, when I was eleven. When I got picked up the prison doctor told me if I'da kept going for another month I'd be dead. I was full of all of this chalk stuff, the doctor said. In my lungs and places. It gets around your heart too."

What gets around your heart, too, is the chalky residue from "poor man's heroin" – a combination of Talwin, a lozenge-shaped prescription drug for low-back pain, and Ritalin, a drug prescribed to tether hyperactive children. Sucked into a needle through a straw. Injected. An upper and a downer, so that the high lasts and lasts.

Talwin is harder to get on Edmonton streets these days and a set, a one-on-one that used to sell for $45, now goes for $100. An undercover drug cop with a 1970s shag and a Scots accent says Ts and Rs are not for poor men anymore. A hooker he knows does Ts and Rs. Like lots of junkies her body is covered in ulcerating sores. Her scabs rub off on her covers at night. White chalk rises to the surface of her skin and cakes onto her sheets. The cop says in autopsies T and R junkies' lungs look like pale pink saucers of cotton-batting. When the junkies get desperate enough, they start shooting up in the veins behind their eyes. The cop says, "Can you imagine having the guts to do that? Can you imagine?"

The street replacement for Talwin, a little round orange pill itself called MS Cotton, burns in the veins. So what with the burning, plus the price of Talwin, street people are starting to crank coke instead. That is, if they crank at all, the cop says. Some smoke it. They're afraid, he says. Afraid they'll shoot up and five minutes later end up doing the chicken. That's what he calls death. "Doing the chicken."

"Ya, I'd crank anything," Ricky says. "Depends on what kind of high I was on, you know."

The cousin's kids come home. One of her five-year-old twins, the taller and braver one, remembers Ricky even though the boy was only two when Ricky went to prison. He leaps on Ricky's lap and calls him "Uncle." The boy's left ear is pierced with a gold sleeper. He hands Ricky a red sucker from his Halloween suitcase. When his twin brother comes in he says, "That's your uncle." The little twin shakes his head. He runs over to the couch and hides behind his mother. He won't move off the couch.

Later, out in the yard, the big twin falls off his two-wheeler into the mud. He says his mommy's gonna be mad at him. He wipes the mud off his hand onto the railing. He's all dressed up in black corduroy pants. He says, "We are going to the Max to visit Danny. Danny's our daddy."

He says, "You can't run in that place or they lock you up."

He says, "We had another daddy before but we don't like him anymore. The police came and took him away."

Ricky says he's been running around the reserve seeing people. Hasn't even seen one fifth of the people he wants to see. He saw his dad, he says. "My dad spent some federal time too, eh. People in there know him too. The problem is he got his head kicked in, and his mind's kinda gone now. He doesn't remember too much. He didn't even remember me at first."

Ricky turns back to the soap. "That's my problem, eh. I know the guys who did that to him and if I see them, I don't know what I might do." He shakes his head. His braid swishes against his T-shirt. "I gotta stay away. Gotta try to stay away. Gotta get out of the prison way.

"I've been in and out of places since I was two years old," he says. "Different places. You wanna talk to me? I could tell you some stories.

"I saw two of my best friends get shot once, hey. Got shot right in front of my eyes. That was quite something, eh. Right in front of my eyes.

"I was living out in Vancouver then. It was a drug deal – these guys were screwing us and we figured we'd show them something. My one friend, he got shot in the stomach." Ricky keeps his face to the TV. "The other guy, he got it in the head. That one, he died right away."

Ricky turns around on the couch. Now he can't see the TV at all. He smiles. He keeps his hands hanging between his legs. He doesn't move his hands.

He says, "So, you wanna hear an Indian joke?"

The joke Ricky tells goes:

"There was this British guy and this Indian guy, eh. The British guy, he picks up this Indian woman and starts laying pipe – you know what I mean by laying pipe? So anyway they get things going and finally the woman goes, 'Whoa. Whoa.' So then the British guy goes out and starts playing pool with the Indian guy. The Indian guy's a pretty good pool player, eh. Hardly ever misses. Takes shot after shot. Finally, after a long time he finally misses. When he misses he goes, 'Whoa. Whoa.' The British guy says, 'What does whoa, whoa mean anyway?' The Indian guy says, 'Wrong hole.' "

I am told, later, that Ricky lasted two weeks. Some girl lent him a charge card belonging to her grandfather. There were a lot of things Ricky needed to get. A lot of things Ricky needed.

THE JOKER IS a social worker, Métis, female. She is plump, and bothered by it. She is on a protein diet and allows herself to eat nothing but meat and eggs and cheese. She lost a lot of weight that way before, she says. She tells the joke to sixteen other women – one black, two white and thirteen Native. Most of the women are single mothers. Most are poor.

The joker is writing on a flip chart in a meeting room in the basement of the Boyle Street Co-Op. The co-op, on the west border of the inner city, has taken over most of the old Provincial Court House and holding cells. The room in which the women gather was once part of docket court, first-appearance central. Docket court's wooden benches are gone now, and the prisoner's box is gone and the cranky judge's dais is gone. Everything has been painted white. There are old photographs on the wall: of the International Hotel, now a dive on the strip; of tepees set up along a city curb; of the Dreamland Theatre – movies ten cents.

The women have just finished eating fried bread and stew, pickles and cheese. The dinner was pot luck. The joker, who has organized this event in her spare time, wants to start a support group for Native moms. She wants to know what the women want from a support group. She tells them she was on welfare and drinking not so long ago; she doesn't want to dictate to them. She tells them about the time she was drinking down at the York Hotel on the drag and came out of the bathroom with her pants on backwards and pinned together with a safety pin. She talks about a boarding room so cold she wore men's socks to bed. About finding a condom when she was a child and blowing it up because she thought it was a balloon, batting it around, batting it till her mom saw her and grabbed it out of her hands and tossed it into the fire, ashamed. About having her children taken away by Social Services. She says she can talk about that now, because it is over. She says she is ready to write down the women's suggestions.

The first thing someone says is Cree. Cree lessons. Somebody else says recreation. Maybe a movie once in awhile. A birthday cake if it's somebody's birthday. Not serious stuff all the time.

Someone else says maybe things your social worker forgets to tell you. Like you can get an extra ten dollars for diapers every month. Or Social Services pays part of the funeral expenses if someone dies. That's good to know, they say.

Another woman says, "Ya – but then you can't have no grave marker. They just keep burying them, over and over."

Everyone is quiet. This woman wears her hair caught up in a silver clip. She has scars like stairs up her arms. "That's what happened to my little sister," the woman says. She sets down her coffee. "When my little sister died, my family went through Social Services. Afterward we wanted to put up one of them headstones, but we found out we couldn't. There was four or five other people there in the ground already where my sister was buried.

"When we found out we tried to have her moved but they told us it was too late. There was already other coffins sliding in on top of her.

"They've just got these little numbers there, eh, on the graves. So I don't know where my sister is."

The joker twists the top of her red felt pen, around and around. "They have filing cabinets for us while we're alive. And then they do that again to us when we're dead."

Later the woman who doesn't know where her sister is will go outside and sit on the hallway floor for a smoke. She'll say, "It was back in 1973. She was only sixteen, eh. She was my kid sister, but I thought of her like my kid. I used to work summers and buy myself clothes and buy her clothes. My parents weren't too well off, but I didn't think of it like that at the time. It hurt pretty bad – that with my sister. We learned next time. When my brothers died, we didn't go through Social Services at all."

Later still, an official from the graveyard denies that any of what the woman said is true. "They can have their pick," he says. "Any site they want. Plus headstones. I don't know where you got this information."

Another woman at the co-op, fine white scars running from her mouth like tributaries, says nothing about what she would like to see from a support group. She is too shy; she will only talk to the person sitting beside her. The woman with the river mouth is excited; her picture is in a new brochure for the co-op, and it's going to be sent all across Canada. The photo shows her standing beside the man she lives with, hugging her three-month-old baby girl. Her mom took all five copies of the brochure she brought home to mail to relatives. She's going to have to get herself some more.

She says, when she's asked, that she has three other kids. All boys. Two from the first man she stayed with. She left him after he dragged her downstairs by the hair and put a gun to her head and threw one child against a wall and the baby straight at her. She went to a battered women's shelter and then a motel and then decided to give her kids up. Told Social Services to send them back home to her dad in BC. But, she says, now that she's stopped drinking for a year she wonders if her kids are OK. If they are being treated as mean as she was, she says, she wants them back from her dad.

The third kid is with a foster mom, she says. She gets to visit that one, anytime she wants. Pretty soon she's going to see if she can get that one back. That one's father is in prison, waiting trial for murder. The murder involved the brutal beating death of an old man, asleep in his bed. She says that guy was a mean one too. That guy put her out to work the streets.

She says she comes to the co-op every day. She was taking school, but had to stop when she had her baby. This man she's living with now, he's an artist. He stays home all day and draws. When she comes home from work, he better have something to show her, she says. She has one of his drawings with her – two red sparrows on a green pine cone. She plays with it, tapping it against the table. He is going to make this into Christmas cards, she says with pride. She says he's not a mean one – he only hit her once, and that was back a year ago, back before they both stopped drinking.

She says, when she's asked, "Me, I'm twenty-five. Just about twenty-six."

She says the people at the co-op are real happy with her, with how she's stayed off the booze and everything. She says they think she'll be able to keep this baby.

The joker, who ate fried bread and chocolate cookies despite her diet, leads off her joke by saying, "We can support each other by helping out each other."

Then she tells the joke, apologetically, as if it isn't a joke at all.

"I've heard it said that the new Indian war cry is 'bingo.'

"Well I'm damn glad you're not at bingo tonight. I'm damn glad to see all of you here."

✪ MAGGIE

ROYAL CANADIAN LEGIONNAIRES, poppies on their stern blue breasts, guard the advance election poll in their lobby. Upstairs, an aging Métis singer, solemn as Sunday, twangs his guitar. He glares through the cigarette haze at a restive crowd and beyond to the wall-length mural of battering seas and sinking battleship that ends the room. Gamblers mill around tables where casino strips are sold. The strips – lemons, oranges, apples exposed – lie in colorful heaps on the floor. Kids swirl underfoot. The singer stomps his boot and drawls out his competition piece. "I get te-ars in my ears," thump thump, "from crying for you de-ar."

Maggie Royer lets loose one of her contagious, rolling laughs. "Truly, usually the singers at these festivals are better," she says. "Now if only they'd play the *Tennessee Flat Top Box*. That's how my ex-husband won me. He played that for me on his guitar and then," another giggle, "oooooh."

Maggie, forty-seven, her jean shirt studded with silver, silver and turquoise rings on her fingers, glittering at a crowded Métis cultural festival in the downtown legion on a dirty December afternoon.

We are at the festival to watch her niece, Lisa, dance. Maggie has been hauling Lisa to dance competitions for years. Maggie's passion for dance began when she went to a powwow and cried because she didn't recognize the music. She vowed then that she, and her children and her sister's child, special to her because "the girl doesn't get a chance with her mother," would regain what she had lost.

It is typical Maggie, this stubborn determination to recapture what has been lost: time, chances, pride. She tells me Lisa can do both types of dances now – Indian and Métis. Jigs. Grass dances. Prairie chicken. Owl. "Doing both – that's what being Métis is all about."

Up on the hardwood stage Lisa is pretty-as-the-fifties in the pinafore and wide blue bows of her dance costume. The fiddler taps and sways. Lisa jigs with her partners, light on her feet.

Her group wins four first-place trophies and then disappears. Maggie is upset; she thinks Lisa has gone off looking for a place to drink.

"Booze. That is how Lisa deals with her pain and loneliness. For awhile there, when she was fourteen, fifteen, we thought we were going to lose her. She tried to kill herself." Lisa is better now. But still, Maggie says, she sees signs of addiction coming through.

The next competitor, a giant who specializes in the country-music hiccup, plinks into the mike. The crowd knots and unravels at the coffee canister, at the casino stands. The room is hot. Congested.

Contrasts abound. The shining hardwood stage and the sinking battleship. Solemn, stomping fiddlers, and blue-uniformed Legionnaires disdainful or uninterested a floor below. A fast-footed girl in a pinafore and crinoline with scars on her wrists, her stiff-backed partner in his broad red sash off to hunt for beer. Maggie, her hands glistening with silver, giggling at the courting rituals of a man who drank, and womanized, and beat her. A man she respects, nonetheless, for loving their five sons. Maggie, whom her son Kicker condemns as selfish, who is stubbornly protective of her niece, of those same sons. Maggie, who had a hard childhood and worse, who married a drunk and was one, who lived on welfare in Edmonton's dumps and dives, who dried out, who won out. Maggie the student. Maggie the social worker. Maggie, gentle and giggly, fiercely proud of her Métis culture. Cheerful, ever. And articulate in her grief and anger.

MAGGIE GIVES ME a tour of her basement suite under a bungalow in a tidy south Edmonton subdivision. The suite is small, chilly. Her kitchen walls are covered in bric-a-brac: little pencil drawings of the city, her bingo daubers in a pouch, her boyfriend's real-estate business card, the serenity prayer from Alcoholics Anonymous. In the living room the bustle she made one of her sons for his Indian dancing. Countless self-help paperbacks. A drawing of three of her kids around the time they were apprehended by Social Services. An old Indian man Maggie carved out of apple, whose wrinkled skin becomes soft and full whenever she's cooking. A blue budgie in a blue budgie cage.

Maggie tells me the story of the budgie, given to her by a white woman friend. The friend came over with her four-year-old son. The two women heard a sudden squawk from the living room. The child, playing with the budgie, had pulled off its tail.

"But you know, that darn budgie lived," Maggie says, laughing. "So I told my friend it was a Métis budgie. It was a survivor."

We sit at Maggie's kitchen table. She's eating dry toast for breakfast; she's on one of her constant and constantly disregarded diets. She won't drink coffee though she loves it; she considers caffeine a drug. If she's going to be an addictions counsellor, she says, her own house has to be swept clean. "A soul is never done sweeping," she says.

This, then, is what she tells me.

"I WAS BORN in 1943 on a Métis settlement by Lac La Biche. When we left the settlement, I was two years old and we moved to my mom's reserve 'cause my mom wanted to be with her family. So that's where I was brought up – on the reserve.

"I was the oldest one of twelve kids. I went to school on the reserve in a day school. But I didn't start till I was eleven. My mom just kept me at home. She finally got a threatening letter that I should go to school or else they were going to cut off the family allowance. I guess she just didn't think of sending me till then.

"The reserve back then was really poor. Like there was no electricity, no hot running water. It was so poor there was only two cars, a Model T and this blue 1958 car. This was in 1958, too, so it was a brand-new car. A guy won that car in a car bingo; they had car bingos back then." Maggie laughs. "He was really famous because of that car.

"And we were so poor, we were so dirt poor. Like, with our food. In springtime we'd eat gophers. You'd pour water down their holes and drown them. My grandfather would pull their guts out and throw them on the barbecue with the potatoes. The hair would just singe off and we'd eat them." She sets down her toast. "I don't know if I could stomach that now.

"The kids in the family used to fight for the rabbit's head. We'd play spin-the-rabbit-head to see who would get to eat it. We were so poor we didn't have any toys. So we played with our food." She laughs. "Mealtimes were fun.

"My dad didn't work. My grandfather had an old-age pension and that's what we lived on. My dad hunted. My mom would make stuff for people – she was very creative – and exchanged around for things. She could look at something in the catalogue, and just cut it out of old rags. The evangelical minister would come down; he'd bring clothes to the reserve and give them away. My mom created a lot of things out of those old rags. I remember her making skirts out of neckties and blankets out of neckties. So when Dolly Parton sings *Coat of Many Colors* I can relate to that." Maggie laughs.

"What I remember mostly, I guess, when I was growing up is, my mom used to make these flowers out of crepe. She'd dip them in wax and water, in wax and water, again and again. She'd make these beautiful flowers for the coffins when somebody died. And my dad would make the coffins. So," she laughs, "I guess you could say my mother and father were the funeral directors, in the Native way.

"I grew up always being around dead bodies and funerals. So I had a very big thing to overcome about death when I grew up. I was very scared of death. 'Cause when I was small I saw a lot of dead bodies and sometimes they didn't smell very good. When it was really hot in the summer they got decomposed because they were kept for three days. I saw really terrible things at times, like when the body would get real big and bloated up. That's what happened to my grandfather's body. Those aren't very pleasant things for a kid to grow up with.

"Now I like to think of death as a beautiful experience. Mind you, I don't want to die. There's a lot of good living to do yet. And I am lot happier now. So I have experienced a little bit of happiness, that if I die now it's not that bad anymore.

"My father's Métis so he hasn't got any treaty rights. He never has. So after my mom married him, there was a new bill that came through that if you were treaty and married a Métis or a white person, you automatically lost your rights. I think I was seven at the time. Later on we found out that other people got over $2,000 for letting go of their treaty rights, which was just incredible when all she had gotten was $115. Which at the time was a lot of money because we were so poor. I remember her buying a whole lot of groceries, like I never saw that many groceries before. And she bought some clothes. But that's all she had gotten.

"I have the opportunity to be treaty now but I don't want to, because of my Métis culture. And now that I know what my culture is and what my identity is, I don't want to trade it off for a treaty number. I guess I would be set for my financial expenses as far as school is concerned, but my soul is at stake here, too. I'd feel like I would be trading off my soul if I suddenly decided to be treaty.

"Because I was Métis on a reserve the other kids treated me like I was second-class. Like every time we needed school supplies or a pencil or something they had to get in touch with the Indian agent, because we were not treaty so it was not provided for us. And at times the Indian agent hadn't authorized it, so there was a big hassle. And the kids would start making really derogatory remarks about, 'Oh, Métis' and 'halfbreeds.' At times it just sounded so terrible. And I didn't understand. I was really confused. I felt like an Indian. I spoke Cree. And here, something was wrong.

"And as I grew older I noticed my own relatives made remarks about 'that Métis halfbreed' again. And they would laugh. But I didn't internalize that statement as a joke or anything to feel good about. So I grew up eventually feeling ashamed. Feeling I did not know what I was. And most of all I began to resent the Indians, because they didn't accept me. So I just wanted to get away from the reserve as soon as I could. I did not like being there.

"Then I came to the city, and here I was being called a squaw. That didn't feel right either because it was not said with respect. It was derogatory, like something dirty. And there I thought, 'Well, what's happening now? I come to the city, I'm an Indian now? While I was on the reserve I was not an Indian. What the heck is going on?'

"When I went to school I was exposed to the evangelical minister's wife. She was a teacher in this school. And I thank God for that person in my life because I needed somebody to affect me in a positive way, and she did. I became her pet because I worked very, very hard. When I think of it, I think I was smart, because she said to me, 'I need you to catch up and you finish these books. If you can do them right, I'll just move you on.'

"I remember I was very proud of myself because I had all that encouragement from her. I skipped grade four. Went on to grade five, finished that. And I was going to be promoted on to grade six but my mom and dad asked me if I wanted to go to school or go to work.

"A fifteen-year-old, you don't ask them a question like that. Deep down, I wanted to go to school. But I also wanted to get away from the reserve. I wanted to be on my own. This was in June, and in October I turned sixteen. Two weeks after I turned sixteen I hit the city.

"Whoa. That was something else."

WHEN THE SMOKE and music at the Métis festival grow too thick, Maggie ferries her fourteen-year-old son across the street to a food fair in a downtown mall. Eddie Jr., who lives with his dad in the country, goes wild with possibilities. Chicken balls. Tacos. Chocolate shakes. Fries. He disappears into deep-fry heaven.

Searching for her son under the glaring fast-food lights, Maggie runs into Ralph. There is nowhere Maggie goes she doesn't run into someone she knows. Ralph, a Sioux, wears two hearing aids. He used to work at Dow Chemical; he was poisoned by chlorine and quit. Now he studies at the University of Alberta. He is particularly interested in the psychology of color.

Eddie Jr. returns with french fries. Chop suey. A yogurt cone. Ketchup packages and paper salt and peppers.

Indians in the country see differently than Indians in the city, Ralph says. Recently he has been dreaming in red. Red means spirituality. He dreamt of the path of enlightenment, red from bleeding feet. A man walked it.

Ralph leans over Eddie's chop suey, his voice booming as though the entire assembled food fair were among the deaf. "Yes indeed," Ralph thunders. "That man *was* Jesus!"

MAGGIE POURS ANOTHER coffee for me. "When I first went to school I didn't speak a word of English. It was very difficult. I didn't even know what 'hello' meant or anything like that. That was really really hard.

"And we were not allowed to speak our language. If we were caught speaking Cree we were threatened with the strap. We used to speak Cree anyway." She laughs. "We'd go and sit in the bushes away from the school and speak our language. But one time this man teacher, he was kind of strict but nice in a way too. And there was a whole bunch of us, it was lunch time, we were all just talking away in Cree and we were having so much fun. And all of a sudden I looked up and here was this teacher. And he says, 'Come in, Maggie.' And I went in.

"He was standing there and he had the strap in his hand. And he says, 'Do you know you're not supposed to speak Cree?' And I said, 'Yes, I do.' And he didn't say anything, he was just looking at me. He said, 'Well go play anyway, but don't speak Cree.'

"And he didn't hit me! So that was OK. But boy, I was scared. I think he must not have believed in it really, the policy. Because if he had believed in it, I think he would have hit me.

"We had an easier time in school compared to the kids who grew up in the convent like my mother. They were very strict in those days.

"I did an interview with my mother. I had to do a paper about assimilation, so I wanted to interview a person who had spent all their life in a convent. And it was so devastating because here's this person who I love so much and I was seeing her go through all the emotional pain. It created some anger, too, towards the people who broke up families and stuck children in convents to try and assimilate them. Why? The Indians didn't need that. They had some very strong family structures and that was busted away from their lives."

Maggie pounds her fist into her open palm. "Where in the world do they develop this bond that they are supposed to have with their families if you stick them in a convent, forbid them to speak their language, forbid them to practice their culture? To top it all, to remove them from the people that they love so much.

"The highest grade they ever had for the Native people in them schools was grade eight. They didn't even prepare them properly for the outside world. And most of all, they didn't prepare them to survive in their own culture. Those kids didn't learn about hunting, they didn't learn about arts and crafts, they didn't learn about their spirituality.

"And then the nuns and priests expected the Native people to go back onto their reserves, or the Métis people to go back into their communities. And be what now? They took them from their homes, and returned them back very empty.

"And seeing my mother talking about that, sitting across from me at the table, and the pain in her face and the shaking of her voice and the trembling of her hands was just so hard for me to witness. That was the first opportunity my mother ever had to talk about the child in her, being away from home, being stuck in a place full of strangers.

"She was taken when she was eight, and they didn't let her go till she was eighteen. And when you reached twelve, you only went to school half a day and the rest of the day was spent doing chores. So it was cheap child labor that they had from those kids.

"She ran away twice from the convent and her dad brought her back. The nuns pulled her pants down, laid her flat on the bed and strapped her. And all she wanted to do was to be with her family who she loved, because she was so lonesome.

"I asked her, 'What did your dad do when you ran away?' And you know what she said? She said, 'He made me feel very ashamed.'

"The residential schools went on for so long. We were weakened as people. Our culture was weakened. And now there are massive amounts of problems in our society with Native and Métis people. I think it's been building up since that time, since the assimilation.

"But it is a very strong culture. They have been trying to kill us, but they haven't succeeded. And they are not going to succeed. Because there are still some strong ones left, thank God, who have been able to teach us.

"And now I'm beginning to be stronger too. There is no way that I am going to lose my culture for anybody. And now I am stronger, I am able to teach my kids. And if they know it they can teach their kids. Who they are."

MAGGIE DAYDREAMS, SHE says, and then breaks her daydreams down, step-by-step, into reality. She daydreams a Native-awareness workshop for her fellow social workers, most of whom are white, and then organizes it in her spare time. She holds the workshop at the same church camp she brought her kids to when she was down and out, and invites a handsome, soft-spoken man named Houston to speak about Native spirituality.

"We as Native people on this continent have the same kind of communication with what you call saints, but we call them grandfathers," Houston tells the social workers. "Unfortunately we are not listening to them, which is tragic. Because they still do communicate.

"Even the trees talk to us with their swaying, but we've lost that now. We don't know what that means. We have lost our foothold. The Native people have lost so much. A lot of it six feet under the ground."

Houston explains that elders are respected because they are closer to the Creator. That women, whose natural spiritual powers are greater than those of men, are associated with the moon. "If you look close into the moon you see an old woman spilling blood," he says.

When Houston breaks for morning coffee and donuts, the social workers and income-assistance workers and the United Church minister with his very young second wife who have sat listening for the last two hours, pour out onto the lawn.

"Gawd," one of the social workers says, hugging her Siwash sweater to her chest. "Goddamn, he's cute in those jeans."

After the break, Houston talks about residential schools. He tells how the RCMP used little caged carts to pick up kids. He tells how there was sexual abuse in the convents, physical abuse.

"When I was in the convent I remember this one little guy was pretty sick. He died. Toby Roberts. One day he was sick and we had to have this bowl of porridge. Bowl of milk and porridge and bread, like we had every morning.

"Toby, he threw up in his bowl. And then them nuns forced him to eat what he threw up mixed in with his porridge the next day.

"I saw that with my own eyes."

MAGGIE IS FRYING bacon to add to her dry toast. "I grew up loving all kinds of sports," she says. "I knew the hockey players from the Toronto Maple Leafs like you wouldn't believe. There were always pictures splattered all over our house, baseball and Charles Atlas, all this body-building and wrassling.

"We used to have that radio, that big battery radio with an aerial outside – it looked like a clothesline. But we were only allowed to listen to it when there was sports. That was all that radio was for – just for sports. I even knew Barbara Ann Scott when she was a figure skating champion." Maggie giggles. "You know I will never forget Barbara Ann Scott. There was even a doll in the Eaton's catalogue about Barbara Ann Scott. I grew up with beautiful memories like that about sports.

"At that time my parents didn't drink. My dad used to, a long time ago, but then he quit. But it was a dry drunk home, which can be very destructive also. My brothers both died so my dad had promised God, I guess, that he would quit drinking if my brother lived. So he did quit drinking.

"But I saw him drunk once. It was a devastating experience for me because I thought he was going to die. It was so horrible I will never forget it. I must have been about five years old. He drank wine and he was under the table and he had gotten sick and this red stuff was coming out of him. And I didn't know what drinking was, 'cause it didn't happen in our home. All this stuff was on the floor and everybody was behaving differently than normal. I literally thought he was going to die.

"And I really loved my dad, I just loved him so much because he affected me in a tremendous way with the sports. I felt like he shared that with me. My dad was a god-like figure in my mind. He could play baseball, he could do anything. And all of a sudden, when he got drunk that time, I began to see my dad as not who I thought he was. I was devastated. And I never ever forgave him for that, I guess. For disappointing me.

"In time I began to realize what a horrible person my dad was, because that was how I thought of him then, somebody very unreasonable and horrible. He was really strict. You did your best just to please him all the time, because if you didn't you would get a licking. At times you got lickings you didn't even know what you got them for. I learned to be a people-pleaser, to make things right. And you just literally shook if he asked for something and you didn't know where it was. I used to pray, like I was really religious when I was young, and I used to pray to God that I would find whatever he asked for. And lots of times I used to find those things and I really thought God looked after me and answered my prayers.

"And because of the religion, too, I wanted to die when I was twelve years old. Just to be with God. It was not because I was so miserable but because I just wanted to be with God in heaven. Death, dying to go to heaven was exciting."

THE ALBERTA NATIVE Health Care Commission has sponsored a talk on drugs and child abuse for social workers. A detective from the sex crimes and child-abuse unit shows disturbing slides. Photographs of children with "glove burns" from having their hands dipped in boiling water. Wrap-around injuries from belts, willows, electrical cords. Bruises in the shape of spatulas. Bruises in the shape of hands. Cigar burns. Cigarette burns. Babies with venereal sores.

Maggie tells me she reacts differently to these grim images now than she once did.

"My father was violent. He used to beat us with sticks one inch thick. I was black and blue so many times. It got so bad he even beat his own father. He beat horses. He beat my mother. My mother is very bitter about it. She feels she wasted her good life on him. It's amazing we didn't all grow up as madmen, torn between these two extremes – my mother who was so soft and loving, so passive, and him. We do have our issues, our problems, but it's a wonder we survived.

"But once you've gone through it, your pain is different. I've done the fourth step in AA. I've done all my crying for my past pain. So it's different for me. Before I used to react to things like these injured children with my own pain. But I've done all my crying now."

"WHEN I WAS sixteen I left the reserve to go to the city. My mother had written my auntie – to save me I guess, because I think my mother really knew inside of her what I was going through.

"My uncle, he came and got me. I was so bushed. I was so bushed and so afraid 'cause I used to see him only periodically and he looked like a white man, when I was not used to white people. So when he come and got me I just sat in the car just the way I got in. That's how I sat all the way to the city. This is over one hundred miles! And I never moved an inch all the time 'cause I was scared to move. When he would offer me a cigarette I would just move my arm.

"So when I got to the city, when I got out of the car I fell flat right on my face. I fell right flat on the ground. I had no control over my legs because of the fact I had sat so still all that time." She laughs.

"He drove me from one part of the city to the other. And I was so awed by all these lights and the cars. I had never ever seen anything like it. It was just incredible. And I just, oh man, like I was so amazed. 'Cause jeez, there wasn't even any electricity where I come from." She giggles again. "It was just really something for me.

"And then when I came home I was so hungry and they fed me, and I ate with my head down. I did not look up. I was so shy. The only one who looked similar to my color was my auntie, because she's dark. And yet she was like a complete stranger to me. She didn't act like an Indian either. My uncle behaved like a white Métis. And I guess she got integrated into all that behavior, all them years she was married to him.

"And my cousins, they were even stranger. They couldn't speak Cree." She chuckles. "I couldn't even argue with them or talk to them because I couldn't sling out my English. They spoke English like, it just slithered out like a snake. And here I was just stuttering because I was not used to speaking English.

"Then my uncle exposed me to the white-man world. Because it was all a push-button world. He taught me for two weeks. I remember that first time when he plugged in the vacuum cleaner and it went 'kaboom!' I was so scared, I just backed up into a corner because I had never seen a vacuum cleaner before in my life." She giggles. "I didn't know what this monstrosity was.

"The phone, I had never ever saw a phone before in my life. I was sixteen, but you know the thing is I hardly ever went to town because my dad was so strict with everything. I wasn't exposed to any of that. So it was really just mind-blowing. I went through cultural shock like you wouldn't believe when I came to the city.

"I used to watch that show on TV about the hillbillies. I knew what they were going through." She laughs.

"I was just lucky. I wouldn't have survived, I don't think, if it hadn't been for my uncle and auntie. I am pretty sure if I had ended up in the city by myself something terrible would have happened. But my uncle took me under his wing. He was very strong, and he was a politician and he was very outgoing. And so he used to tease me all the time and try to make me speak up for myself. He would push me. He would say, 'Speak up for yourself, Maggie. Don't let people walk all over you. Come on.'

"In time I understood he did what he did to help me out. But at the time, sometimes I thought he was just a damn jerk.

"My uncle was the one who taught me about Métis-ism. One day, when I was really angry because he was bugging me, I said, 'Oh you fucking Indian.'

"And he got really angry. He said, 'Don't you ever call me that.' He said, 'I'm a Métis and I'm proud of it. I'm not an Indian.'

"And I just went really quiet and I thought, 'He's saying something here, but I don't know what.' But it just hit me that it was something different.

"And finally I said to him, 'Explain to me what you mean by this

Métis and Indian.' Because I was still very confused about who I was. So he sat down and he explained the difference.

"And I thought, 'Wow, now I know who I am.' Because even when I had asked my dad, that one time I had asked him, 'What's an Indian and a Métis?'

"And he said to me, 'Well this cow came by and did his number two. And then this horse came by and did it right on top of this cow shit. And then this little Indian kid came by and mixed it all up. And that's what a Métis is.'

"That's my dad's education of being a Métis. I guess he was trying to be funny but that was not funny for me. Something happened inside of me. I went away feeling a little shittier than I already did. I would never, ever tell my kids something like that.

"So then when my uncle explained it so beautifully and so differently, I just grabbed onto that. I thought, 'Now I know who I am.' And thank God that he did. I'll never forget him for that.

"After two weeks of learning in a push-button world my uncle got me a job. And here it was a white family. And oh my, my, that was so difficult. I didn't know how to cook the white-man way, or anything like that. And I know that white guy was upset with my cooking, especially that one time because I didn't cook his eggs right." She laughs. "I cooked them really rubbery which is how we cooked our eggs. And here white people have them sunny-side up! I couldn't understand what was wrong with them eggs.

"But I learned. And I got good at it. Baby-sitting and housekeeping.

"When I think of some of the places I was at, I was taken advantage of. But I didn't know the difference. I remember looking after a very elderly woman in one place, and I stayed there about a whole year. She was very sick. And when I think of it now, she was a drunk. Because I was fixing medicine all day. She used to lie on her bed and I had to change her diaper. I was seventeen. I was so naive I didn't know any different. And I was always fixing this medicine all day long. This medicine of beer and wine and whiskey."

MAGGIE CHALLENGES ME to a Ms. Packman game after a lunch-hour, caffeine-soaked Alcoholics Anonymous meeting. The woman is a Packman wizard. Under her practised hand the yellow blob gobbles dots and avoids ghosts with ease, earning apples, bananas, pretzels, the high score.

Maggie's boyfriend, John, a white man and fellow AA member, is playing pool at the other end of the games room. The real estate market is soft; work is slow for him and he is thinking of selling his condo. Maybe the two of them will even move out to the coast.

Maggie tells me about finding John's baby book. It is falling apart, she says. She wants to have it restitched and every individual page plasticized for him for Christmas.

"John's mother wrote in there, when he was three, that he liked to play alone. And that he was fascinated," Maggie giggles, "by cowboys and Indians."

"AND THEN, WHEN I was about eighteen, I discovered boys in the city. I spoke English all the time and I mostly went out with army guys, white guys. I just more or less left all my past behind. I did not want to go back to the reserve. I hated the reserve anyway.

"I got assimilated into the white world for a long time there, to the point where I just about lost my own language. I remember sitting in the bar with a whole bunch of people that I had gone to school with on the reserve. They were all talking and laughing. I had a really difficult time to be in the conversation because I couldn't speak Cree. And I tried and I was stuttering, because it wouldn't come out of my mouth. And I remember feeling really sad. I was so depressed I just walked out.

"So right the next morning, hung over as I was, I got out a Cree book. And I told my mom and dad, I said, 'Don't ever speak English to me again. Speak Cree to me, because I am losing it and I don't want to lose it.' So they did. They spoke Cree to me and it came back. And now I can sling it pretty damn good.

"But my kids, because of my ex-husband, he was Métis but he

was totally brought up white. And he didn't understand a word of Cree. So when I got married into that, he was like a white man. He didn't even eat rabbits, never ate bannock. I remember cooking duck for him this one day, these mallards he'd shot. And he woke up with this real dirty hangover and walked into the kitchen and here I was, cooking these ducks and their heads were sticking up out of the pot. He told me, 'Maggie, you don't cook the heads.'

She giggles. "I said, 'Why not? We always eat the heads.'

"Anyway, because of my ex-husband my kids do not speak Cree."

SESAME STREET IS a strip of shuddering skid row houses owned by a recently deceased Edmonton landlady. It is called Sesame Street because the activity there never stops. The slum landlady, it is rumored, was worth a million and died in a shack. All her houses are for sale, and inner-city workers are worried about where the people now in them will live.

I drive Maggie past the strip on our way to a Christmas party she has organized for Native kids on welfare. She used to live in that landlady's houses, she says. They were dives. That woman charged a lot – usually the maximum that welfare or Indian Affairs would pay. But the good thing was, she didn't care if you were poor and had a whole lot of kids and were Native. She even lent Maggie's husband money sometimes. "She would never lend any to me," Maggie says. "But Edward, that was different. She liked Eddie.

"When we first got married, I looked for a place all day. That's when you really notice the discrimination. I was so frustrated that night. I said to my husband, 'I looked all over and every place I go it's rented out.' And Eddie went out and, because he doesn't look like an Indian, in half an hour he had a place.

"And I cried and he held me and I cried. And I said, 'I tried and I couldn't because I'm an Indian.'

"But that happens even today. Either the places are gone, or these slum landlords, they accept Native people but they are dumpy houses. And because of that acceptance people take the houses.

"But now I'm mad. I don't want to live in a dump, there's no damn way. I mean, this place I'm living in now is no mansion. But there's no cockroaches. And there's no bedbugs anywhere and the paint isn't peeling off and the linoleum isn't coming off the floor.

"I used to accept those things at one time, because I didn't feel good as a Native person or a Métis. I didn't feel good as a individual and so I took places that were no good because at least they accepted me to live there.

"I used to work for that landlady, too, you know. She owned restaurants. I worked in the back of one of them, a diner down in Innercity, washing dishes. I was twenty-two, twenty-three at the time.

"She had this handyman. They were together for years. I think she left everything to him when she died. Anyway, he would go into all these old houses and do the plumbing. And then he'd come back into the kitchen and never wash his hands and work on the food. It just turned my stomach.

"I remember there was this banana cream pie – all soft and horrible. She told him just to put some new banana slices on top and set it out again. 'Those people don't even know what they're eating,' she told him.

"I finally got out of her houses when I took my kids and went to stay with my mom and dad. I went to work at the International Airport. Me and my mom. We worked nights. Oh, I hated it. Cleaning urinals in the men's washroom. I still think of that sometimes. How I'd clean those urinals and think, 'I'm not going to do this forever. I am not going to do this forever.' "

MAGGIE STOPS TO slip on her moosehide moccasins; the chill in her basement apartment has started to seep into her bones.

"My uncle, he may have showed me the good part about being

Métis but I still had a lot of other issues to deal with. Not feeling good as a human being. And to top it all I was sexually molested when I was small. Not by my father, of course, but by another person. I had that to deal with. And I hated myself as a person. I did not like who I was because of lack of education too. I couldn't get jobs that were any good. I had really low self-esteem, I just, oh, it was so low. I always felt like a dog. I mean a dog that doesn't have any esteem, 'cause I've had dogs that had very high self-esteem.

"So I had all those issues to deal with: my upbringing and being called dummy all my life, and being beaten up and verbally abused, and the sexual assault and all of that.

"And so I discovered alcohol eventually.

"Alcohol made me feel like the person I always wanted to feel. It made me feel so good. I was talkative, I was not shy anymore. It was magic.

"My dad always said if people drank they had to handle it like a man. They can't be falling all over the place. If you got drunk you were nothing, you were crap. So when I started drinking, getting drunk was not what I wanted to do. For about ten years I drank and drank and I could always handle my booze.

"But I never went to the dance without having something to drink – a little bit, never staggering drunk – because if I didn't have a drink then I was shy. I could not dance. I couldn't flirt. When I was under the influence I could flirt like crazy and I always got my man." She laughs. "It gave me courage.

"So I kept on drinking and I guess my tolerance level began to get higher and higher. I needed to drink more to get to that effect.

"And then I married an alcoholic. And he was very, very alcoholic, very, very sick in his disease. And with all that emotional stress because of my marriage, I began to drink to relieve depression.

"My husband used to beat me up in the first years of my marriage. One time he broke my nose. I brought a stop to that, in time. But that is what happens when you are physically and mentally abused as a kid; you get the idea you are not worth any other kind of treatment.

"And it seemed like I began to drink much, much more often. I needed to drink more, and quicker. It wasn't once a month anymore. I had quit drinking when I first got married 'cause I laid out my life the way you lay newspaper on the floor so nobody dirties it. I thought, 'Now I'm married, my kids are gonna go to a certain type of school, certain type of church, we're gonna have a certain type of friends.' Because of the fact that I married this alcoholic and because I was not well, I fell flat right on my face. Nothing, nothing worked.

"I couldn't stand it anymore. I drank to relieve my depression, to relieve the feeling of failure. And I felt like a failure all my life.

"I did my heavy drinking when I was pregnant with my kids. And I was so addicted that – 'cause I knew I couldn't sit in the bar with a big stomach 'cause that was not accepted in those days – I did my drinking in the earlier parts of my pregnancy. That is the most dangerous time, because that's when the construction of the baby is happening. But I wasn't aware. I didn't know those things, at that time. It's amazing my kids come away strong and healthy boys. How that happened . . . I think God really looked after me and blessed me with such healthy babies.

"Yet, there were problems with all my pregnancies. I had a miscarried abortion, too, at five months because of my alcohol. I was hemorrhaging all the time and they tried to save my baby and I ended up in the hospital to the point where I couldn't even sit up. They wouldn't even allow me to sit up to eat. And finally one afternoon, they just took my . . . they did this abortion. I guess the baby had died. Earlier in the morning I'd felt it move. And then all of a sudden it was gone.

"And you know. You are aware. I was not put to sleep when they took her.

"That was the most horrible thing. I couldn't get over it for three years. I kept thinking back, 'Where's this baby I could have had, who didn't come to full term because of my drinking?' She still exists in my mind. Like her name is Dove now. At least she has a name.

"And when I saw the documentary about abortions, how they just throw the aborted babies into incinerators, it just made me cry. Because that's where my baby probably ended up.

"And I didn't know. I mean, I could have had a burial for it and I didn't know. I asked the doctor even, whether it was a girl or a boy. He wouldn't tell me. And because I was so passive, I didn't insist. All he said was, 'You don't need to know that.' And I couldn't speak for myself so I just buried my face under my covers and cried.

"You see today, today I would say, 'Yes I do. I am the parent, I need to know that, I need to know what you're gonna do with my baby's body.' Because it was five months, and I felt it come out.

"I've had to do a lot of forgiving to forgive myself. It was a very painful thing in my life. Now I can talk about it, still with pain, but I'm able to talk about it 'cause I know that, maybe it sounds like an excuse, but I was an alcoholic and I didn't know any better. That's how it was then. I wasn't aware of those things.

"And what they did was they stuck me in the ward where all these mothers come in with their babies. And that was the most horrible, cruelest thing that could have happened to me. Because I was mourning. But I couldn't talk to anybody about that. I did not say anything. And they would bring their babies in and I would just, it was so horrible that I would just leave.

"And so, at the end of the line, I just totally felt sick to my stomach. And the more sick I got the more I needed to drink. I drank to the point of losing my children to Social Services.

"I felt so like a failure that I gave up my kids at one point, 'cause I felt I couldn't look after them anymore. It was so hard to get them back again. And then I got them back, and I went and got drunk again because I was so unhappy.

"I just didn't bother going home one weekend. I just left the kids with the baby-sitter. I knew I should go back, but I couldn't. I kept on drinking and drinking.

"And when I did come back, my oldest boy – he was thirteen at the time – he had run away to avoid being taken by Social Services. My next one, Kicker, he was eleven, he was already on the street by that time so he wasn't there. But my three little ones were gone to Social Services. And I didn't know where they were. Social Services wouldn't tell me.

"I stayed drunk after that for one whole month. I couldn't sober up. I drank every day. Every time I tried to sober up the pain of my kids not being there was so great that I just, that I couldn't handle it. Liquor was the only thing. As long as I was drinking I didn't feel the pain.

"And then after a month I thought, 'I gotta get out of this. I gotta, because I want my kids back more than anything else in the world.'

"So I started trying to make moves, trying to regain my kids. But it was very difficult 'cause you got this system now – the courts, Social Services are involved and you feel so disempowered. They got the power and you feel like nothing. You can't even fight them.

"And you cry again, maybe you get drunk again. You suffer such despair, such hopelessness and self-hatred 'cause you done that to your kids. But at times, too, you don't realize it's your fault. Because you're so sick emotionally, you blame everybody else but yourself.

"In the end I ended up in Henwood, this clinic for alcoholics. I was working at the Bissell Centre, that place in Innercity where they help out the people. I worked at the Bissell Centre during the week and did my drinking on the weekends. And when my children were apprehended by Social Services, their social worker at Bissell was the one who made the referral that I go to Henwood. And she come and delivered me there.

"And then, too, I ended up in Henwood because I tried to commit suicide. I guess they pumped my stomach out. I don't remember any of that. But I remember being on a stress line. I remember taking pills and alcohol all mixed together and I was telling them I was trying to commit suicide and they wanted to know where I lived. And I remember saying, 'I'm not telling you that, I don't want you to know that, you're trying to find me,' but all in a foggy state. I can hardly remember that.

"But I guess I must have phoned the child care director at Bissell too. And when I came to, she was standing at the sink washing my dishes.

"You know those people from the Bissell never once to this day have talked to me about that. They just did it for me and they just forgot about it. They understood. Never, ever, not once did those people bring that back in my face. They just accepted me as I was. I was having problems with my life. I went for help, got better, and that was it."

MAGGIE PHONES ME, frantic. Kicker, walking down the street drunk, got stopped by the cops. He called them assholes. One of them clubbed him across the face with a nightstick.

The left side of Kicker's face is swollen now, like a splitting fruit. He refuses to follow his doctor's orders and go for X-rays. She asks me to drive him to the hospital. She thinks his cheekbone must be broken.

She is very angry. "I've seen this happen too much. I know these policemen. I know they can be mean. I know they have a hard job to do, but sometimes it makes them hard.

"I don't hate cops but when this happens . . . I am so sick of not being able to do something. If you don't do something there will never be changes made.

"Kicker's doctor was so mad. I guess he was so mad at what the police had done to Kicker. He tried to get him to press charges. But Kicker was drunk. He doesn't know the guy's badge number. You don't have the evidence of who done it.

"Besides, Kicker is afraid. He said to me, 'Mom, if they would do this to me for calling them assholes, what are they going to do if I lay charges?'

"There's some policemen could do worse than what they've

already done to Kicker. They have killed Indians before. I have seen that happen before in Innercity."

MAGGIE LOOKS AT my coffee longingly. She takes another bite of bacon.

"I've been sober, it's going to be twelve years in May. The first couple of years, three years, it was really stressful for me just trying to survive and be sober. How I overcame it is a miracle to me.

"I remember a lot of pain, loneliness. Like I had to let go of my old friends. The bottom line was, they weren't friends anyway. But they were all I had, all the family I had it seemed.

"Especially one of the cousins. I love her so much and yet I drank with her all the time. She was my buddy. If she had money, she'd phone me up; if I had money I'd phone her up and we'd get drunk together. And when I sobered up, she was constantly bothering me all the time.

"Finally it was seven one morning, she came over and I was trying to get all my babies together. I took her very gently by the arm and I guided her to the door and I said, 'Look, I want to stay sober and it hurts me to say this, but you gotta go out of my life now.' I said, 'If you decide to sober up, you can come anytime and have coffee with me. But other than that, don't ever come back. I'm sorry.'

"It hurt me to say that, 'cause I really loved her. I grew up with her. But it was either that or my sobriety. I could not have these people around drinking 'cause I was very vulnerable. And I wanted to stay sober so desperately because of my babies. I wanted that more than anything else in the world, 'cause I knew that I just about died when they were gone. I was gonna do anything in my power to keep them with me."

MAGGIE DAYDREAMS A support group for Native mothers on welfare and then organizes it, in her spare time, in the basement of the abandoned provincial courthouse. She organizes agendas, food, films, bannock. She tells the women about working one night at an emergency welfare office, part of her training to be a social worker. She went out on a call about a seven-year-old boy, left at home all day and all night to look after his five-year-old brother and a baby. The boy had finally gone to a neighbor's, frightened because his house smelled like gas.

From what the boy told her when she got there, Maggie realized she was related to him. That was so hard, she says. She had to maintain her professionalism, but it was hard.

"I guess he told the workers, 'I'm not talking.' When I walked in he was looking at me. I knew he was sensing out his common ground 'cause everybody else was white. I didn't say anything, just kind of sat there for awhile.

"And then all of a sudden, these tears came to his eyes. So I just went and sat beside him and I said, 'Do you speak Cree?' And he said, 'A little bit.' And I says, 'Well, what can you say?'

"And he says to me, he says the Cree for 'I love you.' And then he said it again and with more emphasis – 'I really love you.' And I said, 'Where'd you learn that word from?' And he said, 'My mom.' And I says, 'Oh, your mom must really love you to teach you that.'

"And that kind of broke the ice. And after awhile he said to me, 'You know what? I got my mom's bus pass and her driver's license because she loses them every time she goes out so I have to keep them for her.' Seven years old and he's parenting his mom.

"And then I just felt angry, angry at alcohol, angry at the mother. And he said to me, 'I don't want to go to welfare. I went to welfare before and I don't want to go to welfare.' Oh, it just broke my heart. I told him we were going to do everything we could so he wouldn't have to go to welfare."

The mother returned before her children were apprehended, Maggie says. Maggie explained to her in Cree what was going on.

"And you could see the girl was awfully worried. There was a pleading thing to her voice. I keyed into that right away. I knew the feeling: the worker's there, she has all the authority and any minute she could just say, 'I'll take your kids.' I knew that feeling. And I could hear it in that mother's voice.

"That social worker, she was really good. She didn't take the kids. The mom was sober, she was coherent. And when we were going out, she was so thankful. And then I gave her my name and I told her I was going to start this support group for Native moms. I said to her, 'I know you want your kids.' I said, 'I know you love them, but if this carries on, you're gonna end up losing these kids that you love.'

"I said, 'I know. I'm speaking from experience.' "

KICKER, THE DAY after he gets hit by a bus, stoned up on pills and drunk and deaf to its horn, on his mother: "She treats my dad like shit. He doesn't deserve that. I like my dad better than my mom. It's not just me that doesn't like my mom; it's her that makes me feel that way. She asks why, she wonders why, she just doesn't get it.

"Like when she was a counsellor? She was counselling all these other people and left the kids to my dad. And look how we turned out."

He snorts. "That's pretty stupid."

"LIKE I WAS saying, Kicker was a hobo at eleven years old. I had totally lost control over him. I never hit my kids but I should have beat him up to keep him in the house. I could have physically restrained him. But I didn't believe in physical abuse because that's the environment I grew up in. And then because I was so mixed up with life I was verbally abusive, which can be just as damaging. And because of the alcoholism, too, Kicker was the scapegoat.

"So Kicker just acted out. He got in and out of trouble. He would stay away from home two, three days at a time. He did a lot of theft. He got into glue sniffing, introduced the glue sniffing to his older brother.

"He finally ended up in a home, in a youth detention centre because I had charged him for truancy. Because between trying to be sober and trying to go to school, trying to make something of my life, I tried to get him to go to school and he wouldn't. A couple of times I literally had to take off from school to go and find him. I put him right in the classroom and half an hour later he was gone again. So that stress, and my husband was drunk all the time, too, and I had all these kids. I just couldn't carry on anymore.

"My oldest son, Barney, really blamed himself when Kicker went into the detention centre. To the point where he just got so stoned on glue one night. And this was something Barney had never ever done. In our family it was always Kicker. And I remember it was three in the morning and Barney was coming in and out of the house, I couldn't sleep, and each time he came in he looked more and more stoned. And I was so stressed out and hurt because the other one was in the detention centre and here, this one was stoned high on glue.

"I remember phoning the police to come and get Barney somehow, to try and put him somewhere, because I didn't know what to do. I thought he was going to die from this glue because he was so spaced out. And I remember I went up to him on the couch and I just hugged him and I cried and I said, 'Barney, we'll work this out together. We'll do it somehow, I don't know how, but we'll work it out together.' And I was crying. And I remember him crying and he said, 'It's my fault Kicker is in Westfield.'

"See, he had taken all of that blame for himself. And it's really, really difficult when you're a mother and you see your children go through the pain. That hurts you so much.

"And I was so hopeless and helpless. There was no end to it. I couldn't rely on my husband; he was in the garage stone drunk and I wouldn't let him in the house. And holding your child, I think he was only about thirteen that time, and they are so high on glue, it hurts. I thought, 'I got to do something.' And that was my one way, to call the police.

"When the police came it took three of them to get him in the car. That was the first time I ever felt anything in my heart. My heart literally hurt, physical pain. I was crying and Barney was crying and they were dragging him out of the house. They were going to take him to some lock-up for kids. And he was just like a little tiny boy – he reminded me of a four-year-old and he was crying, 'Mommy, Mommy.' And here these police were taking him away because I had phoned them. I just felt like grabbing him again and just protecting him. But I knew I couldn't.

"I always remember I was crying and this one policeman, he came back in and gave me his name and he said, 'You know, you're doing the best you can right now. This is probably going to be the best thing for him, what you're doing right now.' I never forgot that.

"Deep down I never gave up on my kids, never ever. Barney, he's twenty-three now, he's struggling with his addiction. I know they're all going to straighten out sooner or later. Each one of my kids is so special in their own way. Like Kicker, I think he's going to make a damn good counsellor someday for younger kids because of his experiential learning. He's been a street kid since he was eleven. He has gone through hell.

"Kicker was the one who, when he was born, he was very huge. When he came out he didn't even cry. He just kind of whimpered and his feet made this punching movements in the air, like a kick boxer. I decided, 'I'm going to call him Kicker.' I was crying because I was so happy. He's a kick-boxer as far as I'm concerned. I don't like to call him Christian. I never have.

"That kid has gone through hell. He's going to have some mighty good experience. Once you are straightened out, all that learning, all that suffering, it pays back. I know from experience."

IT IS A hot summer day. The windows of the parking guard's booth outside the Edmonton Remand Centre are lined with rows of fat plastic bears full of honey. The remand centre is an imposing slab of a prison, the site of a "jail-house rock" party for the local glitterati before it opened. Maggie says Kicker told her lots of guys plead guilty simply to avoid awaiting trial in the centre's cells; remand is too crowded and there is nothing to do in there.

Kicker was picked up with his cousin, Lester, for trying to steal a car. Lester didn't waste any time; he pleaded guilty on his first appearance without talking to a lawyer. Maggie got to Native Counselling Services before Kicker went up on the stand. He reserved his plea. She says it tore her heart to see Lester get nine months; she thought Native Counselling would have told him what to do. Besides, Lester knows the system as well as Kicker does; he knew what would happen to him if he pleaded.

Maggie has never bailed Kicker out before in his life. But this time she is frightened. Her sister laid charges against the cops for smashing Kicker's face. And now he's gone and got himself picked up again. Maggie is terrified he will be hurt in prison, for making trouble for the cops.

The guard who signs visitors in and out of the remand centre has a naked woman tattooed on his forearm and the word "Aries" or "Area" or "Darlene" tattooed underneath; it's hard to read through the hair. He takes his time. He can't find Kicker's name on the inmate list. We're in the wrong place anyway; he sends us across the courtyard to yet another building, for yet another wait.

Maggie and I walk down narrow, winding stairs to the basement room where bail is posted. Both of us are nervous. The woman behind the metal folding window has a bad perm and no reason to smile. A Xeroxed sign beside her phone reads: "No typing accidents in this office for 23 days. No typewriter deaths for 54." She tells us it could be ten minutes before Kicker is released, it could be hours. It all depends on how busy they are over there at the jail. "They're a separate company, eh." We wait.

Maggie tells me about her work at Kikino, a holding centre for kids before they are placed in foster care. One little guy, Métis, told her he was Mexican. Another kid she can't get out of her crafts room. Always wants to take the beads and needles with him. She has to tell him the rules for him are the rules for everybody else. She's sorry.

She said, "I read that kid's file. That kid is only fourteen. He has a really thick file already, and they're starting a second one." She said she found "lots of mention" about how he was aggressive and uncooperative, and only one mention of the fact that, when he was thirteen, he tried to commit suicide. He tied his shirt around his neck. The file said they had to put him into his baby-janes. She asked one of the other counsellors what baby-janes were. He told her it was a straightjacket.

Kicker finally emerges from the tunnel that connects the jail to the bail office. His running shoes flap around his feet. His shoelaces and cigarettes and coins are handed to him in a sealed baggie just before he walks out the door. He stoops in the corner of the bail office to re-lace his shoes. "This is one great day," he says. "This is one fucking great day."

We walk to my car. Cops from the cop shop stroll by. Lawyers. Secretaries. Suddenly Maggie stops. She reaches down into the gutter beside a parking meter, and stands up with a dead sparrow in her hand.

She is thrilled. She fans out the bird's tail feathers with her finger. She is going to put that little bird in her fridge, she says. "This is perfect. You know that little apple doll of mine? It needed a new bustle. These feathers are perfect for that." She giggles; her boyfriend hates it when he opens the fridge and finds dead birds. But then, she says, "That is just too darn bad for him."

Kicker re-opens his plastic baggie. "Them cops ripped off my sunglasses," he says. A pencil falls out onto the sidewalk. He bends over and picks it up. Maggie laughs, "Oh ya, you and all your treasures."

"This here is all the treasures I need," Kicker says. Meaning the fresh air, the clean day, the freedom.

"AND THEN MY other son Shaun, he's fifteen, he's the one who just affects me something else." The blue budgie in the blue budgie cage chirps from the living room. "Extra somehow. He's the one who was sexually molested when he was five years old. And him and I have been talking and I have been counselling him all these years. And we've become really close, because of that.

"With my sexual assault, I don't feel guilty for that anymore. I don't hate that person. I don't feel any pain. I can talk about it. And I think because of that I have been able to help my child go through this.

"I was really young at the time. I think I was about five. I was molested by my grandfather. And I don't think it was a penetration or anything, but it was more or less, very physical kind of, where it hurt, you know, with his hands and stuff like that.

"That was really difficult for me, having him being such a big adult and I having grown up with all that stuff. Self-hatred. It wasn't him that I hated, it was me. I blamed me. When I tried to commit suicide it was that sexual assault and a whole lot of other things mixed in with that.

"It is just so important to be aware when your child's personality starts changing, or their behavior. Something is coming down, 'cause that's how I knew, that's how I found out with my son.

"Like he's really close to his grandmother and he loves going to grandma's. And then one day I was going to leave him there and he got really uptight. And I said, 'Why, I thought you always like coming here?' And he said, 'No, I don't want to stay.' And he was really fidgety and I was holding his hand and I said, 'Why, why don't you want to go?'

"And he said, "Cause I'm scared of that picture, the monster in that room.' And I said, 'What monster?'

"And so he showed me the monster and it was this lion on the wall. And I said, 'It's always been there, you've never been afraid of it.' I said, 'You're going to have to stay here because I got to go to town, there's nothing to be afraid of.' It did something to me somehow inside, but I left him there anyway.

"So the next time I was going to leave him there, he was really uptight to the point of crying. He said, 'The monster, I don't want to go, the monster is there.' And this gut feeling I had just came again. And I thought, 'Well, I'm not going to leave my kid here if he is so scared of that picture.' So I took him 'cause he was crying and I said, 'You can come with me to town.' And he was so happy. He was just hugging and kissing me. 'Thanks, Mom,' and all this.

"I couldn't forget it. Once in awhile I'd ask him, 'What's wrong? Can you let me know? I know something is wrong.' So one day I really sat him down and I said, 'You can tell me anything you want and I won't be angry with you. I know something is bothering you.'

"And I didn't suspect. A sexual assault like that was the last thing I thought of. And he went, 'Oh, it's OK, Mom,' and went off to play. Then all of a sudden, I was sitting on the couch, and all of a sudden he just came and jumped beside me and whispered in my ear. And he said, 'Uncle Frank was kissing my bum.'

"I just went, 'Oh God.' And I told him, 'No one has to know. Just go play, OK?'

"I told my husband, 'I got to go over there, I got to go there right now.' I asked him to drive me. And he sat there like a dog on log. He didn't move. He didn't say anything. I had expected him to jump up and go half-kill my brother and he didn't. He just sat there.

"And I think that's where something happened to me inside about my husband. I thought, 'You! This is your child. How could you just sit there, how could you just sit there? How could you not say anything? I need you and he needs you.'

"Anyway, I got Barney to drive me to my mom's place. And my mom and dad were there and Frank was sitting at the table. I just whispered over to him, 'If you ever fucking touch my kid again, I'll kill you.'

"And I whispered just like that because I couldn't start hollering because my mom and dad were there and I didn't want them to know. I guess that's where I done wrong. I should have showed my anger, but I protected everybody else.

"I've never even talked to my ex-husband about this, in all the talks we've had. He doesn't know me at all. He doesn't know the things I go through with my kids. And I didn't want to explain. I was so disappointed when he didn't come with us. But I understand, too, now that he has his own, he had sexual experiences when he was small that I'm sure he has not dealt with.

"I look at it that way now, but at one time I didn't. I felt so abandoned."

MAGGIE'S THREE YOUNGEST sons, Ian, Shaun, and Eddie Jr., live with her ex-husband out in the country. They've been with their dad ever since Maggie started school several years before; when she graduated she didn't reclaim them. She feels the country is a better place for them to grow up. And they are teenagers now; she says she can't handle them anymore.

"I had a very difficult time with my kids when they were here visiting, because of that arcade by my place. It was open till two in the morning. And one night something told me to get up, and I did. And I went to check the kids sleeping in the living room. And the old bit about making their sleeping bags look like somebody was in them? They were gone. Oh, I freaked out. 'Cause I don't want my kids to stay out late.

"Shaun is the one who is going through that adolescent stage right now. He's fifteen and getting really, I don't know, unsettled. So I packed them up one day and I says, 'You're going back to your dad. You don't want to listen, that's what the consequence is gonna be.' Then I dropped them off at the farm. And I said, 'It may seem like I'm abandoning you, but I'm not.'

"My heart just didn't know what it felt like when I dropped them off, but I thought it would be best for them. 'Cause Shaun done it the second time, stayed out again. And this time it was four thirty in the morning.

"And I thought, 'No more Kickers. No way.' "

"SHAUN, BECAUSE OF his sexual abuse, he was even talking about suicide one day, because of the assault. He was only about twelve. I took him out to supper to McDonald's that day, and him and I talked. He's very isolated at times because he can't mingle in with the other kids. 'Cause he doesn't fit. I know that, that's how I was. He was feeling so alone; he can't connect to other kids 'cause there's something, I don't exactly know what it is, but you feel so different.

"And I said, 'I think we have to move, try and move to the next level now, up to the point where you have to be able to talk about the act itself.' And he tried. And he started spitting up on the ground and he said, 'Mom, please let's not because I'm getting sick to my stomach.'

"And so I didn't pressure him. And I said, 'I respect that, but do think a little bit. Eventually, you will be OK.' And I told him, I shared with him about my experience.

"And I said, 'That has happened to me, and it's a big, long, hard struggle, but the more we work together it will be alright.' So, he'll be eventually OK. I know it."

AFTER THE SLIDE show the detective from the sex crimes unit flips on an overhead projection listing sexual abuse indicators. VD in young children. Physical trauma. Pain around throat or genitals. Offensive odor. Pregnancy in young children. An unusual interest in sex for the age. Seductive. Runaways. Fearful of women or men. A child who doesn't want to go home.

During this Maggie doodles on a paper napkin. A tepee. A flower. A sun.

"ALCOHOLISM. YOU KNOW you're over your alcoholism when you can enjoy a sunset. When you're drinking and the sun goes down all you can think of is the sadness, the depression. Another day gone. Wasted. I remember the first time I saw a sunset and I saw its colors. All those beautiful colors. Like flannelette – all streaked with pink and blue. I could see how beautiful that sunset was, and I almost cried.

"It scares me to death when I think about if I hadn't become an alcoholic. I wouldn't have this awareness about myself, 'cause I had to go through shit to come to learn, to feel this way about me. I'm an alcoholic and I'm glad I'm an alcoholic. 'Cause it made me respect life and it made me aware. If I had an opportunity to change all that and have it a little bit different, maybe better, forget it. I'll go through it again because what I have now is very valuable to me. I'm glad I'm an alcoholic.

"I'm sure up and down the block here, if everybody was honest, everybody gets affected by booze one way or the other. They may not be drinking themselves but they have a relative, or a husband, or something. It's not just in the Native people, it's also in the white people, because it's such a big problem in our society today.

"I'm a slow learner. It took me somewhere in my thirties before I knew about myself, about how to deal with my disease. But that's a good part, too. Because, when you start working inside yourself at a later age, it prevents you from getting old and depressed because it's such a renewed kind of thing in your life. 'Wow, I'm alive. I feel good!' And even though you're in your forties, thirties, it makes you feel like a new person.

"I don't feel old, and I don't feel all used up. I feel re-energized. I feel life is exciting."

✪ KICKER

TWO THIRTY SATURDAY morning. Early September. The phone rings. Kicker. Yes, again. Kicker.

Kicker, hung over, looking for the hair of the dog that bit him. A dirty November afternoon. The moon is pale against a pale grey sky. Kicker stares up, his forehead pressed against my car windshield. "The moon is a dried blood beast."
Me: "Who said that?"
Kicker: "Jim Morrison. I don't know where he got it from. The moon doesn't look anything like that. To me."

When the phone rings, Wendy has just started to snore. Lightly, like an asthmatic breathing. I jump out of bed and grab the receiver. Wendy doesn't wake. Lesley in the living room stirs.
Kicker: "I'm sorry to wake you up, man. I got beat up. I got nowhere to go."
Me, whispering: "Kicker, I've got two people staying with me."
Kicker, panicky, insistent: "I got nowhere to go."

Kicker, all twenty-two years of him, all 5'6" of him, all black Metallica T-shirt, Guns-and-Roses medallion of him, in his basement apartment next door to a freeway and three floors below his grandmother's suite, where he lives with his fifteen-year-old girlfriend, Meagan. Meagan is pregnant. Social Services wanted to send her to an unwed mothers' home, Kicker to the Single Men's Hostel. Kicker's mother, a social worker herself, intervened to plead that the two be allowed to live together. Meagan's mother had to sign custody of her daughter over to Kicker. She did it without question.

Kicker's Iron Maiden posters decorate the living room. A dove, a present from his grandmother, flaps from cupboard top to curtain rail and back again. Kicker snarls at it. "One of these days," he says, "one of these days I'm going to get hungry and eat that damn bird."

Kicker: "I think I got to go to the hospital. My lip is still bleeding, man. It's been bleeding for the last two hours. Won't fucking stop.

"Five guys jumped me, man. Believe it or not they were Indians. Five fucking Indians jumped me."

Wendy and Lesley are staying at my place for one night. They are up from Calgary to audition actors for Wendy's first feature film. "Midnite" in the film's title is spelled incorrectly on the advice of a psychic Wendy paid to check the name for luck. Even though the psychic now approves, Wendy wants to change the title. She has considered, but rejected "Love and Spawning." Likewise "Tube-Tied." She is after her friends for more ideas. This film is a comedy, she says, and the title must make that clear.

Me, rubbing my face: "Kicker, where are you?"

Kicker: "7-Eleven."

Me: "Which one?"

Kicker, impatient with my stupidity: "This one, man. Here on 97th Street."

Me: "Where on 97th Street?"

Kicker, mumbling: "I don't know, man. Phone number here is. . . . "

Kicker, the gritty November afternoon. His Uncle David, his age, has just beat him up. A zipper scar now closes Kicker's chin. A tooth is cracked. His nose has grown a broad red ridge where it met his uncle's boot.

"I got into a scrap with my bloody uncle, eh. That was some

scrap. He's a square head – he's never even done any time. But he got the best of me because I was hammered. I don't think he was even drunk, him. He kicked me in the jaw – fucked up my molar. Kicked me in the nose too. But I'm feeling pretty good, eh. I'm OK.

"I went to the dentist. I hate needles in the mouth, eh. I told the doctor, 'Just pull it out, man. No needles.'

"My uncle really burned me. But I beat him up once before, so I guess we're even. We're still friends, eh. But when you think about it, it's pretty weird. My own uncle." Kicker stares up at the pale sky. "We're blood."

I'd spent the afternoon watching Wendy and Lesley do their casting at the Edmonton franchise of John Casablancas' modeling studio. John Casablancas offered Wendy the use of a video camera and space for free, in return for giving its acting students a chance to audition. The students had no hope of making it into Wendy's film. In fact, she didn't even turn on the camera while they read.

Later, Wendy discovered she got the video's on and off switches mixed up. The only things she recorded the entire day were an hour of an empty chair while she and Lesley went to lunch – and all the Casablancas people.

Me, cold now in the dark: "Kicker. I need to know which avenue you are on. Can you go out and look at the address?"

Kicker: "Ya." There is silence. Then the clatter of the receiver being picked up again. "This guy's a real fucking jerk here. I don't remember how he say, one two seven ninety seven ninety, I mean one two seven two. . . . "

Me: "Don't leave."

Kicker hates "Kicker." It is what his girlfriend Meagan, his mother, his brothers, the cops all call him. The cops consider it his alias and include it whenever he's charged. He hates it so much that, when I ask him one day where it comes from, he won't tell me.

"Didn't my mother tell you? No? I hate that name. It's a tough guy's name. Kick-er." His voice is gravelly and mocking. It turns mocking and sweet. "Then, Chris. Chris. I don't like any of those names. That's what I always say when I'm on acid. Someone calls me. 'Hey, you're calling me?' "

"Do you have a middle name?"

"Edmund."

"Do you like that name?"

"What? I don't even know what the hell it means. I remember this one time I was talking to this lady from Social Services. She wanted my full name. I said, 'Christian Edmund Boucher.' She said something about, that it sounds like royalty. I was scratching my head there for awhile. 'What the fuck does that mean?' "

"Did you ask your parents where it came from?"

"Where I came from? I came from down the chute."

"No. The name 'Edmund.' "

"I don't know. I don't ask questions. That much."

I ask his mother. Maggie says she decided he was "Kicker" the moment he was born, whimpering, punching at the air with his feet like a kick-boxer. Then, when he was little and she was still drinking and her kids were going to Sunday school without her, Kicker came home and told her that none of them – not her, not his brothers – were going to heaven. Only *he* was. He was Christian and only Christians go to heaven.

I GET DRESSED and tiptoe out of my apartment. I drive down Jasper Avenue. The police have picked someone up at the corner of 105 Street, across from the city's "Needle Park." The cop-car lights are rolling. I can just see the top of the arrested man's head in the back seat. He looks short. Everyone in the back of a cop car looks short.

This is the second time in a week I've seen police make an arrest on this corner. Last time it was two women. A policeman tried to push one of them into his car. She wouldn't budge. He grabbed her purse. He tried sitting on her to shove her in. She bounced back out again and again like a pop-tart.

I turn north off Jasper Avenue and drive up 97 Street. This

street is Edmonton's borderline. To the west is downtown. Rose-colored, $13-million Canada Place. The Law Courts, an inverted concrete pyramid. Provincial Court, glass ascending. To the east – the neighborhood Kicker's mom calls Innercity. She says it with no "the" and all as one word, like Westbrook or Glenora or any other Edmonton subdivision. Here are the city market benches where men who drink Lysol and Scope warm themselves. The China Gate, a ruby-and-gold confection guarded by two lions, an archway leading straight into the drag, the strip, the core. Risk your hand in the lions' mouths to rub the brass balls caught in their throats, the gate promises, and good luck will follow. A Ukrainian bookstore. A drugstore selling decals that proclaim, "My other car is a piece of shit too," and "Sex Instructor – First Lesson Free." The SOS Army Surplus. Dan's Exchange. Dan promises to buy, sell, and trade anything of value. Of value to Dan, going by the showcase, is a Pierre-Trudeau candle with an ape body, a wax owl, and two pairs of velcro-clasped running shoes.

Blocks and blocks north, after Sonja Born Gifted Psychic, after Jing Jing Fashion, after St. Josaphat's, after the Slavic Pentecostal Church, 97 Street changes character again. Up here it is lined with franchises, Honda dealerships, Fasco Rentals. Kicker's 7-Eleven. I pull in. My headlights catch a man taking a leak against the store's back wall. He looks at me and moves back into the shadows. The store lights are harsh and turn the pimple-faced clerk behind the counter green. I can't see Kicker. The clerk asks if I need help. His red 7-Eleven uniform exaggerates the vegetable tinge of his skin. He looks ill.

Before I can answer, Kicker walks around the corner of the sandwich bar, a half-eaten hamburger in one hand. He's been watching the monitors on Heavy Metal and Trojan, the store's video games. He is walking like a sailor. He always walks like a sailor. His rolling strut is part attitude, part stubby legs bowed like a cowboy's. His sweats are ripped at the knee. His right eye is rimmed in red. His nose is cut, his hand covered in blood. The five anonymous Indians have split open his face. Below his mouth a thick flap of severed flesh smiles like a third lip.

"This hamburger is too salty." He fingers his torn mouth. "I shouldn't have got him to put on the salt."

Kicker. Christian. Edmund. Boucher. His grandmother, Grace, with whom he lives when things overwhelm him, when he needs help, more than he can get, remembers:

"Kicker was always more interested in hoboing around than getting into trouble. We used to call him "the littlest hobo." One time he was gone for three days, eh. Maggie was so mad. She said he's really going to get a licking this time.

"My sister wanted two of my boys to be in Klondike Parade, for Native children and Métis. They never showed up. So my sister came to Maggie's house. There was no kids home. Here Kicker walks in and Maggie starts screaming at him. But he first screams, 'No, no, no. Let me be a Métis in the parade.'

"That parade, it saved him from a licking. Yeah, he put a vest on and a little black hat. I guess he was putting on more of a side-show than the parade itself." Grace laughs. "Maggie still gets a kick out of that. She still laughs, whenever she tells that about Kicker."

"The quiet ones are always the ones you worry about, and Kicker was quiet," Maggie tells me. "Kicker, he's a perfectionist. Of course, that comes from his insecurity. He's a good person, Kicker. But I can see how he has a mean streak. He can have a really quick temper if he wants."

When Kicker was a kid he reacted to her drinking, to her husband's drinking, by just leaving, Maggie says. By the time he was eleven, he had run away for good.

None of her kids have ever been violent. Kicker, never. As a kid – even now – his criminal charges were all petty thefts and drunks. One time he stole some booze from a fancy bar. Didn't take any of the money, just the booze. She found the bottles and reported him to the police. "I don't know if I did the right thing or not," she says.

"I always wanted to make my kids feel responsibility for their actions."

The Youth Detention Centre, YDC, a juvenile lock-up, did a psychological assessment of Kicker. They wrote him off as just a street kid, Maggie says, so tough that his hands were scarred from street fighting.

"I was so angry at them, because they had all the power and I had none of the power. I'm just this welfare mom. I felt about a quarter-inch high. But I told them, them scars weren't from street fighting. He'd just hurt his hands when he was just a little kid."

She was even angrier when they said he had a learning disability. "I knew he was a smart kid. He'd always been able to fix things. He burned himself once with electricity by putting a hot wire in his mouth, but he'd always been able to do electrical and magical tricks.

"And he's self-taught to play guitar, and he's good at it. I had bought a guitar once, a seventy-five dollar acoustic guitar with a beautiful face. 'Here,' I said, 'do something with this, somebody.' And he started from there, he practised on that guitar and practised. And now he can play.

"I even bought him a two-hundred dollar guitar once. But because of his addiction to alcohol, he went and pawned it. I'm still going to give him a guitar someday. I don't want to give up on him. I told him, I says, 'You know, you got a talent.' And he does.

"During the tornado, you know, Kicker was stoned that time, too. But he had his little Bible with him. He believes it protected him. My son always carries his little Bible with him. Always."

"Did my mom ever tell you the story about the time she hit my dad over the head with a frying pan?" Kicker and I are in one of Edmonton's pink and green po-mo malls, rimmed with plastic jungle flowers and hung with moulded acrobats. Kicker is eating Chinese food.

"My mom and dad, they were both drinking at the time and

they were in a big fight. And my dad grabbed my Auntie Sarah by the throat and he was choking her. And my mom ran into the kitchen and grabbed a frying pan and hit him over the head." Kicker laughs.

"I guess your dad let go of your Aunt Sarah."

"Ya, he let go.

"My mom and dad were always split up, as far as I'm concerned. They used to fight all the time, eh. That was when we were living on Boyle Street. They used to make me and my older brother, Barney, fight with each other, too. Just for fun. My dad would say, 'Here drink this,' he'd make us drink it and it'd be straight whiskey, eh. I was six or seven at the time. There'd be a whole bunch of them there and they'd make us fight, just for fun.

"I remember when I was about four. It must have been around Christmas 'cause they were all drinking. I remember my dad got me drunk. My mom, she didn't mind. I was chasing this little kid around the house, eh. I ran into the end of the door. Bang! I didn't know what the hell happened. Started crying.

"I remember Barn always used to cry when my mom and dad fought. He really used to cry and whine a lot, that guy. I never cried. I was too scared to cry."

Kicker in his basement apartment three floors beneath his grandma's suite. The dove has folded down on a cupboard far out of reach, cooing.

"How d'ya like this place? It's a typical Indian place, eh. Lots of cockroaches. I'm just kidding. I don't mind cockroaches anyway."

He lights up a cigarette. "I smoke a lot when you're around. You make me nervous for some reason. I feel like you're observing me. I feel like a fucking guinea pig or something."

To distract me, he pulls out his collection of poster books. The drawings are all Frank Frazetta-like: steroid-plumped monsters, eerie landscapes and thrusting, scantily armoured women; fantasies common to comics, to heavy metal, to sci-fi.

"These guys are really great artists, eh. You ever dropped acid? These things, like Ten Years After, you look at them when you're straight and they look like nothing. But when you're on acid, they're like – whoa."

He has cut out and framed his favorite poster – a bearded, long-haired old man smashing through a brick wall. In the old man's raised hand is a staff of stars.

"I really like this picture, eh. That's why I framed it. That guy? I think it's Moses. The stars," Kicker says, "the stars, that's the universe, man."

SATURDAY MORNING. THREE o'clock. The pimple-faced clerk watches sullenly as Kicker rolls like a sailor out of his 7-Eleven. Kicker asks for a ride to the hospital.

The first time I took Kicker to the Charles Camsell was the first time I met him. It was late June, and a prairie thunder storm had just blown through the city. His mother said Kicker's face had to be X-rayed; the doctor thought the cheekbone might be broken. She was certain Kicker wouldn't go to the hospital unless someone took him. She wanted me to see his face for myself.

We picked up Kicker at his grandmother's. The left half of his face was the size of a grapefruit, the swelling flesh threatening to crack open his skin like a rind.

He fell off the wagon, he explained. Two cops stopped him walking down the street. They hassled him. He called them assholes. One of them punched him and then handcuffed him and threw him in the back of the police car. He called them assholes again. Their answer – a nightstick across the face.

He woke up the next morning in the Single Men's Hostel. He couldn't remember the name of the cop who hit him, or his badge number. He was too loaded, he said, to remember anything about the guy at all.

I find a phone booth and jump out to check the address for the Camsell. Kicker asks, do I mind if he throws the hamburger out the car door – he can't eat it. He rolls down the window and chucks the burger out. Then he puts his hand into his pocket and pulls out a plastic-covered Batman air freshener. Perfect, the package states, for cars, RVs, campers; anywhere a fresh, clean scent is desired. "That guy at the 7-Eleven was nice," Kicker says. I think for a confused moment the pimple-faced kid gave Kicker the air freshener because he felt sorry for him. Then Kicker pulls out a stack of ten, fifteen Batmans. He asks, do I want one? He says, here, have one, and props it up on the dashboard.

"I had this address for my friend, eh. I just went up to this girl at this bus stop and asked her if she knew where this address was. These five guys come up to me and ask me am I hitting on her or something. Then one of them hits me, *here*" – he points to his cheek – "and *here*" – to his bloodied chin. "So then I hit him back.

"I can't fight so good when I'm drunk, man. I wish I wasn't so short. They were younger than me too, eh. Five of them.

"I was just at this party at this girl Gina's. Gina's a really nice person. Even though she does T's and R's, you know, Talwin and Ritalin, first thing in the morning. If that's a good person. And then I was just asking for directions, eh, and these guys jumped me.

"That girl tried to help me too, eh. She tried to say, 'Hey wait! He was just asking for directions.' "

I ask, "Were they drunk too?"

"Of course," he says, staring at me. "What do you think?"

The week after we take Kicker for X-rays, Maggie phones, upset again. This time Kicker was picked up with his cousin, Lester, for trying to steal a car. Kicker's in remand. This is not out of the ordinary. The problem is her sister went and laid charges against the police for what they did to Kicker's face. Now Maggie is afraid of what will happen to him while he's in jail. She is so afraid that she is prepared, for the first time in Kicker's life, to bail him out.

The day Kicker is bailed out his balloon face has collapsed, leaving a permanent dimple in his left cheek like the neck of a pouch. He says his auntie will never get anywhere with her charges. He sings: " 'I fought the law and the law won.' "

"Your mom was afraid of you going to prison."

"Yeah, I know. That's one of the reasons why I didn't want any of this to go in the paper. A book is OK, but not the paper." He imitates a cop's voice. " 'Christian Boucher. Keep an eye out for him. Next time he comes in here, give him a few smacks for me, too.'

"I'm not scared of cops, no way. I never forget a pig's face. Only the nice ones. Them I forget."

The day after his mother arranges his release from remand, Kicker swallows ten Mandrax and some Halcion, hypnotics prescribed for insomnia. He overdoses.

His explanation: "I just couldn't help it, man."

At first he says he found the drugs lying around. Then he says, "No, actually you go to a doctor and tell him that you're depressed. Then you go to another doctor. It's called 'double doctoring.' That's RCMP stuff. I wonder when they'll arrest me for that."

He tells me this a few days later, after he has had his stomach pumped, after he has been in hospital yet again, this time getting his forearms sewn up – twelve stitches to close one, thirteen the other. He'd been beat-rolled by three punks in a back alley.

He was drunk at the time, he says. He was rolled for his money. "I had a lot of it, too. I stole a lady's purse yesterday. Well, I didn't actually steal it, she dropped it. She didn't even realize she dropped it. There was no ID in it, so I couldn't give it back to her."

As he talks he shakes. He smells like booze. He says the shakes are from Mandrax. He says he needs something to cure his hangover. Like what? Coffee? Food? No. Like Jack Daniel's.

"There was one older kid, he was bigger than me. The other two, they were Negroes, niggers, coons, whatever you call them. They must have been part of a posse. The Chinamen, Vietnamese, they don't bother the Indians as long as we don't bother them. The Blacks are in posses."

I ask, "Are you in a gang?"

"No, no way. That's not my style. I'm just a hobo, you might say."

"Jeez, you do have the shakes, don't you."

"Mandrax give me the shakes. Mandrax, they're like Halcion. You take them, it's like a drunk high. It's a sleeper. But if you take about – I took, what, nine or ten, something like that – well, I couldn't even walk. Fuck. I didn't want to sleep because I'd waste the high, right? That's what I thought. When you're sitting down like this, you're OK, you're not shaky or nothing. I don't know why they make you shake. I guess probably because I took, take too much of them. Got knocked out.

"In the hospital, all's I know is tubes in me. Pumped my stomach. My arms? They're all right. Got my stitches. Nothing spectacular."

"People are going to think you tried to commit suicide."

"Let them think what they want. When was it, last night? I went to the York. This guy, he was a nice guy, too, he said, 'I see you tried to kill yourself, eh? Here, have a drink on me. Smoke some hash and knife it.' We went to his place. Downed some beer and whiskey. He was pretty depressed, too, by the looks of it. There was so many people in his place. It is only eight blocks from the York, eh. City's core, you might call it. People coming in, crashing out, screwing, leaving, doing T's and R's and all that shit. Pretty goddamned depressing."

A few days after he gets out of jail, overdoses, gets rolled, Kicker calls. He is feeling real bad. A friend of his just got killed. "I think it's the time of year. Everybody's getting their arms broke or beat up or getting killed. It's the time of year for it."

I pick him and Meagan up. Meagan is tall and slight and wears a pair of black sweat pants, almost worn through, and cracked plastic shoes. Her hair hangs over her eyes, which she circles in black pencil, and she cakes white make-up on her skin. Kicker says he hates that white stuff; it makes her look half-dead. It is a long time before she speaks to me. When she does, months after I first meet her, what she says is: "Where's your glasses?" Nothing more.

For awhile Kicker and Meagan lived with her mother and stepfather, and six or seven of her mother's kids. Kicker joked that he told people they didn't need the address. "Just look for the Indian house. The filthy one. The one with dirty di-a-pers in the front yard."

"Meagan's stepdad, he's an asshole. He stays at home. Does nothing all day. Her mom, too. And when they drink, they drink. They fight too. I had to break them up the other day. The cops came. She hit on him. He hit her back. I had to get in between them. You know, the usual drunken stuff.

"You wanna talk about life, go talk to Meagan. She's had a rough life. She still is having one. Her real dad died in a car accident. Don't ever tell her I told you this, 'cause she'd kill me if she knew. But her stepfather abuses her. He sleeps with her, man. Nah, not with the other girls. The other ones are his. She's the one you should talk to. She's had a hard life.

"I don't know, man," he adds, just under his breath. "I guess I think I love her. I just kinda love her."

Meagan calls the girl who died her sister. She was, in fact, Meagan's sixteen-year-old cousin, but to Meagan she was her sister. The girl was just in town, just that morning. She drove back up north and went into a bar and came out and drove her truck straight into an oncoming Winnebago. Meagan is silent. Kicker repeats, endlessly, "I was just talking to her. I was laughing with her and joking with her. Now she's dead. I can't believe she's dead. I guess people are born to die. Aren't they? I guess I was born to die.

"I feel like I want to cry right now. I must have cried for about an hour or so, maybe longer. We're not here forever. The way she died, though, that was pretty hard."

The arms of Kicker's jean jacket are stiff with dried blood. He is shaking so bad he can hardly pull his cigarette out of the pack. Meagan, otherwise silent, laughs at him when he can't get it lit. He pulls a mickey out of his jacket and pours the dregs into his coffee.

"I guess my life is this bottle. At least this gives me something to hold onto."

Later, after the girl's funeral, Kicker says: "Meagan cries in her sleep at night, eh. She won't admit it, but I've seen her. That was her closest friend. That was her sister.

"But life goes on, right? With or without us."

July. Kicker appears on his car-theft charge to plead not guilty and set a trial date. He watches an old man go up for drunk driving. The prosecutor unrolls a copy of the man's record, letting it fall with great drama to the floor. The lawyer smiles. "Your Honor, this record is longer than my kid." Kicker is angry. "Fuck," he whispers to me, "they think it's a fucking joke."

Afterward I suggest we go eat. He says he's had a few raisins that day, so he's not so hungry. I tell him it's OK, I'm hungry. We eat Egg McMuffins. He says he did a dine-and-dash yesterday. Thirty-eight bucks for a hamburger that he ate real, real slow, and then some beer and some vodka and whiskey. Don't tell his mom, though. "I guess old habits are hard to break."

He looks around the McDonald's and asks if I know how they kill chickens. He says his auntie told him they line them up by their feet and stick their heads in boiling water. He says thinking about that makes him want to puke. He calls George Bush a war pig. He shows me the scar on his thumb where the cops pulled the skin back during one of his arrests.

He asks if his mom ever told me about a woman she used to drink with named Kate. Kate was in a wheelchair. When he was a kid he used to push Kate wherever she wanted to go. Into the bar, wherever. She used to beg. The only people who always gave her money were other Native people. She did pretty well at it. Some guy gave her a watch once.

He grew up around the city core. The place where he used to play marbles is a hooker street now. He ran away, he doesn't know how many times he ran away in his life. He ran away from lots of places. Why? For the adventure.

"It was a good time in my life.

"I was, what, twelve. Compulsive care. It's a lock-up. Can't go out or nothing. I tried to run away from there. Zigzagged. Backtracked. I had frostbite that night. There was no way out. I turned myself back in.

"I don't even remember why I was locked up there to start with. When I was a kid, I got into a lot of shit. I think that time it was because me and Lester broke into a hardware store. There was a twenty-six in the desk and I just guzzled it. Then I took the truck, there was a truck in there and I smashed it into a telephone pole.

"The guy who owned the hardware store, that was his truck. He must have heard the smash. He opened the truck door and I fell out right on my ass. He says, 'Get out.' I was already out on the fucking ground. He kept pacing back and forth saying, 'I don't want to hit him. I don't want to hit him.' All we took was his whiskey and his fucking truck. Probably mad 'cause we did front-end damage.

"I puked in the cop car that night. 'Cop!' I said. I started yelling, banging on the window and everything. No cop. The cop was getting the story, eh. Doing his homework, getting his brownie points or something. I puked on their side." He laughs. "Didn't get none on me.

"How old was I the first time I ran away? Um. . . . " He pauses to consider. "That's a long time ago. I think I was about six. Somewhere around that. Six, five. Slept in somebody's tent on Boyle Street. In the backyard. There was a tent in there, blankets. I had a good sleep. It was hot. The sun was shining. Last day of school. I was happy. When you're a kid, you don't need nothing," he turns his head away from the tape recorder, "except love. And then when kids grow up, life is so much different. You're on your own.

"I got about a grade-four education. I'd say it'd take me maybe three years and I'd be able to write. Like, every time I'd go back to school, eh, I'd get it down in my head. But then, it's like reading a book. When you read a book and you get down a few paragraphs, you forget what the hell it said. Alexia? Is that what it's called?"

"Dyslexia?"

"Yeah. Like say I'm writing my name, sometimes I'd put an "h" in front, put the "c" behind it. Dyslexia. Yeah, I get pretty mixed up. I only read the books I like. One book that was pretty good was, I Was An Animal, But I'm All Right Now. Did you read it? It's a story about Eric Burdon, you know that guy from The Animals? He did a lot of drugs. Acid. All kinds of stuff.

"Me, first time I ever sniffed glue I was about nine. My friend, Ronnie, he started me. At first I didn't want to, man. I thought it was pretty heavy stuff. But this one time he got some glue and he started to sniff. It was over in Jasper Place, that rich part, you know? Over by the museum? They got this big fountain, with all these colors. I finally started to sniff and I looked at this fountain and it was all these beautiful colors. I thought, 'This is great, man. This is paradise.'

"I sniffed from there on. One time in YDC I was sniffing with my roommate. I hallucinated. It was as real as though you were looking at this room. I thought I saw the devil. Not the devil, this little demon about this tall. He had these big black eyes, eh. And this bald head. And his skin was real ugly. I musta passed out or something 'cause this guy got on top of me and was slapping my face. I thought it was this demon on top of me, trying to choke me. I started screaming and screaming. The staff had to kick the bedroom door down. Man, I was freaked. It took me months before I'd sniff again.

"My dad, he was always the one, even when we were little, who cared most about us. I remember this one time when we were little, they found my glue-sniffing bags out in the garage. My mom just freaked out and started lecturing me. My dad took me outside and said, 'You know, if you ever need somebody to talk to, I'm here. I understand.' That was real nice of that man.

"You don't know my mom very well. My brother, Barn, man, he hates her now. Calls her a bitch. My dad calls her a bitch. She can be real mean. Real moody.

"My mom always overreacts because she doesn't want the responsibility for us, from my perspective." He laughs. "Perspective is a pretty big word, eh. She just wants to care about her own career and shit. When she was a drunk she was a hell of a lot nicer, I can tell you that. I think maybe because when you're drinking you're really depressed and who else do you have to turn to except your kids.

"Now she just doesn't care. One time she left us to sleep out in the car in the middle of the winter time. And this wasn't that long ago either. She just didn't want us living with her anymore. I went out and bought these forty hits of acid. Every time you do acid you gotta do a bit more because you get immune to it, eh. So I did these six hits of acid just to keep from freezing to death, just to keep myself awake.

"But that's, how you say, ancient history. You gotta hit those streets. You gotta hit those new horizons."

Law Courts Building, August 24. Kicker's trial date on the car-theft charge. It is also the day crews are filming the courtroom scenes in a Farrah Fawcett made-for-TV movie. Farrah is playing a mother whose three children were shot one night on a deserted road. Though she claimed they were shot by a stranger, the mother is on trial for the crime herself. According to the movie, based on real life, she tried to murder her children for the love of a man.

On our way into the courthouse Kicker and I walk past the huge ITV trailer that, I assume, is housing Farrah and company. Kicker is talking about his lawyer, who "everybody seems to like." The lawyer is legally blind. "The first time I met him? I couldn't figure it out, man. This guy wouldn't look at me at all. I thought, 'This guy is prejudiced,' 'cause he wouldn't look at my face.

"My lawyer was telling me I should get nicer clothes, get myself a suit or something for today. I say, 'Why act phoney? You should just go out the way you are.' That's what I say."

Kicker is living up to his principles. His shiny black jacket is decorated with skulls. His hair covers his eyes. His medallion praises Guns and Roses; his ripped T-shirt extols The Clash.

He is shaky and red-eyed, and he spends a lot of time in the can before the trial begins. When he comes out for the third or fourth time he says, as if by explanation, "I've got a runny nose. I've got a runny nose again, man." Then, "I don't know why I get so fucking nervous before court."

The car Kicker is accused of trying to drive home is a 1989 Chrysler Daytona, worth $14,100. The cops say Kicker and Lester and a third guy, Teddy, tried to push-start the car in the dead of night while the owner was asleep in his house. Lester has already pleaded guilty to the charge and is serving nine months. He is going to appear today and testify Kicker had nothing to do with any of it.

The prosecutor is a tall, bouncy man whose clothes don't fit and whose joints seem disconnected. If he weren't a lawyer he would have to be a stand-up comic; no other profession would suit his floppy physique as well. The clerk mutters to him, "Gawd, I hope this only takes half an hour." And Kicker's trial begins.

The car's owner testifies. Yes, a Daytona can be push-started, the arresting officer testifies. When he discovered the car it was halfway into the alley, with Lester and Kicker pushing from behind. Under cross-examination he adds that, with the wheels angled as they were, pushing would have returned the car to the driveway.

Kicker goes up on the stand.

"We were coming home from a party. Lester and me and Teddy. I was about half a block ahead of them. I walked back 'cause I noticed this car in the alleyway. I wanted to see what these guys were doing.

"Lester, he was pretty drunk. I told him, 'Put the car back.' We were trying to push the car back into the driveway."

The prosecutor cross-examines. "Mr. Boucher, if you were concerned about keeping your cousin out of trouble, why didn't you just leave?"

"I just wanted to help Lester from not getting into trouble because he was drunk."

Lester, a handsome kid with the over-developed upper body of a weightlifter, is brought in from jail to testify. He admits to being "half-cut" that night. Why were they pushing the car back? "It was blocking traffic." Why was Kicker pushing? " 'Cause I just got out of jail that day, so he wanted to help me."

Kicker's lawyer sums up. "At best the prosecution's evidence is equivocal. The wheels were straight on. Under cross-examination, Kicker said he knew pushing the car was not the right thing to do to help his cousin stay out of trouble. But he wasn't around when the two individuals decided to try and steal the car."

There is a disturbance in the courtroom while Kicker's lawyer makes his argument. A sparkling blonde with a huge mane of hair, accompanied by a lesser blonde carrying a tennis racquet and a California man in white shorts, tiptoe into the courtroom. They sit a few minutes, a blonde, tanned block radiating wealth and health, and then leave.

The prosecutor is beside himself. His loose limbs threaten to fly apart. He pounces on Kicker's lawyer. "Was that Farrah Fawcett?" Kicker's lawyer, being blind, does not know. The prosecutor turns to the cop at the back of the courtroom. His whisper is strangled. "Was that Farrah?"

The judge stares down at the prosecutor. The prosecutor collects himself. He starts jabbing his pen in the air. "Sir, why not just leave the scene? Staying around makes no sense, especially if Mr. Boucher wanted to get his cousin out of problems. His story is ludicrous."

If the judge knows the identity of the radiant blonde, he is keeping it to himself. "Pushing at that stage would have put the vehicle back. I am giving Mr. Boucher the benefit of the doubt. Mr. Boucher, I find you not guilty."

Out on the street again, Kicker says, "All that, you know, it was a lie. Why not lie, the cops lie! Hey man, it just feels good not to be in jail.

"No more crime, man. At least not until I drink again. In 1988 I got caught four times. But I was doing a lot of crime that year, man. Every day. Hey, I had a habit to support.

"I *am* trying to stay out of jail. If not, man, I could have money every day. I'm trying my hardest. I don't know. It's fucking hard."

Kicker phones the next day. He's feeling shitty. He needs somebody to talk to. I drive to the address he gives me. A young woman, maybe eighteen, opens the door. She is wearing a blue baseball cap, backwards. "You want Kicker?"

I have interrupted a party. There's a bottle of Silk Tassel whiskey on the kitchen table. A tape player. Cards. Kicker's Uncle David is there, his jaw swollen like he's sucking a huge plug of tobacco or he just lost a tooth. He is, in his words, "only half-cut." There's the girl who answered the door and Meagan, and then there's Kicker who's a lot more than half-cut. He is stumbling and incoherent, his eyes punch-shut. He's done some acid.

"Come on in," David says. "Fart, do whatever you want." He's been going to school, he says, so this is the first time he's partied in a long time. The baseball-cap girl says, "Bullshit." He says, "Yeah, it is." She says, "Bullshit." He glares at her and cups his hand, as though holding a dripping mound of shit.

He wants to know if I'm Kicker's lawyer or probation officer. Meagan says, no, I'm a friend of Maggie's. I explain I'm there because Kicker phoned. David says, coyly, "Well, maybe I should phone sometime." The girl in the hat shakes her head. "Nah. Come on. Two different worlds."

"No," David says. "Same shit. Just two different piles."

Kicker chugs Silk Tassel. He mumbles, barely decipherable, "Thanks for coming," and falls to the floor in a clattering heap. Meagan giggles. His uncle drags him to the couch. A baby, the child of the baseball-cap girl, totters up to where Kicker has passed out, face down. The baby whimpers. He holds onto his bottle of apple juice with one hand and, with the other, pats Kicker's hair. Kicker, stoned, drunk, reaches out through his druggy haze. He strokes the baby back.

Kicker phones the next day to apologize for being drunk. I say it doesn't matter. He is already drunk again.

Kicker in his basement apartment with his cooing, cowering dove, flipping through his heavy-metal, muscle-babes poster books. "I don't have any artistic talent, eh. The only talent I have is playing the guitar. I love to play the slide guitar. I can't read music though. Jimi Hendrix, he couldn't read music either.

"I read Jim Morrison's poetry. I could understand about half of it. That guy's my favorite singer. I read that book about him three times. They say he died in a bath, of a heroin overdose. But no one ever saw his body, eh. So some people say he's still alive somewhere.

"You know The Doors' organ player? He used to burn incense when he played. Said it was for 'the communal brain.' The communal brain – that means the minds of all the people coming together. That guy, that guy was one intelligent guy, man."

Late September. Kicker phones. "I got into another scrap, did I tell you already? Remember I was drunk that time when you came to pick me up, when I had that cut lip? Well about two days after that I went downtown to the Cecil. Me and Meg. I was scoring a gram of hash. The sleaze-ball who sold it to me sold me some mud. I was drunk, eh. I usually check it out, break it up, make sure it's for real, but I was drunk. So when I found out I went back to that scum-bag. I told him, 'Give me my fucking money back, man.' And he said, 'No way, man. You bought it.'

"Then he gave me this punch, this little sucker punch right on my fucking lip right where it was cut. Then he took off. Meagan was yelling at me, 'Let him go. Let him go.' I was just yelling at him, 'That's not a cool thing to rip someone off like that, man. I'll see you in jail.'

"I will see him in jail, too, eh, because I remember his face. And he's gonna end up in jail, too, selling drugs right there on Jasper Avenue."

A rare Edmonton October day, hot and sunny. Cars in the parking lot look licked and shiny. Meagan leaves a message on my answering machine. She says Kicker told her to ask if they could borrow twenty dollars for groceries. And Kicker has been charged with assaulting a police officer. It is the most I have ever heard her say.

A beige sectional replaces the chenille-covered mattress that served as the couch last time I was at their place. An orange fake fireplace, attached to nothing, looks weirdly out of place in one corner of the living room. Meagan and Kicker have been playing cards. Kicker bought coffee for me. There's no cream.

"Gotta get a lawyer on the 30th. I went to court, you know, and looked my name up on the docket. Assault on the first line. And then 'police officer.' And then his name. If it was assault on anybody else there wouldn't be the name. I don't see what difference it makes. Cops are just like everybody else.

"Man, I was home-free there for awhile and then I fucking woke up in the drunk tank. I thought I was just in there for drinking. So I asked this guy and he told me, 'No, assault.'

"Little wimp cop. Cry-baby cop. He says I hit him seven times with his nightstick. It sounds like I'm beating him to death. Ha. He could have shot me. There was two of them.

"I'm not looking forward to going back to jail. Jail sucks. I'm getting used to the idea, though. You gotta get used to it. You can't sit inside chewing on your fingers all day worrying about it."

Meagan is watching a soap opera with the sound turned off. Kicker laughs at her. "What ya doing? Making up your own words?" She lunges out to kick him. She misses. Kicker laughs again.

"I been working out in the country with my dad. Doing stucco and stuff. He paid me two hundred bucks. I went and rented a room in the Bonaventure and I drank it up. Man, booze is expensive.

"The country was boring. I came back because my arm is hurting. I have to go to the doctor's. I got arthritis, eh. I've had it since I was a kid. I was about three and I spent the night in this haystack and I got really cold and really wet. And the next day I woke up and my legs just ached, man. They ended up sticking me in the hospital. I had to take like six aspirins a day. It's not too bad now. But this time, man, it's moved. It never used to be in my shoulders. Shit, I don't know what it's going to be like when I'm old. I hope I don't get it in my hands.

"Did I tell you Lester got another three months? Last year he and me were in a gas station. I even had money and everything. He stole a pair of sunglasses. They added three months on. Consecutive. Three months for a pair of six-dollar sunglasses. Justice sucks, man.

"I miss Lester. I grew up with him, eh. He's my best friend. Guess I gotta get in there with him and try it out. See all my friends. All my friends are in there. I got a lot of friends inside." Jim Morrison. "I got friends inside."

Kicker walks into the living room. He picks up a dictionary. "Hey Meagan, what's the definition of prick?" She shrugs. He reads: "A small, hard thorn." She breaks into a giggle, covering her mouth with her hand.

"November 30th for my trial date? It's not a long way away at all. It seems like a short time to me." Then, "Don't tell my mom about the twenty bucks, eh. Don't tell my mom."

November 30. Kicker is nowhere to be found at the court house. I watch a defence lawyer argue for an absolute discharge for a kid who stole a roll of quarters from an open safe full of money. The kid is a cadet. A member of the biathlon team. A volunteer at the Calgary Olympics. The boy, in his razored hair and dress shirt and tie, is painfully nervous. His mother sits at the back of the courtroom, shaking her head at every fine word of the defence lawyer. "Yes, believe him, sir," her nodding head says to the judge. "Please, my son is a good boy."

I go in search of Kicker and find him slouched outside the courtroom doors. He looks terrible. His hair is tied back in a greasy ponytail, his grey jacket is filthy. His eyes are veined and red, and he smells of last night's drunk.

Meagan is with him. She is starting to balloon. Kicker says he thinks she's going to have twins. "She's getting huge. I can't sleep with her anymore. She hogs the whole bed up. She's getting ugly. Hey, just kidding."

Kicker's lawyer is nowhere to be seen. Kicker insists Doyle is a good guy. He trusts him; Doyle got him off before. We wait. We wait. Good-guy Doyle does not show.

Kicker tells the judge his lawyer was supposed to be there. He asks to have his trial set over to the afternoon so he can find him.

The prosecutor, tiny and tidy in his precise brown suit, does not believe Kicker has a lawyer. He thinks Kicker is just stalling. "Your Honor, Mr. Doyle is not the type not to show up in my experience." He points out that three police officers have taken the day off to appear as witnesses. He outlines the expense involved. He suggests the trial proceed.

The judge seems swayed, ready to believe that Kicker is lying. He frowns down from the height of his dais. "I'm not inclined to put this off, Mr. Boucher. I suggest you call your lawyer and have him here." He grants a brief adjournment.

One of the three police witnesses offers Kicker a phone. Kicker turns it down. "I just want to plead guilty, get it over with, man. I just want to get the fucking thing over with. Serve my time. I won't get any more than six months. It's a bullshit charge anyway, eh. The judge is already mad at me. I hate getting up in front like that and talking. I fucking hate it."

I turn to Meagan. Meagan can persuade Kicker to stop screaming, drunk and obnoxious, at a passing stranger he thinks is staring at him. "What the fuck you staring at, asshole? Hey, asshole!" And Meagan can shut him up. Meagan can convince him to walk when he is so stoned his legs prefer to crumple under him. Meagan can deal with him. Meagan can cope.

"Tell him to phone his lawyer," I say to her. Kicker overhears me. "Fuck it. I'm just going to plead guilty." And hunkers down on the courtroom pew.

I think, "To hell with it." I call Doyle's office. Mr. Doyle, his secretary says, had another pressing matter this morning. A Ms. Mayer from his office is on her way over.

Ms. Mayer arrives just moments before court is recalled. The prosecutor, suddenly gracious, says that, as it now appears Mr. Doyle is representing the accused, this puts a different complexion on things.

Court is adjourned till two o'clock.

Two o'clock. Kicker has gone home and showered and washed his hair, but his eyes are still bleary and the new scars on his chin and cheek and nose gleam bright red. He reeks of booze.

By the time no-show Doyle shows up, ten minutes late, I am furious. He shrugs me off. "Things happen," he says, laying his arm over Kicker's shoulders. "Things happen."

In the courtroom, one of the three police witnesses, disgusted with his wasted day, pretends to mimic Kicker. "I'd plead guilty but Legal Aid is paying so why not waste everybody's time." Doyle huffs in. He does what he's there for; makes his deal with the prosecutor, a guilty plea in return for probation and a fine. He bows to the judge. "I'm sorry about this morning, sir," he says. "Something happened. I don't know what." The judge jokes back, "It may say something about your age."

The joke eases tension in the courtroom for the judge and lawyers. Where there was confrontation there is now camaraderie, an understanding that, after all, this adversarial stuff is just part of the job. Kicker is outside of the joke, outside the charmed circle, in the back of the courtroom, at the bottom of the process. After all, for him this is everything. Especially personal.

The prosecutor reads an abbreviated set of facts. "Police officer attended on complaint of a noisy stereo. Mr. Boucher punched and kicked the officer six or seven times. An attempt was made to use the officer's nightstick. It was a very quick assault, sir."

Doyle speaks. "The record is property-oriented, Your Honor. The situation is simply that he was drunk. The gentleman – it's not his normal habit. I suggest a period of probation, sir, with perhaps the condition that Mr. Boucher receive some alcohol counselling."

Meagan exhales. Meagan, who has been silent throughout, breathes. Kicker, who is sentenced to twelve-months probation and a $300 fine, will not be in jail when she delivers their baby. Kicker will be with her when she has their child.

Kicker shakes Doyle's hand. We walk out onto the icy three o'clock street. I am relieved. Kicker is not. "I was ready to go to jail," he says, gruff, boozy, disappointed. "I was all fucking prepared."

As it turns out, Kicker is not in jail the dry December day Meagan gives birth to their son. Kicker is three floors below her in the Charles Camsell General Hospital, getting his stomach pumped out.

"I got to quit. Get counselling. Next week. That's the second time I OD'd. I woke up and Meagan was there. They pumped my stomach. I was popping pills, man, on the bus. So I got to do something.

"You get half high, you just want to get higher and higher. It's a VD doctor who gives me the pills. He's a fag. Mandrax are sleepers. Put you to sleep forever if you take too many of them.

"Just about broke on through, man. Before my time is due."

EARLY SATURDAY MORNING, a little after 3 a.m. Kicker slumps down into the car seat, shuffling his Batman air fresheners like cards. From time to time he stops to wipe off the blood dripping down his chin.

"Those Indians that beat me up, I feel sorry for them. You see, they gotta make themselves feel better than everybody else. Maybe their mother gave them a beating once," he sneers, "or something when they were kids. I'm not like that. Well, maybe I am, a little.

"I'm a good fighter when I'm not drunk, eh. But I only defend myself. Not attack."

214

Me: "Kicker, if you want to live to be an old man you gotta quit drinking."

Kicker: "I know."

Me: "Your luck's not too good when you're drinking."

Kicker: "That's not luck, that's God."

Me: "God is trying to give you a message, Kicker – quit drinking."

Kicker: "Nah, that's bad luck – that's Satan talking."

January. Kicker lends his bus pass to his cousin. His cousin gets drunk and gets rolled and loses it, along with Kicker's wallet and all his ID. Kicker needs the bus pass to travel to the junior high school where he is working off his court fine by scrubbing walls. If he does not finish his hours by the end of the month he will have to go to jail. He gets a new bus pass.

Two days later he phones me. He has no bus pass. This time he lent it to his uncle who got drunk and lost it. I ask him why he gave it away again, when he knows how badly he needs it. His answer: "I just can't say no, man. When people ask me for stuff, I just can't say no.

"I'm bored. Meagan went to bingo. She's a bingo addict. I'm watching the baby right now. Crying Brian. At first I was in a state of shock when he was born, eh. But now I love him. He plays by himself but he needs some toys. He's got nothing to look at here except out the window. He likes looking out the window at the trees.

"I think Meagan's going to leave me, man. Because of me OD'ing again."

February. Kicker tells me they lost their baby. Lost their Crying Brian. They decided to party, and Meagan's cousin volunteered to look after the kid. He and Meagan went out and got half-cut. When he woke up in the morning he walked into Brian's bedroom. Brian wasn't there. Kicker freaked. He thought Social Services had apprehended the baby while they were out drinking. Or that the "effing neighborhood cop" had snuck in, in the middle of the night, and taken Brian away.

Kicker phoned Social Services. They told him they didn't have his baby; he should call the police. He called the police. They told him they didn't have Brian, and threatened to report him to Social Services for losing his child.

Kicker was going crazy. He was about to phone his mother to find out whether she had stolen his child when Meagan's cousin came back. He forgot, Kicker said. He got so drunk he forgot he had given Brian to Meagan's cousin. For safekeeping.

A week later. "I don't want to talk to my mom. I don't want to talk to her ever again. She took Brian away. I had to call the police on her.

"Ya. My Uncle David was here all by himself, 'cause me and Meagan went and rented a room, eh. Cause this one cop comes here all the time and checks if we're drinking. If Brian's here and we're drinking, he'll take him away, he said. So, David was here by himself, straight, and she come in here and just took Brian. She wouldn't give him back to us so we had to call the police on her.

"We got him back, eh. Now I don't want nothing to do with my mother. Nothing more at all."

March. Kicker calls from jail. It was an accident, he says. He accidentally launched a rock through a car windshield with his slingshot. He pleaded not guilty, but still got fifty days. He is serving his time at the Fort.

"It was stupid. I was doing all right. Then I started taking Valium. Went out, took a walk, seen this ghetto blaster in this car. Thought I might as well grab it. But I got lucky or something, 'cause I realized somebody was watching me through this window. So I threw the ghetto blaster back in the car.

"The cops told me that I'm lucky I only got possession and mischief, 'cause I threw the thing back in again. I said, 'Great, so can I go home tonight?' Nope. No such luck."

Meagan phones while Kicker is in the Fort. She needs ten dollars to buy Brian milk. She feeds him sweetened evaporated milk, straight from the can, and it is expensive. She says she wants to pawn his dresser for the ten dollars, and will I help her move it.

When I get to their apartment, she has emptied Brian's dresser of its sleepers and sweaters, and has dragged it out into the middle of the living room floor. She is set to pawn it for milk.

Kicker phones from the Fort. He wants Meagan to come visit him. But she needs picture ID first. Can I take her to the Money Mart, where they cash welfare cheques and stuff, and get her some ID? It'll cost ten dollars. Meagan has trouble thinking of the two references with phone numbers she needs to complete her Money Mart form. She has no idea how tall she is, or how much she weighs. She tells the teller 5'8" and 180 pounds, an estimate at least fifty pounds too heavy. She has trouble signing her name; she was in a fight the night before and her right thumb is sprained, maybe broken. A nasty red cut runs down her shin from knee to ankle, her arms are nicked and I wonder if the wounds come from a knife. When I ask her if she's been to the hospital, she says she's OK.

When Meagan's picture pops out of the instant-photo booth, it is all dark hair and pale skin, bangs shadowing her eyes. Her grin is sweet; toothy and excited. This is her first-ever picture ID. She is a fifteen-year-old kid. This is an adventure.

Meagan and Brian and I drive to Fort Saskatchewan to visit Kicker. She has dressed up for this; pulled her hair off her face with a headband, put on long shining earrings. We manage to find the old jail, but not the new one. I can't see the McDonald's Kicker said was the nearest landmark. By the time we finally get to the new Fort, visiting hours are over. We turn around. Just outside Edmonton, Meagan asks how I know where I'm going. I'm surprised. I point to the sign overhead. "There," I say. "I just follow the road signs. See, where it says South, Edmonton?" "Oh ya," she says. It is then I realize she cannot read.

We pick Kicker up from the Fort early the Saturday morning he's finished his time. It will be a brilliant spring day; the light is already yellow and gleaming. A few prisoners are out in the ditch in front of the jail, picking weeds or broken glass or garbage, I can't see to tell. A work truck full of prisoners sprays dirt at us as it leaves the yard. When the jail door opens to let Kicker out, Meagan is in the washroom, so she misses him. Kicker dives onto Brian and chucks him into the air. He says he's afraid Brian has forgotten who he is. He's pissed off, because Brian grew so much hair while he was inside and he couldn't watch.

Two days later, Kicker wants a ride to the hospital. He has OD'd on pills some guy in the Fort gave him as a going-away present. He's taken them all, all thirty of them, all at once.

"Ya, I took them. To get high, man. I'm all red. I'm fucking all red all over. I can't call the ambulance. I don't have no medical. Stomach pumped, man. Stomach pumped."

Meagan, busy with Brian and the baby carriage, does not watch as Kicker is wheeled away from emergency down a long hospital corridor. She does not watch as he calls out, "Don't tell my mom, eh. Don't tell my mom."

May. Kicker decides to go to the country and work with his dad. It's a question of survival, he says. "Edmonton really sucks. Every time I come into the city I do crime. Either the city or jail you can always get drugs. Easy. I want to go stay out in the country for the summer.

"I'm a city boy but I like the country. The country is really beautiful. What's the word for it? I know, I only got a grade-four education. Knowledge, right, what good is it?"

We stop at a gas station. He jumps out and cleans my windows. He says he is going to have to leave Meagan. She is getting too bitchy. The other night he had to hit her. Straighten her out. He can't take it no more. He's going to have to leave her, and leave Brian, too.

"It's sad, man, but that's just the way it's got to be. That's just the way things are.

"She was sleeping with this other guy while I was in jail. She still is. I know she is and she keeps denying it. She used to work at the International Hotel, eh, and there's this real old guy who works there. She says she goes and visits him 'cause he's a friend.

"Never tell her I told you this. Never tell her. She'd kill me, man, if she knew I told you. She used to be a hooker. Down on 97th Street. When she was like eleven, twelve.

"So now she goes out with these guys and she comes back two hours later with a case of beer. They are old guys, too, man. She does it with them for a case of beer."

Kicker. June. "I just got hit by a bus. I mixed my pills, my booze. I lost a tooth. Got my lip stitched. I didn't know nothing. They just said, 'You got hit by a bus.' I freaked, man.

"Road rash. That's what they call me now, my cousins and that. Because I'm always falling on the pavement on my face. Getting my face scratched up.

"No more drugs for me. No more pills. No more booze. That's what I said this morning. I said that yesterday, too. That's it, that's all. This is bullshit. Getting hit by a bus, what's next? A train?"

A week later. "I'm getting paranoid in here. Here? The subway station. It's too clean for me. God, I hate to ask you this, but could you give me ten dollars? It's for my friend. He needs help. It's not for what you're thinking. It's not for, not for booze. I swear on my grandma's grave. It's for some medicine. Ya. For him. If we don't buy it he'll steal it. I don't want him to do that. Like he's kinda mixed up in the head. And he's one of my good buds; I grew up in school with him. This place is sick. It's too clean in here. Like I'll give you, what do I have on me. I, I have a ring.

"No, it's not that I want to buy drugs for this guy. It's medicine that he needs. OK, I'll tell you what it is. Cough syrup. He's got to have it, man. If he doesn't have it, he'll steal it."

I ask my question. There is a long pause. "Ya. He wants it to get high. It's not like it's like booze or anything. OK, OK, forget it. It's alright. This, this cough syrup shit makes you want to kill somebody. I'm just like, I'm shaking right now. This place is too bloody clean for me. This place is making me paranoid. Everybody that walks by is looking at us.

"OK. At least I told you the truth. I lied to you before, but you already know that, eh. That twenty bucks you lent me? I said it was for food. Well it was for food, but we starved anyways. We bought booze. But we survived. We all survived. We always survive."

Kicker. Christian. Edmund. Boucher. July. "These pigs fucked my wrist. They treated me like I was a fucking terrorist. Fucking pigs. Doctor over here at the Camsell, he said, 'You better have it casted.' He said my fucking wrist is sprained or fractured.

"I was just at the fucking Safeway with Lester and Meagan. This cop, he must have been an off-duty cop or something, man, he called his buddies. They said, "Sit down, sit down on this concrete." Outside the Safeway. They said I stole some meat but I didn't steal some meat.

"They cuffed me and they fucked my wrist. They fucking bend your fingers back, right all the way back. Oh that hurted, man. They told me to sit down on the cement. I said, 'Forget it, man, you have got nothing on me.'

"They took Lester and me to fucking Londonderry Station. Left us in there for two hours. They kept coming in, saying, 'Your buddy spilled his guts. Your buddy. He told us everything.'

" 'Ya, right.' You know what they ended up charging us with? Disturbing the peace. That's a very stupid charge. We weren't doing nothing! I got two witnesses. But you know Meagan, she'll crumble at the stand.

"You know what we went to the Safeway for? A baby bottle and a bag of chips. A baby bottle and a bag of chips.

"Londonderry, I got the boots before there, man. You should see the boots. Boots on your forehead. You have to curl up in a corner. They make sure that they don't break your legs. They make sure you don't talk.

"Then they got the phone-book treatment. They grab a phone book. They put it on your head and they grab the butt of a gun. Or wherever they want to hurt you. They use the butt end. They got the football helmet. Centered. So they don't wreck your face, they don't kill you.

"It's a pretty sad story. Alberta is the saddest. Maybe cause it's got the big cops, I don't know.

"These things that go on behind the people's eyes."

SATURDAY MORNING. EARLY September. Four a.m. Wendy and Lesley in my apartment and the John Casablancas students in their beds and Wendy's psychic in Calgary and all her friends with their funny movie titles, all those people are asleep right now in this city or somewhere, all already halfway to tomorrow. Kicker with his sundered face, in the closed world of my car on the way to the hospital, is still working on making it through today. He pulls out a zip-lock baggie. He tells me it's pot. Then he says, "Nah, just joking, man. You think I'd have something like that?" He rolls himself a cigarette.

"Sometimes I wonder what's the meaning of life. I don't know, man. Sometimes I think it's a test. If you can make it through all this pain and shit. You know what I mean? Just like those Pakis believe. Reincarnation. I sure don't want to burn in fiery hell.

"Sometimes when I think about Meagan I feel real sorry for her." He stares at me. "Fifteen and pregnant. Fifteen and pregnant."

We pull into the hospital parking lot. Kicker refuses to go in through emergency. "It's just a split lip. It ain't no emergency, man." I push on the metal handle of the main hospital door. It won't move. We walk back down the sloped sidewalk, down the stairs to the hospital's underground emergency entrance.

It is then that Kicker takes me by surprise. He reaches out his arm and gently pats me on the shoulder. "You're a good person," he says. "You, you'll be on the roll call."

I turn to him. I say, knowing that it is true and knowing, too, how futile is the truth, "You too, Kicker. You're a good person, too."

"Nah," he says. He laughs. "Not me. 'Cancel my subscription to the resurrection.' " Jim Morrison. "Cancel my subscription to the resurrection." And walks in through the emergency doors.

✪ HELEN

BUFFALO STROLL THE field outside the yellow door. The sky is slate-grey; it is drizzling and cold. Helen's daughter, Jennifer, sits on my knee in the warm afternoon kitchen, smelling of little girl mustiness and chocolate cookies, blood from her after-school nosebleed spotting her white blouse. We flip through the Sears catalogue. Jennifer has been working on a list for Santa of everything she wants for Christmas, though it is not yet Halloween. She hands me a pencil. "I forgot I want this," she says, wriggling, her small bones digging into my thighs. "Write it." Louder. "Did you write it?" She points a demanding finger. "I wa-a-ant you to write this down."

Jennifer, who is six, swears like a trooper and has eyes like plates. She has three older brothers: Darryl, age ten; Peri, the eleven-year-old adopted son; and Freddy, a teenage giant, fourteen and already over six feet tall. She owns four Barbies: the bottle-blonde version; a brunette; the bouffant Super-Star model; and a black Barbie with an Afro.

Helen, who is thirty-six, had a bubble-cut Barbie and a kewpie doll with no legs. She had two sisters, and a half-brother she's never met. Both sisters died; one a baby with a too-small stomach, one killed in an alley at age five. After the second death Helen's mother, who had already given up her first child – her son – for adoption when she was a young unmarried woman, after the second death Helen's mother, overcome by grief and history, took to her bed. And stayed there for the rest of Helen's childhood.

Jennifer squirms. I stare at the fridge, lost in what I have been told. Barbie with a bubble-cut. Barbie, dolly with missile breasts. Kewpie, dolly with no legs. Weed who cannot speak. Weed who cannot hear. Assault.

HELEN LIVES ON a reserve an hour outside Edmonton. Three days a week she drives her Cherokee 4x4 past the buffalo in the field, past a lake, down and up a treed valley and into the city to university. She says she doesn't mind the drive; it is the only time she is alone.

"These last few months have been a real transition for me, being new on campus. So I've just been tired, just dead tired. But I am finding that the drive is good for me. I actually like that hour on the road; it gives me time to collect my thoughts. It gives me a chance to be alone."

Helen is studying psychology and says she has found in feminism a kind of spiritual home. She wants to combine psychology, feminism, and the traditional Native spiritual beliefs her father, a respected elder, taught her, to help heal the women on her reserve. Ninety per cent of those women, Helen says, were sexually abused as children.

"MY SON, FREDDY, caught me crying the other night." It is early morning. I've just arrived, bearing two boxes of cookies. Though it is only an hour past breakfast, Helen peels back the cellophane wrap and digs out a coconut crisp. Food is a problem for her, she says. She uses food for comfort. She has always used food for comfort. "I've always been fat, eh. Always insecure about my weight. About how I looked." She looks lovely, with her open smile and soft brown hair, but I'm afraid that to say so would be an affront. When she was thirteen she was wider and taller than her mother. Her parents took her to a doctor hoping to find some illness to explain away her chunky body, her doughy limbs. No one guessed, no one understood what she was feeling.

The rain outside hints of snow. Helen's living room is full of trophies and ribbons: hockey prizes and baseball prizes her sons and her two ex-husbands won, and the trophy she herself won for being Mother of the Year on her reserve. Freddy is home sick with the flu. She has just finished one set of exams and is avoiding starting on a paper. The other three kids are at their off-reserve school. A plumber bangs on pipes in the basement; the reserve is installing a new water tank. The well she had been relying on has run dry.

"I rented this video with Barbra Streisand the other night. I thought it was going to be a musical." It wasn't a musical. Barbra Streisand was a hooker on trial for murder. She'd been abused by her kindly stepfather, and she was nuts.

"I was crying through this movie, eh. Freddy asked me why I cry so much sometimes. I cry a lot sometimes, it seems for no reason. So I told him." She says it is important that her children, especially her sons, understand.

"WELL, I WAS born in Edmonton and I lived there and grew up there most of my life. And when I was born I was almost not given the opportunity to be with my father. My mother was contemplating giving me up for adoption. Being a single woman in 1953 and having a baby was not too well-accepted. And she didn't have much of an education, or a way of supporting herself, let alone a child. She had already given up a brother. I had an older brother, she gave him up.

"The story is, I guess, that my dad went to see her after I was born and she told him she was going to give me up. And he didn't want her to. He begged her not to. And she said, 'Well, if you want me to keep her, you're going to have to help me raise her because I can't do it alone.'

"I often wonder how much real love was between my parents to start with. They felt that they had to get married, with me born. I used to have a problem dealing with that, because I used to think that maybe my mom really didn't want me after all."

Helen's father was Cree, from a reserve in northern Alberta. His childhood was hard. His mother died when he was five. His own father had his favorites, and Helen's father wasn't one of them. He was given first to his grandmother to raise and then, by law, to the nuns and the priests at a Catholic residential school.

"He was in residential school, I don't know how many years," Helen says, "but he has about grade two, grade four education. And even that, I don't know what that's worth. I don't even know if that was even a grade. It may have been just a number they gave him.

"He told me a few things about residential school when I was a child but I didn't really believe him, eh. My mother was trying to raise me Catholic. I was trying to believe in God and the Great Spirit. That they meant love. I thought religion was about love.

"But I was in a convent, too, from age nine to eleven. My mother was sick, in and out of hospital all the time, and my dad was away a lot, so they sent me to a convent in Edmonton for two years. I believed him then.

"A lot of what my father can do, his ability now, is because he educated himself. Like when he sobered up, he decided he was going to learn to read better and to write better. That's how he got his education – from reading Alcoholics Anonymous literature. He said he read the Big Book with the dictionary. The book and the dictionary. And he went from there."

Helen's mother was a pretty blond French girl from small-town Alberta. She left home young and hitchhiked to Montreal.

"I can see my mom now being a unique woman, an outstanding woman of her time," Helen says. "I mean in the '40s what woman, single woman, young woman, would hitchhike all the way to Montreal by herself and back?

"She did that. At the time when she told me the story, I never really thought it was any big deal. But now when I look back at the way women were treated then, it was something. It was really something out of the ordinary.

"My grandfather was an alcoholic. I hate to say it, my aunties would hate me for saying this, but he would sexually abuse the whole family. I know that now. And so she had a hard life. It's no wonder she was the way she was."

The way she was. The asthma. The ambulances. Buried under

her wool blankets. Buried, blankets up to her chin.

The marriage was not good. In one of Helen's recurring dreams her father is taken away by police. In the dream she is standing by her baby sister's crib and she is frightened.

"I don't know where my mother was, but I remember seeing these, to me they were shadows, like I didn't know if they were police or who the hell they were. They were shadows, dark figures. And there was a struggle. And it upset me."

Her dream confused two incidents. One when her father, who physically abused her mother, beat her mother when she was pregnant. One when Helen was four, and the police came and took him away for assaulting a taxi driver.

It was while in jail on the assault charge that her father was introduced to AA and sobered up. After that, she says, the physical abuse stopped.

"In fact I only got the rarest spanking. It was only if I, well I remember one incident where I told my mother to shut up. I thought I was so brave. I knew I did something wrong 'cause I ran away. But he caught me." She laughs. "The fast way to learn to respect your elders."

Her father was one of the first Native men in AA. He was involved in the first Native Friendship Centre, in setting up Native Counselling Services, in the Indian Association.

"Through it all, you know, he had his glory, but I think Mom and I were the ones kinda left out. Because, when I was thinking back to the times when all these things happened to me, where was my dad? Where was he?"

The things that happened to her. The things that happen. Starting with the deaths.

"I DID HAVE a younger, two younger sisters. And my youngest sister died when she was eight months. She had some kind of stomach disorder – they knew that only after a long time. Her stomach opening was too small and she couldn't take solids. And she was at an age where she needed them and she became so weak that she caught pneumonia. She died.

"My mom had that happen and then the following spring she had an ectopic, a tubal pregnancy. And, and then, not long after that, we lost my other sister. She was five years old. I was six and a half. She got hit by a truck.

"It was in the back alley. I was at school. She used to go visit an old lady across the alley-way from our house. And she was coming home from the lady's, and there was a garage and there was a fence and she came from in between. And I guess there was a big gravel truck and I guess he must've been hauling or something, to a house or something in the area.

"He didn't even see her. He said he felt a big bump and for some reason, before he went over her with the back tires, he decided to stop. He said he didn't even see her.

"I heard that really broke that man. It was about ten, fifteen years ago that we heard a little bit about him. He never drove again.

"The hardest part was — a few days before that we had a fight, her and I. I was going to go visit some of my friends, but I didn't want no little sister tagging along. 'You can't come,' I said. 'No.' And she kept on insisting. And I told her, 'No, you can't come. I don't like you, I hate you. You're not my sister anymore and I wish you would go away.'

"And I lived with that, with saying that to her. I lived with that for a long time. I couldn't even tell anybody that I had said that to her. I couldn't even tell. I felt so guilty; I thought that by some miraculous magic or something I made her go away. And I lived with that for a long time.

"I don't remember very much about her funeral or anything. Although my mother told me that when they buried her, I went crazy at the cemetery as they were putting her down. I told them I didn't want her to, don't put her in the ground, don't put her in that dark hole where it's cold.

"When my sister died, that to me was when our family fell

apart. My dad was just newly sober; it was a very difficult time for him so he really needed his program. He stayed sober. He said he almost drank.

"But for my mother it was the last straw. She . . . I guess the story is that my dad blamed her. Where was she when my sister was outside playing? Is that why it happened? Why wasn't she looking after her better?

"And I guess she thought he was right. She took that blame on herself and she lived with that. And their relationship just deteriorated after that.

"And in the process they forgot they had another daughter. My dad not as much, because I think he sometimes tried to make up for it in his own ways. I remember when I was seven years old, my first birthday after my sister died. He gave me a bouquet of roses. And I have had a bouquet of roses, or carnations, for every birthday since. I think when he passes on, that's going to be one of the hardest things for me, when my birthday comes and there's no roses.

"But my mom, like she really, she just turned into herself. Psychiatrists couldn't help her. They just didn't know things in those days they know now. And she had a doctor who was more than willing to give her pills for whatever illness she had, or that she could create for herself. So she spent a lot of time sleeping. I never knew from day to day whether she was going to be there for me, or if I had to be there for her.

"She was what they call a hypochondriac. That's the term they use now. But now that I understand a little more about psychology, her mental . . . well I don't know, they said she was unbalanced and everything, mentally, emotionally unbalanced was the word. And I think that because she wasn't able to get the right help to deal with her problems – my sister, her past and everything, she couldn't deal with those – it made her sick. It made her ill, physically ill because she was holding all that stuff in there.

"I mean, she's sixty now and she's only now, for the first time in all her life, talked about her father. That's a lot of garbage. It's no wonder she became so ill when my sister died. I mean, how much more was a person supposed to take?

"But for me, it was like my childhood was taken away from me. I felt I really didn't want to have to take care of her. But I had no choice. It was like I didn't have a childhood anymore. Like I was always old. I used to feel sometimes, even when I was twenty years old, that I was forty. I wasn't really ever young.

"And then having been sexually abused."

THE FIRST ASSAULT was by a cousin. A teenage boy who came to stay with the family for the school year. "At an age when he was just starting to feel his needs." He came in September. He left a month later.

"I think he was afraid. 'Cause he wasn't there very long. But over the years, because I had blocked the whole thing out, I couldn't understand why he left. But now I understand. I couldn't remember until two years ago, eh. But when I went through hypnosis, then I remembered.

"I remember him with my sister. My younger sister before she was killed. And she was lying on the bed and he was playing with her. There was no penetration. But there was touching. And he took off her panties. I remember that. And when I did the regressions, I found out he had done the same to me.

"And sometimes I think, when I think about it, that perhaps it was better that my sister died when she did. Who knows what it would have done to her life, if she had lived to remember. Who knows how she would have handled it.

"My cousin, he's never been brought to court or anything, and he has over the years, I know he has . . . like even, I have a couple of cousins who are younger than I am and I know that he probably molested them as well. I'm sure, not only did he molest cousins, but maybe even his own sisters. He was the oldest boy. That wouldn't surprise me. Wouldn't surprise me at all.

"The sad thing is, I think about how much I used to be angry with him. And then I realized he's a victim too. Somebody else did that to him. And I even . . . because the families were smaller and closer a long time ago, I often wonder whether the gentleman, I can't call him a gentleman, the man who molested me when I was about eight, might not have had access to a lot of these other kids too. Even to my cousin.

"And yet even that man himself, being deaf and dumb, he was a victim too. Somebody knew that he couldn't tell."

THE SECOND ASSAULT. Helen was eight. She was living in Edmonton and went up to visit her auntie and uncle on the reserve. She went over to her friend Brenda's house. It was raining. It was raining so hard she couldn't make it back home to her auntie's. She started to feel sleepy. It was the middle of the afternoon. She went upstairs to Brenda's bed. She lay down on Brenda's bed. And then she was raped by her auntie's brother, a man who was deaf and dumb.

"That was the one I really blocked out. I had no clues. I had no idea. I had no idea."

Memories only started coming back to Helen in her early thirties, in dreams. "I would wake up feeling horrible. I would remember the room. How the room looked and everything. I remember lying there in the dark. I was scared. I remember feeling so alone and scared."

Her dreams became more intense. For a whole month she woke up in the middle of the night, sweating and crying. Then one night the phone rang and interrupted her sleep.

"I woke up and I remembered. I remembered lying in bed, there was me and Brenda, we were lying in bed and this man, his nickname was Weed, we called him Weed, he was standing over both of us. He was standing on the side of the bed. Looking down at us. And smiling.

"And I woke up and I was still feeling that scared feeling. Like I had my blanket pulled up right up to my chin. I woke up like that. I woke up and I was like that. I had my blankets up to my chin and I was lying there stiff as a board. And I remembered.

"It was during the day. And I had gone upstairs to sleep in Brenda's room because I was tired. And he came in. And I couldn't do anything. I mean, what can you do when you are eight or nine years old? At that time I was a skinny little girl. I was just eight years old. I was just a skinny little girl.

"I think part of the problem I have with my hip was as a result of that incident. Because I have a hip displacement. And when I had my children, I had to have a caesarean. What happened was I couldn't open up. My pelvis wouldn't spread wide enough. So I had to have caesareans. Nobody knew. I didn't even know. Didn't know nothing.

"There was only one clue that could have helped me remember. To understand. If I had known, if I had understood how to look.

"See, I remember when, I think my mom had started working, she had been working for awhile. After my sister died she didn't work for a period. She was going through severe depression, the whole bit. Then for awhile there she did work. And when she worked I remember spending time home alone by myself.

"And I used to, I had a Barbie doll. And I had this other little, tiny little doll, they used to use them as kewpie dolls. The old-style kewpie dolls, with feathers stuck in them and everything. Long hair, ponytails usually. Not like what you see now. It was a whole different type. Real nice soft rubber flexible dolls, eh. Really nice little doll.

"But she had no legs. I don't know what happened to her; I don't remember what happened to her legs.

"But I used to play with these dolls. And I used to, when I was by myself, only when I was by myself I actually played out what had happened. And I told my therapist about it and this is why she knew that there had to be more. What happened to me with Weed had to be more than what happened with my cousin, because what I did when I played with my dollies involved penetration.

"You see I used to use a little stick pin, eh. I used to use that on my Barbie doll. I used to poke it in there, eh. I used to act out the whole thing. The Barbie was being actually attacked and raped with this stick pin, with this pin.

"And then this tiny little doll, this Kewpie doll, was the little girl of this big doll, of the Barbie doll. And she used to always come to the rescue. She used to fight off that terrible person who was doing this terrible, terrible thing to her mother.

"So I was acting it out. It was just that my parents never caught me ever doing it. So they never knew.

"And I used to feel terrible. I used to think there was something wrong with me when I got older, that I did that with my dolls. I used to think," Helen whispers, " 'What was the matter with me? Why did I play like that with my dolls? That wasn't nice,' you know.

"I used to be so ashamed."

The rain has turned to sleet; the weather is growing ugly. "He's dying now, that man. I found out the other day that he's in the hospital and he has cancer of the throat and he's pretty well going into the last stages now.

"At first I felt – good for him. Got what he deserved. But then I realized that, that for him having cancer in the throat was guilt, stress, and anger, feelings that were repressed and could never be expressed.

"So the things that he must carry around inside him. It's just terrible, the things he must carry around inside.

"Those were the things that blocked out my childhood. Those events. I realize the reason I never spoke about it was because, at that age, I didn't know how to explain what happened. That's why I never told.

"I used to blame my mom and dad. I used to think they should've known, they should've seen something was wrong with me. They should've known.

"But they didn't. And I didn't have the words. I realize now it was because I didn't have the words.

"Those are the incidents that blocked out my whole childhood.

They have affected me, my whole life."

THE KITCHEN DOOR bangs open. The three youngest kids are home from school. Jennifer, her long black hair flying, runs in holding a piece of foolscap to her face. It is spotted with blood. A little girl bopped her in the nose getting off the school bus. Why, Jennifer won't say. Peri, with his round smile and spiky hair, bounces in chiming the names of all the kids at school who have flu just like Freddy: Mona, Tommy, Ralphie, Susan. Darryl dives at the cookies on the table. Several cookies later Darryl says he doesn't feel good.

"You don't feel good too, eh. Another one. Oh my God. Go lie down, take a pail with you. You'd better get a pail, I don't want you puking all over the house."

Peri grabs a fistful of cookies. "You know what, Mom? You know how men get divorced in Iran?" There has been a speaker at school who travelled to the Far East. Peri dances around the end of the table with excitement, a wispy tail of hair trailing down his back. "All you have to do is turn around twice and like that, you're divorced. Pretty cool, eh." He grins and his round face spreads like light.

Helen asks him, does he really think it's cool? What about the woman? He thinks about it. Sheepish. "Oh ya," he says. "Oh ya."

Jennifer wants juice. She chants it: juice juice juice. Darryl wants milk. Jennifer wants her dollies, wants to haul them out for the unknown lady's inspection. The plumber emerges from the basement; the hot water heater is hooked up. Helen claps her hands. "Hot showers," she says. "Oh thank God, we can all have hot showers again."

When the cookies are all devoured, the kids disperse through the house, absorbed into rooms I haven't seen. Jennifer goes to fetch her Cricket doll who sings and talks, and all her Barbies. Peri disappears to his big brother's sickbed to watch TV. Darryl grabs Donkey Kong and sets himself down on the couch. The ape, hanging by one hand, recklessly lets go of the vine and falls, falls, falls. The game whistles and bings and burps. I stare at the fridge. Helen makes camomile tea, sweetened with honey.

WITH HER CHILDHOOD memories erased, conversation became difficult, she says. "Other girls used to talk about sex. Not me. They used to talk about their boyfriends and stuff. I wouldn't say a word."

She was scared of boys. She only would date boys younger than she was; they were easier to control. She was not sexually active. She didn't sleep with any boy till she was seventeen. "I consider it my first time, 'cause it was to me. It was my first time being with a boy.

"It was a disaster.

"We were living in this great big house, just my dad and I. My parents had separated off and on over the years, but they had separated for good by then. My dad went away to work for a week. And I was scared by myself in the house at night. I phoned my mom, but she wouldn't come. She wasn't well, it was cold outside, it was winter, and she didn't want to come out because she was scared she would get chills.

"So here I am all alone in this big house. About eight o'clock the phone rings and it was him. His name was Richard. Richard Romeo." She laughs. "He hated that name, eh. But I loved it.

"We had split up about a month ago before that because I wouldn't have sex with him. Never heard from him again until that night. I was so scared of being alone I told him to come over. But I didn't know he was going to bring me a case of beer and a couple of twenty-sixers. And so we landed up drinking.

"All I remember was waking up with him the next morning. And then he held me in his arms, and he asked me if that was the first time. And I said, yes it was. And he couldn't believe it. He didn't think it was.

"After that I never saw him hardly again. I wouldn't have

anything to do with him. I totally rejected him.

"Perhaps being under the influence of alcohol, he might have made me feel something. And I even questioned that, you know, even then I used to question, 'Why would he say that, why would he say ask me if it was my first time? Is there something wrong? Why would he think that I had been with anybody else? What have I done?' I couldn't understand."

Jennifer runs into the kitchen. She is carrying a big blonde doll in one hand and its legs in another. She is very stern. "This doll's leg breaked," she says. "Mommy, this doll's leg breaked." Helen takes the pieces of doll from her. She keeps talking, pushing one leg and then another into the doll's hips, twisting and turning the fat pink joints back into their plastic sockets.

"MY DAD, I don't think he had a clue of how much I drank. I remember in early spring of grade ten I dropped out of school. This was the second time I'd dropped out of grade ten and it was because I was drinking. He had gone on a two-week trip and for those two weeks I was drunk every day. We cleaned up the apartment and sold all the beer bottles before he came home. And we got drunk for another day on the money we made from selling the bottles.

"I remember I used to even go around carrying a mickey underneath my belt, in my pants, eh. That was the only way I could go to a dance because I used to be so shy. So afraid to meet guys. So if I had a drink, feeling a little bit good, it was easier.

"I was sniffing for awhile too. We sniffed nail polish remover. Before they put the acetone in. I don't remember how we started. But it was a regular thing we did, me and my cousins. We used to go shopping. My dad used to sign a cheque, and we'd go get groceries. The clerk was dumb. I mean we used to put ten bottles of nail polish remover on the counter amidst the groceries. You'd think she'd have enough sense to know like, 'Hey, this is not normal.'

"Anyway, during that time I decided, 'Well, maybe if I go to a different city and go to school maybe I won't have this drinking problem.' So I relocated. I went to Calgary and I lived in a boarding house and I went to school and I did really well. I quit going to the bars. I was sixteen, and I was doing good.

"Then I met up with an old boyfriend that I had when I was about fifteen. Harry. Harry had joined the armed forces. He was stationed in Winnipeg but he was on a month's leave, visiting his brother in Calgary. I ran into him, by accident, at the Calgary bus depot.

"So I started drinking again, with Harry. And the next thing you know, I skipped school to go see him, to spend time together. Finally, after Christmas I quit school completely to move to Winnipeg to live with him.

"My dad came and visited me in Winnipeg a couple of times. The last time he visited me was just about May 8th. I remember this really well because that's when I decided to quit drinking.

"When my dad left to go home, I felt so lonely for him. Harry and I, we were OK. Not great but OK. But it wasn't good enough. And I missed, I wanted to go home with my dad. But I didn't want to say that to him. I didn't want to feel that he was controlling my life anymore.

"So when my dad left I went on a two-day drunk. I woke up the morning of May 10th and I was so sick. But my mind was so clear and it suddenly dawned on me, 'Helen, what are you doing? Is this your solution to your problems, is you go out and get drunk?'

"And I realized that this was wrong. All the things I had learned growing up with my dad being in the AA program, I knew that if I didn't do something right now, I was headed for a real severe problem with drinking. So I decided that morning I was not going to drink ever again. I was not going to touch another drop. And I have not had a drink since that day.

"But it was hard. Harry, for some reason, all of a sudden he started changing. He'd want me to drink with them. 'How come you don't want to drink? Have a drink.' I'd become a party pooper, so to speak.

"I remember one time he got a little abusive because I wouldn't drink. We were with another couple and he actually kicked me under the table, kicked my legs – he had on cowboy boots – right in the shins. Because I wouldn't drink. And I got up, I went in the bathroom. It hurt so much I was crying in the bathroom. I couldn't believe he would do that to me.

"Then, the weekend before his birthday, we had a small party. A couple of friends I had made from work came over, some of his buddies from the army came over. He was dancing with my girlfriend and it was a little too close for comfort for me and I said so. I got pissed off.

"He beat me up afterward, eh. He got really mad and he beat me up. I had a black eye. I wouldn't even go to work until it cleared up. And his birthday came a couple of days later and I baked him a birthday cake. He felt like an asshole, eh. But I was scared of him. I really, I was afraid of him. He said he wouldn't ever do it again."

They stayed together another month and a half. Harry was to be stationed in Cyprus, peacekeeping. She told him she couldn't stay in Winnipeg if he wasn't there.

"So we went to Lac La Biche to his mother's place. He told them we were married. We weren't. We had wedding rings because we were supposed to get married but we hadn't officially gotten married yet. But he said, 'We'll wear our rings while we're at my mom's, eh.' So I agreed with him. And everything was OK until he went to the bar. He came home and he started getting abusive again.

"The next day I left. I didn't care what he told his parents, how he explained anything to his mom or his sister and them. Didn't matter to me. I wasn't sticking around anymore. I wrote him a letter, sent him back his ring." She laughs. "And that was the end of that. I've never seen him since."

JENNIFER'S NOSEBLEED IS back. She sits on a kitchen chair, her head tilted back, her mother holding a cold cloth to her forehead, reassuring Jennifer that everything will be alright.

Helen looks out her kitchen window. "I still haven't taken my carrots out yet, my potatoes. Boy, am I late for my garden this year. Late with everything this year."

It is four thirty. The kids are getting hungry and if Freddy is going to eat before he plays hockey – if he plays hockey – she's got to make dinner. She lends me a pair of gum boots and we go outside to dig potatoes out of her garden. She relies a lot on her garden – that plus the moose meat her father and her second husband catch every fall. The living allowance Indian Affairs pays her to go to school is less than she would earn on welfare, she says. "Where's the incentive, where's the incentive they give you to go to school?"

Her first husband, Freddy Sr., hasn't helped her out much. He's broke – he's got a new wife, new kids and he never was any good, she says, with money.

I scrub the potatoes in the kitchen sink under the newly hot water. She talks about Freddy, who is the father of both Freddy Jr. and Darryl, and about Hutch, her second, common-law husband and Jennifer's father. Neither man is in her life anymore. She is struggling to get used to being alone.

"When I started having sexual relationships with men, boys, I was always afraid that I wasn't good enough in bed. I was always afraid of having sex. Like I didn't feel nothing. When I was with those guys I used to wonder, is this is all there is? I never got anything out of it. I never felt anything. I didn't know what to do. I was totally ignorant, totally naive.

"That was one of the problems I had with my first marriage. It was a bomb sexually. I used to blame myself for that. I figured that's why my husband screwed around on me. I know it wasn't all of it. Maybe part of it.

"I started coming out of that with my second husband. I had a good sexual relationship with him. But even he used to tell me sometimes, 'When we make love,' he said, 'I don't think you're there.' He said, 'What are you thinking of? Where are you?'

"You know I didn't even realize it. And then I stopped, and I really started looking at it. And I realized that was how I dealt with it, my past. Being a rape victim, you go out. You leave. You just . . . leave. It's just unreal.

"I don't know why I married Freddy. I think I did love him in the beginning, but I don't know if it was the right kind of love. The kind a man and wife should have. I think it was more of a friendly love. He was fooling around on me already then and I found out about it, but I married him anyway. Stupid.

"I think I married him because I wanted to be married. I felt like I was getting old. You know, 'Twenty-one years old, I'm getting old.' He was nineteen. I was stupid.

"After he divorced me, he got married again right away. When we were still together his girlfriend used to call the house all the time. Come over. They were pretending to be just friends. He had to marry her, eh. She was pregnant.

"Hutch, he was Freddy's best friend. When I was going through all this with Freddy he used to be so good to me, eh. So kind. Six months after I split up with Freddy I started going out with Hutch. Hutch was faithful for one year. Then he started drinking again. Then he wasn't faithful anymore.

"We split up two years ago, me and Hutch. We didn't have anything to do with each other for three months and then it started all over again. He happened to come visit me at a time when I was lonely, depressed, 'poor me,' you know. And I was very vulnerable.

"It was really bad when we got back together. A real seesaw. We wouldn't even live together a week and he'd be gone again. Finally it got so he wouldn't even bring his stuff over. And then gradually it got to be he'd only come to visit for an evening. He'd come and visit Jennifer and then he'd stay and we'd visit with each other, have sex with each other.

"At first that was OK for me, but then he started going out with another woman and then another one. I can't believe he actually juggled three women. Unreal.

"I remember one time it drove me crazy, it damn near did. If I wasn't in therapy I don't think I could've handled it. In fact that's part of the reason I was going to therapy because I felt that I was going crazy. I had suicidal thoughts. I even thought of killing all my children and then killing myself. And I knew that wasn't right. I knew, 'There's something wrong, I've gotta get help.' And I did.

"I started saying no to Hutch after that. When he would come over and he would make advances toward me, I'd say no to him. The problem – I think it started opening my eyes even more – was that he couldn't accept my no's sometimes, and he would force himself on me. At that point he started killing the feelings that I had. Even our sexual relationship was not good anymore, you know, because he couldn't respect me.

"I don't know. I don't think I'm ready to go out with anybody else, but who knows. I keep being told that I'm still young. I feel young yet."

WE SIT DOWN to dinner. Pork chops are stacked high on a platter; the potatoes, whipped with milk and butter, steam. Freddy emerges from his bedroom looking tired and pale, the faint hair of a first moustache dark across his upper lip. He doesn't want to play hockey tonight and phones his dad to tell him not to pick him up. Darryl and Peri exchange fart jokes and burp with their armpits. Jennifer is delighted. She burps into her milk.

At eight, Helen sends all four kids to bed. The three boys, with varying degree of protest, obey. Jennifer out and out refuses. She decides she is hungry. She pulls a package of fruit twists out of a kitchen cupboard.

"No, that's for school lunches," Helen says.

"Pul-leaze."

"No, that's for school lunches."

A wail. "Mu-umm"

"You know what, you can have a slice of cheese. I know you

don't want any but that's all you can have."

"I don't *like* cheese."

"Since when? Since you wanted fruit wrinkles." Helen laughs; Jennifer's lower lip has drooped and the child is scowling. "Oh you look so pathetic. You know what. It's bedtime. It's bedtime. Jennifer honey, go to bed."

Jennifer, miffed, stomps dramatically into the bedroom. She pulls on her Cricket doll. The doll sings and sings and sings.

HELEN LEANS BACK on her couch drinking fresh tea. She returns to Helen, age sixteen, who has just left Harry of the hard-toed cowboy boots trying to explain a set of wedding rings to his mother.

"When I came back from living with Harry in Winnipeg, I moved out with my dad to Smallboy's, out in the foothills. Smallboy's was a group of people, most of them from Hobbema, who had decided that, if they moved back to the bush and lived the old traditional life, it would be better. But it wasn't better.

"I stayed in Smallboy's, just, oh almost two years. And while I was there I saw a lot of things that I thought were not right. They had moved back to live an old traditional life with all the old bad habits. They'd just taken their garbage with them. So it didn't work.

"That's why I didn't stay there long. I found it stagnating. I couldn't see a future with it. I couldn't see a future for any of those people. How are they supposed to live? Welfare? Crazy. I mean they want to go live a traditional way of life but they're pulling welfare. It was stupid.

"They had some good things, like they had powwows and stuff, different types of ceremonies. But the actual everyday living, the real nitty-gritty of life was not really traditional.

"They gossiped just as much as anybody else. Some of the younger people went out and got drunk just as much as any place else. They had drugs, too, just as much as any place else. They, there was even incest, cousins going out with cousins and stuff. Well what else, there was nobody else around. It was too isolated.

"I lived with my dad out there. And I realized, even before I went to Montana with Kevan, that I couldn't live there. That's why I guess it was easy for me to go with Kevan to Montana.

"I've questioned why, why did I stay with Kevan; I must've been crazy. But then it comes back from having been raped before. Then you have what they call a learned helplessness. You don't feel that you have any control, that you can do anything to change the situation.

"It was only when my life was actually threatened, and I had to get out. I had the courage enough for that one.

"This guy, they called him Kevan. Not Kevin but Ke-e-van. I was with him two months, one month in Canada and one month down south. I met him at Smallboy's. And he was a nice-looking boy; he was nice." She laughs. "Maybe that's what I fell in love with. He was about 6'3", black, blue-black hair. Big brown eyes, beautiful complexion, not a zit. And he was nice to me at the time. Kids liked him too. I don't know why that is. I always find that odd, how some men can be such assholes to women and kids love them." She laughs. "Well, I'm not going to go by how kids feel too much anymore."

Jennifer wanders out of the bedroom. "Mom, you come. The bed doesn't feel very good."

"How come it doesn't feel very good, it's empty without Mommy? Ya. OK. You can lie down here." Helen pats the couch. "But don't put your Cricket on. I don't want to hear her chattering. OK? I don't want to hear Cricket.

"Kevan asked me if we could live together. And I felt that was OK. I didn't realize that there was anything wrong with him.

"Little did I know. He was like night and day. In the camp he was so nice, he was so good, he was ideal. But when we left he was just ugly, just totally opposite. It was unreal.

"We didn't even leave the camp a day when he started getting abusive with me. The first night away from the camp, in North

Battleford, he went out drinking. He came back to the hotel room. He was obnoxious. He was rude. He brought a friend with him. I started questioning, what kind of man is this, because instead of going to the bathroom, he just opened up the window. He pissed out the window. Anybody could have been walking down there; we were on the second floor.

"So then it was getting late and his friend left and he wanted to have sex with me and I didn't want to because he was being cruel, he was hurting me. He just ripped my nightgown. Right there. Just ripped it.

"And I thought, 'Uh oh.' Now I knew I was in trouble. The thing of it was, I didn't know how to get out of it. I didn't know how I was going to get home. I didn't have no money, I didn't know anyone.

"And so I landed up going down to the States with him to his parents' place."

Jennifer butts her head, gently, into her mother's stomach. "Can I have some of those brown things?"

"What brown things? Cookies? They are all gone. Oh, I know which ones you mean." Helen gets up from the couch and finds Jennifer a bag of graham wafers. "You know what, Jennifer, it's nearly nine thirty. I think you better shut Cricket off and go to sleep. You're going to be tired in the morning. You're going to be telling me, 'I'm too tired, I don't want to go to school.' "

"But I don't want to go to school!"

"I know you don't. But you still have to go. Besides, how are you going to make Halloween spiders if you don't go to school?"

"Paper."

"But I don't have nothing to make spiders with."

"*Paper*!"

Jennifer is marched back to her bedroom. Helen returns, smiling at her fierce little daughter. She is proud Jennifer is willful. She is happy she's a fighter. She needs Jennifer to be able to stick up for herself.

"It was hard at Kevan's parents' place. The place was not clean. After about two or three days being there, I started getting itchy, getting little bumps. And one time I woke up and my eye was just puffed out and I had welts all over my body. They had bed bugs. It was gross. So I started sleeping with the light on every night because that's the only way to keep the bugs away. And I dreaded it when Kevan would come in and turn off the light. After he'd fall asleep I'd put it right on again. I couldn't sleep in the dark there.

"Anyway, he started going out drinking and he'd leave me home. But the thing I didn't pick up on was, when he'd go out and if I wanted to eat something, I couldn't find a frigging knife. I couldn't find a fork. They would literally just disappear. All the knives, even the butcher knives, everything just disappeared. But they would be there in the morning, the utensils would be back in the morning.

"When he'd come home drunk, he got abusive. He used to slap me around. And he'd want me to perform certain acts of sex with him and I couldn't because at that time, I was very naive. I didn't know anything and I used to be so scared. It was difficult for me.

"He used to tell me that if I ever told anybody – I mean people knew, like his mom and them, they all knew he was abusing me, they didn't do nothing. But he told me if I told anybody I'd get a worse licking. Or if I left him he would find me and he'd kill me. He'd actually shoot me.

"He took my glasses away. He just mutilated them. I couldn't even see. I couldn't function right. And I couldn't drive. I needed my glasses to drive.

"That last night I made the mistake of going out with him. He was with some friends. There was a couple and another guy. The girl came in and asked me to come. She said, 'We want you to come, he never brings you anywhere with him. You should come with us. We're going to go to town.'

"And I asked her, 'Are you guys drinking?' And she said no, that they weren't. But the reason for going to town was so that they could buy booze.

"He wanted me to drink and I wouldn't. And the more I refused the more adamant he got. He started slapping me around in the car. And the couple said, 'Don't do that to her, don't hit her or anything.' He told them to mind their own business. So they did. They just turned around in the seat and minded their own business.

"We were driving around the reserve and I had no idea where I was. It was dark. I was totally lost. Even if I had taken off from him I wouldn't have known which way to go. The roads were back roads, gravel roads. Could've been in the middle of a farmer's field for all I knew.

"Finally, the couple wanted to be dropped off. So we drove them home. And then there was just the three of us. Me, Kevan and his friend.

"And then Kevan decided he wanted to have sex. I didn't want to. 'Not in the car,' I told him, 'not in front of your friend.' That was out of the question.

"But that didn't stop him. He started beating me. And I landed . . . he raped me. He raped me in the back seat of the car.

"And the next thing you know he tells his friend, 'Do you want to have some too?' He just slapped him on the back of the head and told him, 'Come on, I'll let you.' And he gets in the driver's seat and he's starting to drive away and this guy's in the back and when I try to resist him, well he just turns around and whacks me one too. Just knocked me dizzy. I just about blacked out.

"I couldn't believe it. Kevan's friend, he raped me too. There was nothing I could do.

"After, after his friend was finished with me, we went home, to his parents' house. And Kevan dragged me out of the car and into the shed and he started hitting me. He told me, 'If you say anything, if you wake up anybody or tell anybody what's going on, you'll get more of this.' And he hit me really hard and I fell over.

"I remember this real clear. I hit a bar, a steel bar round like this, eh. I even remember how it felt. I fell back and then I sprang forward, like it just, like it had spring action to it.

"When I went into that shed the next day and I saw what that thing was – it was a bar attached to a roller, and that roller had spikes on it *that* long – I thought, 'Oh my God. He could have killed me. He almost killed me.'

"And he had a knife. I don't know where he got it from because, like I said, in the house those things disappeared. After we left the shed we went into the house, we went in the bedroom and he had this knife and he threatened me. He told me if I woke up anybody in the house that he would use this knife on anybody, anybody who tried to interfere.

"He wanted me to perform oral sex on him. That was something I had never in my life done. I was scared. I didn't know what to do, I didn't know how. He was trying to force me, pulling my head down to him, down on him. He was standing up and I was on the floor. And I couldn't. Even though he was threatening me. He had that knife and he was pushing it through my hair. He was pulling it through my hair, pulling on my hair. My hair, pieces of my hair were falling out. And then finally he gave up. I just couldn't, I couldn't do it.

"So he said, 'Do you think you can do better in bed then?' And he just forced me to have regular sex with him.

"Then he got up to leave, with the same threat, he threatened me again. But this time I didn't care.

"I didn't even finish dressing myself. I just grabbed something and covered myself and I went into his brother's bedroom. His brother was living there as well. I went running into his bedroom pounding on the door and I woke him up. I told him, 'I can't take this anymore, I can't handle it. Keep him away from me.'

"He told me, 'OK, when I tell you, you go out the front door and you go down to the creek bed and you hide there in the bush until I come and get you.'

"So I hid. And when it started getting light enough, I started following the creek. I came further up around the back of the house and they had a sweat lodge out there, eh. And it was cold, I was shivering and I crawled into the sweat lodge, I didn't know what else to do. I wanted to be warm and safe, that's all. So I stayed there for a long time.

"Kevan's brother drove me to their sister's place. Her husband was a cop, reserve cop, band constable they called him. They locked up the house, the kids went to school, they had to go to work and they told me, 'Whatever you do, do not open the door for anybody.'

"I was all alone. That was the hard part. I didn't have anybody to talk to. I was scared and numb. I didn't know how I was going to get home. I was feeling totally helpless. Totally helpless to do anything for myself. All I managed to do was to take a bath, put on some clean clothes. And I paced. I couldn't even sleep. I just paced up and down the house.

"When I finally did go to sleep is when everybody was home. And then I could sleep. Then I was able to sleep.

"They gave me a mattress on the floor in one of the children's rooms. And I was sleeping there and I remember hearing them. I guess I had on a short-sleeved nightgown and they saw the bruises on my arms. I remember her saying to her husband, 'Come here! Come and look at this! Look how bad her arm, look how bruised it is. What has he been doing to her?'

"What happened was Kevan used to punch me. For no reason. Like he'd be standing beside me and I didn't know what to expect. I even had after-effects from that. Like anybody who stood beside me who went like this," she reaches out her arm, "I moved. Because that's what he'd do, he'd just lace me one right in the arm. And that's how that bruise got so bad and so big. And I still have, it looks like freckles that I have on my arm, but that's the scar that I have from that. You can see the little vessels inside the bruise.

"They drove me back across the border, his sister and her husband. Smuggled me back across under a blanket in the back of their van. After I got back I never saw or heard anything from him since. Nothing at all.

"I've heard a little bit about him now. At that time I was still there, part of what I heard, when they were talking, was that he went berserk in the house after I ran away. He did some damage to the house and everything. In the process he wrecked all my stuff and he just went berserk. Just tore up the place and everything, eh.

"Then over the years, I heard that he finally did have a wife. They had children, a couple of kids. But she died, very young. She died."

Jennifer, alone in bed with her Cricket doll, yells, "Mom." When she gets no response she yells again. "Mom. Mom. Mom!"

"What?"

"I feel lonely."

"Ya, you do, eh."

"I want you to come here."

"Ya, I know. But you slept there before by yourself. Mommy will come with you after. I always do."

"I can't wait.

"Well you'll have to wait." Jennifer starts to cry in loud, gulping sobs. Helen turns back to me, chuckling. "She'll get over it. She'll have a good cry and then she'll go to sleep.

"When I came back I went back to live at Smallboy's. I was sick. I was really sick. I had diarrhea, couldn't eat. And my diarrhea was just black green, dark dark green, black almost. I wonder now if Kevan hadn't injured me somehow, inside. I couldn't do anything. I just slept. I remember this old man, he's passed away now, he lived across the road from me, him and his family. He used to come every morning and he would make fire for me. And he would make a pot of tea for me and he would try to get me to eat. I'd eat a little bit while he was there but when he left I just pushed it aside. I couldn't eat.

"The thing I couldn't understand, and right to this day I don't know, you know, I don't know where my dad was. I never told him anything. I never told anybody. The thing I remember the most was this old man coming. He never asked me. He never made any indication that I had to tell him anything. But he was there. He was there. And just knowing that he was there was comfort for me."

"I THINK WHERE the turning point for me was, before I finally left Smallboy's, before I even knew I was leaving, before I made the decision to leave, they had a dance.

"It was called a give-away dance. They have a tree, they put a tree in the corner and they hang ribbons on it, their offerings, eh, something like the prints, the cloth that you bring to the sweat. And everybody comes and they bring their possessions.

"It was a way of giving away the old in order to bring in the new. So while you were dancing, you prayed too. You prayed for something that you wanted. Whatever it was you wanted. I remember when I was dancing I prayed for some direction. 'What am I going to do with my life,' for a new life, a better life. I didn't know what I wanted. I just knew that I needed something different.

"So I gave away a lot of my stuff. Even, I had made a dress for myself – it was made out of wine-red velour, beautiful dress, I just cherished it, it was for a special occasion, a Christmas powwow I had made it for. Man, I loved it. And I gave it away. I gave it away.

"I think that was my turning point because after that dance, after that give-away dance I left Smallboy's and I never went back."

Outside Helen's living room everything is dark and quiet. The scudding clouds obscure the stars and moon; her house is wrapped in a black, wet bag. The children, even Jennifer with her Cricket and her waxy bag of crackers, are asleep. There is no sound here in the country, no light. Helen, too, falls silent.

"I'M NOT LIVING as traditional as I'd like to. I would like to live more traditionally. Yet, my dad tells me that it's OK. I used to think I wasn't doing right because I wasn't going to sweats. I wasn't going to a lot of feasts. I wasn't associated with a medicine man. I wasn't having pipe ceremonies, lodges and things like that.

"But after my dad explained to me the role of the woman, I didn't feel bad about it anymore. I realized I am living a traditional way of life without even thinking about it. And the main focus is the fact that I am maintaining my home. I am sober. I am drug-free. I don't neglect my children. I don't run off to the bingo every night.

"I guess you could say, the way my friend tells me is, I'm a devoted mother. My dad said, 'You can't do anything about Hutch. But those kids need you and you need to be there for them.' Other than that is going to school. My dad's all for me going to school. He helps me out if I'm in a crunch for funds too, eh. He's there. I'm so glad that he is.

"So now I don't feel like I'm not doing something I should be doing. The only thing I wish is that I could do more so the boys can learn about the culture. They get some exposure from my dad but I wouldn't mind if they got more.

"I try to teach them. I try to teach them to understand nature. To understand and respect the plants, that they can't just anytime go into the bush and chop trees down for their bows and arrows without giving something first. Even for the garden, before I plant my garden, I put tobacco in the ground and I pray to Mother Earth to bless my garden so that it will grow and give us nourishment. I try and teach them that way.

"I try and teach them responsibility. I can't teach them to go hunting, so the only thing I can teach them is how to work. So that's why I give them the responsibility of the chores. I used to give them a straight allowance, but now they have to earn it. So it works, it balances out.

"Peri, he used to do everything for Darryl, eh. Darryl would still be playing and Peri'd be cleaning up all the toys. Never complain about it. He's wonderful. A wonderful child.

"Peri is Freddy's nephew. His mother committed suicide. That's how we got Peri. He was passed from sister to sister for awhile. Finally he came to our home and once I got him I said, 'I'm not giving him away.'

"At first my dad was against Freddy and me adopting Peri. He didn't feel that we should, that we had enough kids of our own. But later on, once I made the final decision, my dad says, 'When you take a child into your home that's not your own, you will be blessed.' And I have been. I have been.

"See, Peri was born because his mother got raped. She got raped by her brother-in-law. And she would never tell. She was nineteen at the time, eh. She was not on birth control. She didn't go out with men. She was not the type that men looked at. She was very fat, big fat cheeks, like Peri. But she was jolly, oh she was a nice person.

"What happened so she committed suicide was not the rape though. She had an accident. She was driving her dad to the store here. And I don't know what went through her head, why she felt she could do anything. But what happened was, the truck was standard. And they parked it and they had gone in the store and I guess it started to roll. And she ran out of the store and she tried to stop the truck.

"They used to have this great big boulder sitting by the gas pumps. And her leg got pinned between the truck and that boulder and just really got mangled up. They wanted to cut her leg off because gangrene had set in. And she couldn't cope, she couldn't cope with that. That and everything else.

"Peri wasn't even two years old yet when she killed herself.

"Peri, he had asked me about his father. I think it was because he was looking for somebody, eh. He knows he has a father, he knows how babies are made, so he knows he's got a father. All that I could tell him was that the relationship between his mother and dad was not good and they went their separate ways. That's all I told him. Someday maybe I'll have to tell him the truth.

"He found out through kids at school when he was seven years old that he was adopted. They told him in a very cruel manner that his mom shot herself. That I wasn't his mom. You know how kids can be, they can be mean. He was really heartbroken.

"I sat down with him, as soon as I found out what had happened, and explained everything the best I could. I told him, too, that he might not understand everything that I'm saying now, but when he got older he might. That he would then."

Peri beaming, dancing with excitement, his wispy ponytail whipping the air like a thin black lasso. When he gets older he might understand. He will understand, then.

"I THINK OF the Native people's history as being a rape. Everything was stripped from them, their culture, everything. What they have left is a mixture, a hodgepodge of Christianity and Native culture. I don't go for that. That's why I just won't talk to some people about what I believe. Their Christian beliefs overshadow or put superstition into Native belief that shouldn't be there. That's difficult.

"I don't really know how my father got started back into the Native culture. All I know is when I was about fifteen, the next thing you know we were doing these things that were very strange to me. But I liked it. It felt good. Like I felt, I felt a belonging somehow.

"The first time I went with him any place was down south. We went to Wyoming to see a medicine man. And that's how I started going to sweats. And learning a little bit. And it was beautiful.

"I really, I think that's where I had a sense of who I am. Because I remember going through an identity crisis of wondering, 'Am I white? Am I Indian?' And that helped me to realize that I'm a human being. It doesn't matter whether my dad's Cree or my mother's French. That's irrelevant.

"I realize now that somebody was actually looking after me. Even now I feel like somebody is looking after me, taking care of me, helping me.

"You know, if I hadn't been taught to get help, how would I know how to get help? Somebody's guiding me, somebody's watching over me. And it feels good to know that, because I used to think I was so alone all the time. Even when I was with my spouses and that, a lot of times I used to feel so alone.

"I remember, and I'm only starting to understand the significance of it now, I was given a shawl by that Wyoming medicine man's wife. And she told me to use my shawl when I'm feeling bad.

"But I never did. I never did until I started therapy. My

therapist started teaching me how to take care of myself, how to console myself, how to make myself feel loved and cared for. When she mentioned ways to do this, one of the ways was to have tea, get inside of a blanket or a shawl or anything like that, hold a cushion, buy yourself a teddy bear to hug.

"But when she said shawl, my mind went right back to that time when that old woman gave me that shawl. And I thought, 'That's right!' I had something here all this time, and I never used it. It used to just hang in the closet. I never wanted to use it 'cause to me it was so beautiful, I was scared to dirty it or to wreck it or to pull the threads on it. And I've had it since I was seventeen; that thing is sixteen years old.

"Another thing the medicine woman gave me, too, was a pipe. And I never understood that either. I've got it and I've kept it and I have used it on occasion, a very rare occasion, because I think I was afraid. I was afraid that there was more to this than I'm willing to accept or deal with. And I'm beginning to understand now what my gift is.

"And I will need my pipe, not for anybody else but for me. In order for me to keep strength, to be strong. 'Cause I want to help other women. I want to help them and children.

"Men . . . I guess I can't exclude them. I used to think I could. But I realize now that I can't. How can you? I mean a family is a family. You can't just help some and not the others.

"It's a little difficult. But I think in time I'll get over that. 'Cause I still feel anger towards men. Toward any man.

"But in time, I think, that will heal itself."

✪ BICYCLE

There's this old guy riding a bicycle east from Enoch down Highway 16 toward the Alamo Motel. The Alamo Motel squats brown and square just off the highway, ugly, near empty and for sale. By the time you're at the Alamo, you've almost made Edmonton. Just the Windmill, the Parkland, the Royal Scot, the Siesta, the All Star American Bar to go and bingo – you've hit the city.

The old man has a way to go yet before he reaches the Alamo. He's wearing a grey raincoat and a peaked cap and his bicycle is tinny and rusted. His head is bent, staring down at his pedals, and in my rear-view mirror I can just catch his knees pumping – up, down, up, down – going like billyho.

The old man is coming from Enoch, the Stony Plain Indian reserve fifteen minutes west of downtown Edmonon, about ten minutes away, by a back road, from West Edmonton Mall. In fact the mall, some say, is built on reserve land sold off by a shortsighted band council years ago.

Some on the reserve claim the name "Enoch" was given by a Catholic missionary whose inspiration was a Sodom-type town in the Bible. It's not as bad as it sounds, they say; the town, the one in the Bible, pulled itself up by its boot straps and that's what the missionary had in mind for Enoch. Some say the reserve is named after Enoch, son of Cain, second from Adam. Or after Enoch, seventh from Adam, a prophet who walked the earth with God for 365 years and begat many sons and daughters. Someone else says in the early 1900s a man named Enoch Lapatac enticed a few families from the Papaschase Reserve onto this new, fertile reserve to farm. Lapatac was the reserve's first chief, they say; the name follows.

The last story is true. The boot straps story is the one Sky believes. As a consequence, so do I.

Sky and I pass the old man on the bike pedalling down the right shoulder, the wrong side of the road, going with and not against the cars like he is supposed to. Sky was born in North Dakota in 1955 but grew up in Manitoba and spent twenty years in Prince Albert and Stony Mountain penitentiaries. He ended up in Edmonton because when he was released, finally, he happened to be in the Edmonton Maximum Institution. He lives on Enoch because he couldn't handle the city after a few weeks of living in his car, sleeping on concrete, watching his people, he said, picking out of garbage cans.

I'm driving because Sky's got no car. His 1977 grey El Dorado with red leather interior was stolen, just two days after he spent a thousand dollars installing a new motor and a stereo. Sky had big hopes for that car, once it was fixed up.

Sky believes the two kids who stole his El Dorado started out intending just to lift his black leather jacket, the one he bought from the bleached blond Christian wolf-trainer at the Leather Ranch at West Edmonton Mall. This woman told Sky that when she is not selling coats or training wolves she writes books about how to train dogs, although she is having some trouble with her publisher right now. She also show-jumps horses and sews saddles by hand. When Sky walked into the Leather Ranch she saw his deerskin shirt, the one he designed himself, the one he wore at the Sun Dance, and approached him to design shirts for her. She said she'd sell his shirts at the new store she and her partners, silent partners, are just about to open. Just as soon as the negotiations over space are complete. By God, she tells Sky, she knows her leathers. She tells him she believes in God.

Sky says he knew right away he could not trust that woman. She would pay him for one design, then copy it herself and make lots of money and never pay him again. It's happened to him before, he says. God or no God, he doesn't take her up on her offer.

The kids who broke through a basement window to steal his

leather jacket, Sky says, found car keys in his pocket and forgot about the jacket. Then they found his medicine bundle in the car. They opened it. They took out his sacred pipe and smoked hash in it. Then they drove the El Dorado across fields, sped through small towns. When the RCMP started chasing them on the highway outside Morinville, they lost control of the car and drove into two concrete pillars. They ended up on the TV news. They hurt themselves bad. Now they're in jail.

Sky says that, at first, after his car was stolen, he was pretty much numb. After he got over being numb he started to wish those two kids had broken their necks. Then he started to think about being in a Manitoba prison when he was a kid, serving his first federal time. So he went to a sweat lodge and made offerings to the grandfathers for those kids, asking that the kids would learn something and something good would come of him losing his pipe and his medicine bundle and his car.

Sky says he realizes now he was thinking about those possessions too much – his medicine bundle and his car. They were the only two things he owned, he says, so the grandfathers, the spirits took them away to show him the foolishness of cherishing things over people.

Sky's El Dorado is parked now in a muddy tow yard outside an Edmonton bedroom community. The medicine bundle and the stereo are gone for good. Sky has to pay the towing charge plus daily fees to get his El Dorado back. The tow yard is run by an ex-con, a man who oils back his hair with Brylcreem, a man who fancies black leather studded with silver spangles, and gold skull rings with diamonds for eyes. The tow yard office is papered with tire-store madonnas. Sky's car sits in the mud smiling – the concrete pillars the two kids hit convinced the front end to grin, and hay pokes out from under the grill like unshaved stubble.

It's the end of October and none too warm. Sky and I are on our way into the city because he wants to pick up some fish and chips from a strip-mall restaurant before we fetch his car. We've been to the restaurant before; in fact we watched the San Francisco earthquake on the restaurant's TV. Sky took the earthquake with a shrug. It is simply one of the prophesies come true, he said. The white man does not respect the earth, and the earth takes her revenge. The french fries were served in their skins on wicker plates. A hand-lettered sign posted beside the till read: "Fish is brain food and the smarter you are, the richer we are." Sky likes the place, and I don't mind.

It is driving down the highway from Enoch to the fish and chip joint that Sky spots the man on the bicycle. "There's that old man," he says. Sky leans forward to look at the man's reflecion in the side mirror as we pass. He laughs. "Yep, that's him."

I think, incorrectly, that I know which old man Sky means. I am often wrong when I assume I know what Sky means. I think he means the man we were supposed to go talk to about residential schools but who wasn't at home in his motel-strip reserve house when we pulled up. I say, "You wanna stop for him?"

Sky says, "Nah. The old man's OK. Just keep going." He leans back, pulls his long hair out from where it's stuck between his shoulders and the bucket seat, and settles in.

Then he tells this story.

"That old man, he's a drinker, eh. One day he was feeling really sick from his drinking. Real hung over. So he says to his son, 'Son, you gotta ride the bicycle into Edmonton and buy me some beer.'

"The son says, 'Forget it, old man. You want beer you can get it yourself.'

"That old man, he's still feeling pretty sick. But he really wants his beer. Trouble is, he's feeling so sick he doesn't know if he can ride the bicycle. So he pulls it out of the shed and hauls it into the kitchen. He gets on that bicycle and rides around the kitchen a few times. That seems to work OK. So the old man figures he'll just ride into the city and buy his own beer.

"The old man gets onto the highway and starts riding. He rides along for about three miles. Everything is going fine. The old man is feeling pretty good, all things considered. And then the bicycle chain falls off.

"The old man doesn't know what to do. He doesn't know how to fix the bicycle chain. Edmonton is still a long ways away. But he knows he wants his beer. So he decides he'll push the bicycle into Edmonton, buy his beer and then figure things out.

"He's pushing the bicycle along the highway when pretty soon a car stops. This young guy gets out and says, 'What you doing, old man?' And the old man says, 'I'm going to Edmonton.' The young guy looks at the old man, and then he looks at the bike. 'Come on,' he says. 'I'll give you a ride.'

"So the two of them, they try to put the bike in the trunk. It won't fit. They try to put it into the back seat. It won't fit. They try tying it onto the roof, but the young guy only has one rope and the bike won't stay put.

"Finally the young guy says, 'I'll tell you what, old man. I'll tie the front of your bike to my bumper and I'll tow you into Edmonton.'

"The old man isn't sure this is such a good idea. 'No thanks,' he tells the young guy. 'You drive too fast.' And he grabs the handlebars and gets set to start pushing again.

"But the young guy says, 'Don't worry. I'll drive real slow. If I start to go too fast, you just ring the bell on that bicycle and I'll slow down.'

"This sounds not too bad to the old man. So they tie the front of his bike to the young guy's bumper and the two of them start into town, the car towing the bike with the old man perched up there behind the car, sitting on the bicycle seat holding onto his handlebars for dear life.

"So, before too long another car pulls up beside the young guy and starts gunning it. This other car jumps ahead and falls back, and guns ahead and falls back. The young guy just can't resist. Pretty soon the two cars are dragging, racing down the highway side by side. By the time they make Edmonton they've hit at least ninety miles an hour. Maybe a hundred. Maybe more.

"Just outside of Edmonton, just past the Alamo, the Windmill, the Royal Scot, an unmarked RCMP cruiser picks up two speeding cars on radar. The cop turns on his siren and straps on his bubble light. He gives chase and pulls the speeders over. The cop writes out the tickets, then walks back to his car and radios in.

" 'You won't believe it,' the cop says into the radio. 'I just picked two guys up for speeding. And the damndest thing. There was some old Indian on a bicycle behind them, ringing his bell like crazy, trying to pass.' "

When I stop laughing, Sky looks out the car window. He tells me: "I used to know a lot of stories like that. At one time I knew a lot of stories like that."

✪ SKY

SKY DRAWS A cougar, an eagle, a bear, a buffalo. The hand holding
the pencil is black with tattoos, the skin scarred where Sky tried to
scrape off his inky designs with a razor blade. He is thirty-five and
muscular and handsome in his meticulous jeans and white
undershirt. His long hair shines under a red beret; he has been
rubbing his hair with bear grease and it is thick and healthy. His
nose is smeared across his face and he has almost no teeth. The
missing teeth bother him; he thought of asking the grandfathers to
give him new ones, just as they had given a man who lost all his
ribs in a fight new bones. But then, Sky says, he realized the sweat
lodges, the ceremonies, the Sun Dance, were not for selfish
requests. He wants, above all else, to do things for his people.
And he respects, above all else, the grandfathers.

Sky is getting known around the reserve for his art. In fact he is
asked to paint murals on the walls of the counselling office where
he works, patiently talking to people about their boredom, their
drugs, their suicides. A white man, the boyfriend of a woman on
the reserve, sees the murals and tells Sky there is a market for his
drawings. He offers to put up the cash to have the drawings made
into greeting cards, saying he and Sky will split the profits. But
first, the man says, he will enter Sky's drawings at an Indian art
show in an Edmonton mall.

Sky, always reserved, always quiet, gets excited. He has been
looking for ways to raise money to buy tepees, and this is perfect.
His dream, since prison, has been to set up a camp out in the bush
for Indian kids where they could go to learn to hunt, to practice
their spirituality, to "remember the history of the ancestors, to go
back to that way of life, and build from there." He believes

remembering the old ways is the only hope for Indian kids. The only hope for all Indian people.

The Wednesday night Sky has been told the art show opens, he and I walk up and down the cavernous Edmonton mall looking for his drawings. All we can find is new cars, gleaming with spit and polish, parked at intervals along the corridors. It is cold; the stores are empty and echoing. We look for someone to ask about the show, and find only a car salesman sitting at a tiny table, smoking a cigarette and tapping his business cards.

Sky goes up to talk to him. I wander, idly, up to one of the cars. Fancy. Low-slung. A whole lot of chrome. I glance at the placard. "Speed," it says. And underneath, a black and white reproduction of Sky's cougar.

Sky's bear advertises a 4x4's "Power." His buffalo, to sell a sedan-model, is "Class." His eagle, "Style."

Yes, the boyfriend was a car salesman. Yes, he ripped Sky off. No, Sky was never paid for his drawings. No, they were never made into greeting cards. No, Sky never saw the originals again.

Sky on the stage of the Provincial Museum, following a speech by Stephen Lewis commemorating Human Rights Day. Sky had understood he was being invited to speak about the history of Indian people in this country. When he got to the museum he found he was the representative Indian in attendance, lined up on the stage alongside a representative of one of every other category the event organizers could conceive of. Each person has thirty seconds to speak. When Sky gets to the microphone, he points to a school class of Chinese children in the front row. "That is the only thing here that is real," he says. And walks off the stage.

When I first meet Sky it is winter and he is living in his car. He has been ripped off by two employers who find it easy not to pay people with criminal records, knowing no one listens to the employment complaints of ex-cons. He tells nobody he is living in his car, fearing someone will offer to help him. He says he was told all his life he was a leech on the system, and he refuses now to rely on anyone.

I do not find out he lived in his car until long after he has moved out to the reserve to work with one of the elders, sickened by the concrete, sickened by the sight of his people picking through garbage for food. Over the three years I know him he moves farther and farther away from the city, finding even the reserve too much in the end. After ten years in federal penitentiaries and five years of struggling to stay out, of relying on his pipe, the sweats, the Sun Dances, the company of elders to keep his anger at bay, the only escape for Sky is the bush. The animals. The ancestors.

And even they, in the end, are not enough.

"FOR SOME REASON when I was young, I didn't really like my father that much. I think it was mostly when he was drinking. He would beat on our mother. Not on us, too much. When he wasn't drinking, he wasn't too bad of a person. He seemed to do what he could for us.

"When I was eight, my parents split up. Our mother took the girls and left us. I guess our father was supposed to take care of my two younger brothers and me, but he just never came back.

"They left the three of us in this house. I'm not really sure how long we were there because we were pretty small and keeping track of time wasn't something we were too aware of. A month, two months, I don't know. People used to come around but they could never find us because we would hide on them. We were waiting for our parents to come back, I guess.

"We did eventually get caught by our aunt and uncle. They kept us for five, six years. I grew to hate my aunt and uncle. At first they treated us all right. Then, after awhile, if we didn't play with their kids we were whipped. If we didn't cook their meals, we were whipped. If we didn't make their beds, we were whipped. They whipped us with these round black extension cords. They would whip us till our backs and our legs were bleeding.

"That went on for quite awhile. The bitterness and the anger inside me got so bad that I thought what I would do is, I would kill my two younger brothers and then I would kill myself. So I brought this gun inside the house when our aunt and uncle were away. I took this gun and I pointed it at my younger brother's head. I was looking at him and I couldn't shoot him. I just thought, what's the use.

"So I put the gun away. We stayed there another week and I decided I would leave and somehow talk to people and see if they could help us. Help my brothers get away from there too. So I took this gun and this knife and I had a little lunch bag. My aunt and uncle were watching TV. I hammered nails into some boards and I stuck them underneath the front and back tires of their car. My brothers were crying so I decided, 'Well, what's the use, I'll take them.' So we climbed out the window and we left.

"It took us about twenty-four hours to get where we were going. We found our mother and our sisters and they seemed to be happy to see us. I didn't know, then, that we weren't really wanted there. I didn't know that for quite awhile. We stayed at my mother's place for a few days and then our aunt and uncle showed up really early one morning. They caught us sleeping and they talked to us and joked with us and laughed until we left our mother's place.

"And then, when we got back, we got whipped again.

"Even before we started running away, our uncle came home one night drunk. He started chasing us around, throwing stuff at us and swearing at us. And he was looking for his gun. We were pretty scared. We had no shoes or socks on or anything, but I shoved my brothers out the door and we started to run through the night in the snow. We froze our feet, running this half mile. We got to this other aunt and uncle's place and they took us in. They helped us thaw out our feet and they put us to sleep.

"Early in the morning, our aunt and uncle showed up. They were laughing at us for freezing our feet. Then they took us back to their house. And when we got back there, we got whipped again.

"That's where a lot of the ideas of running away, I guess, came from, and of shooting ourselves. My shooting them and shooting myself.

"There was one time when our aunt and uncle, this was around Christmas, I think, they had my brother's arm and they were swinging this cord and whipping him, and I got pretty pissed off. I ran over and grabbed hold of the cord. My aunt and I were tugging over the cord. Finally I let go. My aunt almost fell over. And then she jumped up and started screaming at me and started whipping me. And I decided I wouldn't cry. I wouldn't let her make me cry.

"So it got worse. She hit harder when I wouldn't cry. I had welts all over the place. I was about twelve, thirteen, something like that. That night I decided. No one was ever going to make me cry again.

"After that time, I would always hold it inside. I guess a lot of that was building up over the years. That anger inside. People used to tell me, 'You're like a time bomb. You're walking around ready to explode.' Older prisoners, some of them would say, 'You're dangerous.' And I never knew what they were talking about when they would say that to me."

He smiles, covering his missing teeth with his lips. "It's funny. Out here people tell me all the time I'm the gentlest person they know.

"When they finally did let us go into the foster care system, I was about fifteen. When they took us away, they split us up. I guess it was because I was always taking my brothers with me when I ran away. They put me in Winnipeg and they put my brothers in other directions."

FOSTER HOMES. SKY says little about them. He mentions a German family who beat him with belts, an abusive home he ran away from by jumping out a second-storey window, hitting a garage roof and falling to the concrete driveway. The chief thing he tells me about foster homes is: "My mother and father went to residential schools. My sisters went to residential schools. Any time I asked them about it they would just shut up. But there was a lot of sexual abuse in those schools. A lot of physical abuse. Just like the foster homes and group homes I was in. Except in those homes they didn't care if you spoke your language. They only cared if you ran away. As long as you stayed put they didn't care. As long as you didn't phone your mom and dad, didn't try to tell them what was happening to you. But otherwise, it was just like those residential schools."

"WHEN I WAS sixteen I started to get to know my way around the city a little more because of the homes I was being put into. And I'd run away and I'd get involved with some of the kids who were getting into trouble. I was hanging around with them, but I wasn't doing the things they were doing. But I'd end up getting locked up in this detention center with them.

"This one Indian guy who was working night shift in the detention center, him and I used to talk all the time. And he told me, 'If you want a place to stay,' he says, 'come and stay with us.' It felt really strange going to this guy's place without being forced. And I stayed with him for quite awhile. He never abused me or anything.

"But I would go out and I would do things just to get him mad at me. I didn't want him to get close to me. I wouldn't let anyone get close to me. 'Cause everybody who was ever close somehow disappeared. And whenever they disappeared, it hurt. So I didn't want it to happen again.

"When I was sixteen, I was with a bunch of other kids and I stole this convertible for a joyride. The cops chased us. I drove out of the city and I put the pedal to the floor. We were doing 115 miles an hour. The cops said later they weren't sure how we stayed on the road. And I turned off the road, and I stopped. I waited for the cops to pick us up because I was getting kind of scared.

"When I stopped, the cops pulled up behind us and the people I was with said, 'They're right behind us. Get going!' So I pulled out again and I turned down this gravel road. I had this car to the floor again. We were doing about a hundred on a gravel road."Then we hit the train tracks and the car skidded all over the place. I hit the ditch. And when we hit the ditch, one of the people in the car slammed her head against the window. I guess her head started bleeding on the inside.

"I said, 'Get out and run,' but I didn't know, then, she was hurt. The other kids told me, 'We can't.' They said, 'You run.' So I started to cut through this bush and then I heard gunshots. A branch not far from me snapped. I started to run again, but I tripped and I fell. I just lay there.

"And the cops came. Grabbed me by the hair, and dragged me back to the car by the hair. They got me to the car and then they gave me a severe beating. Beat me in the face with their guns, I guess. My face was swollen. I couldn't see out of one eye. The other eye, I could barely see out of it.

"That girl died in the hospital. They charged me for criminal negligence causing death, auto theft, dangerous driving, all these charges. My grandfather and grandmother came down to visit me in this juvenile centre where they had me locked up. And my grandfather gave me something and he said, 'It will help you in court.'

"They ended up staying the proceedings on the criminal negligence and trying me for auto theft and dismissing all the other charges. They sent me to a boys' home, this lock-up, until I turned eighteen.

"What my grandfather gave me, I'd rather not say."

"AFTER I GOT out of the boys' home, I ended up with a girl I'd met running away from foster homes together. I had just turned eighteen and it was just after Christmas. This girl's brother, Len, always used to try to get me to break into places with him. And I wouldn't go. I was working. I was doing this job assembling furniture frames. But for some reason, this one time I decided to go with him.

"We found this house where nobody was answering the door.

Len kicked in the door and I followed him in. This old guy came dashing around the corner and kind of screamed. So Len hit that old man in the head. The old man fell to the floor. We turned around and we ran out of the house. That old man and his wife came out screaming after us, hollering that we had broke into their home.

"And something felt wrong to me. I didn't feel right. I didn't feel like being in the city. So I told this girl I was going to leave. I went out and I stole this car. And I drove out to the reserve.

"My mother was drinking. And I found out that she had given up my younger brothers and sisters. That she had given them up to be taken to foster homes. Something inside me snapped. I turned around and I started beating on my mother. I gave my mother a licking.

"I jumped in the car and I left. I went over to my sister's. My father was there and we were all drinking and I started arguing with him. I took this knife. I was going to go after my father.

"Then my mother showed up. She was drinking and she had some bruises on her face from me beating her up. She started to scream at me, so I hit her a few more times and she fell on the floor. She was bleeding. And I had no feelings for her. For my father, for anybody. It seemed all my feelings had disappeared.

"Then there was a banging at the door. It was the RCMP. And they held up this picture. They said, 'Do you know this guy?' I'm not sure where they got my picture, somehow they had a picture of me. They said, 'We have a warrant for your arrest. You're wanted in Winnipeg.' And I asked them, 'What for? I never did anything.' I was thinking of the car. I thought maybe they were looking for me for a stolen car.

"They said, 'You're wanted for assault causing bodily harm and a possible charge of non-capital murder.' The whole room went quiet. I'm not even sure what went through the minds of my relatives. But my mother turned around, she was all full of blood. She said, 'I want to charge him too.' But the cops didn't charge me for hurting my mother.

"They put the cuffs on me and locked me up in Winnipeg. The city police in Winnipeg, they took me into this little room to question me. And while they were questioning me, they beat on me. One had me pinned on the floor. The other one was nailing on my knees and ankles and he was digging his thumbnail under my fingernail. They gave me a licking. They left quite a few marks on me.

"When I got to court the crown prosecutor got me out on a bail bond. And while I was out, she lowered my charges to material witness and to two counts of break and enter. And I didn't get into trouble. I found a job and I started working.

"But everybody on the street was starting to say I was putting the finger on Len. That I wrote a statement against him. That I was a rat. Len, he was through the boys' home, group homes, all these homes they put me through, he was through them before I was. And all the kids used to admire him because he could handle himself in a fight.

"I was supposed to go to court as a witness in his case; they were holding my case back until after his was finished. So when I had to testify against him, I told the courts that when we broke into the house, Len was behind me. I said I had gone in first and that I was turning around looking back at Len, talking to him while we were walking up the stairs. And that I got surprised by this old guy coming around the corner, so I turned around and I hit this guy and he hit the floor.

"So I took Len's place in what happened. I explained it in that way.

"They ended up dismissing the charge against Len and convicting him for a break and enter. 'Cause he'd already spent a year in custody waiting for his trial, they gave him one day in jail and then he was released.

"Why did I do that for Len? I grew up protecting my younger brothers and people in the same position I was in. To do that for Len was the same thing. In that type of life you protect one another from the system that is keeping us down, that destroyed our lives when we were younger.

"That's why they call a person a rat who goes to court and testifies against someone. In jail those people don't last very long. It's like they took sides with the system.

"You see, that old guy died two weeks after he got hit. He had a blood disease. Leukemia. I ended up going to court next. And I ended up with two and a half years for the break and enter and I was sent to the federal prison.

"Len, I hear he's dead now. I think he was sniffing glue and all sorts of other stuff. People told me he would sniff and then dive off something. Land on his head. Black out for a couple of hours and then wake up and sniff again. I saw him in Stony Mountain in 1983. He was having trouble with his speech and with his walking, even way back then."

"STONY MOUNTAIN PENITENTIARY. Federal prison. They put you in this little tiny cell for the first couple of weeks with all the other newcomers, and you see all the other men in population. You have heard all these stories about provincial jail and you have heard federal prisons are worse. And you are really scared. Ready to fight anybody.

"This little confined area they keep you in, the prisoners call it 'the fish tank,' and the guards call it 'orientation.' They give you these IQ tests. They sit you down and ask you to spell a lot of words *this* long. I think I fluked and got one right. Then they ask you this long list of questions, like what you are afraid of and what you are not afraid of. And then they make you look at ink blots.

"They decided I was inferior intelligence. So after that they let me get away with quite a bit in population – the fights and the drugs. They figured I was too stupid to know any better.

"Then, being small when I went into that place, I was told people would take advantage of me. I was told the different things that people would try to do. Sexual things. Different things. So I was always on guard when I first went in. I decided I was not going to let anybody hurt me in there. So when people came around and tried to pick on me, I would fight back.

"Sometimes I would get hurt pretty bad, sometimes it would be the other way around. But whenever I got hurt, I would go back, I'd take a weapon, anything I could get my hands on, and I would wait. Sometimes it would take a week, a month, whatever, but I'd wait. I'd make sure I got that person alone. And I'd catch him off-guard. And I'd hurt him, to the point where I'd leave a scar. Sometimes it would be physical, sometimes it would be a spiritual scar. And I'd let that person know that if he ever harmed me again in any way, I'd kill him next time around. And when I'd say that, I'd be dead serious. And everybody I said that to, they believed me. And they would leave me alone.

"It went on for quite awhile. Three years. And then finally people just started to leave me alone. They would say that I was crazy. I don't think I was crazy. I believe I was just protecting myself.

"It's kind of strange the way people will respect you if you are looked upon as being violent, dangerous. And when you hold that type of reputation inside the jail, you try to use it for your own benefit, to manipulate people. And you don't realize that type of reputation can get you killed. Because there is always someone else trying to get their own reputation. And they believe that if they can take you out, and when I say 'take you out' I mean kill you, or do as much damage to you as possible, then they will gain respect. So by getting a reputation like that you live a dangerous life inside the jail."

"MY FIRST SENTENCE was two and a half years, but it kinda stretched out. After I was in that prison for a little over a year, I was given this temporary absence to go out into the city on a pass.

"I came out on that pass two, three times. And then I decided one day I wasn't going to go back. I was staying with my brother in the city and I guess I was the centre of this little group of people because they looked up to me for surviving what I was being put through in prison. And everything had to do with being accepted. We weren't accepted in a lot of places in that city because of who we were. So being accepted in that little crowd gave me a good feeling inside. So I didn't go back to the prison that night when I was supposed to. And I was out the next week, all over the city.

"I got picked up for assault and for auto theft, for dangerous driving, impaired driving. A lot of little charges. They sent me back to prison for another two years, or two and a half years, I'm not really sure now.

"Then when I did start working on the rest of my time, I started to get more involved in the drugs inside the jail. I needed to escape from the reality surrounding me. I thought I was handling the drugs a lot better than I was, I guess. At first it was just smoking, pot or hash. Then it became the needle. Seeing these older people in jail doing that, I looked at them as though they were more experienced in life. And when they offered me drugs, I thought I was being lifted up in status. I didn't know I was being pulled down a little further.

"So I started to inject drugs.

"The guards say they live in danger when they're with us in the prison. They ask for danger pay. They create their own danger by the way they treat the people inside there. Just like if you capture a bear in a cage and you walk up to it with a stick and start poking at it, trying to keep it quiet.

"I've got scars around my eyes from the guards. This one day, I was so caught up with sticking a needle in my arm, so caught up with these pills that took me away from the prison, that my arm seemed like it was cut. It was all black-and-blue. And I didn't see it. I was too busy trying to find a vein that would take the needle. And we were drinking this home-made brew. I was pretty loaded on this stuff.

"This friend came and told me there were a couple of people giving him a hard time. And I was high enough and my feelings were angry enough, just waiting to be let loose. So I said, 'All right, let's go and see them.' I used to hide this big metal pipe underneath my bed. So I took this pipe out and I stuck it up my sleeve. I was pretty loaded on this brew. And we went to look for those guys.

"One of them saw us coming and he started smiling at me. He says, 'How's it going?' 'Just great,' I told him and I walked up to him and I kicked him, right in the groin. He bent forward and I hit him with that pipe right in the side of the head. He dropped to the floor. Then he got up and started running. He ran right up to the guards. But when you are on that speed, it doesn't matter who is around. Nothing matters except what you are going to do right then and there. And you do it. So we went and gave the other guy a severe licking with this pipe.

"As I was walking away these guards followed me, because they didn't want to try to grab me while I was carrying this pipe. When I got back to my cell there were four people sitting there, drinking this brew. And when I walked into my cell the door slammed behind me. The guards locked all five of us in that cell.

"And then this friend, he came running to my cell. I was up on the top tier, fourth tier. He told me, 'There's five, six guards downstairs and they are all arguing about you,' he says. 'They want to see who is going to get you first. And they are armed. They've got clubs.'

"I started to smile. I said, 'OK.' I had no choice, the door was locked.

"So the five of us just kept on drinking and smoking in my cell till eleven o'clock. Eleven o'clock the guards locked everybody up. And as soon as everybody was locked up, the guards all lined up on the fourth tier and they all lined up on the third tier. And they all had their clubs.

"They said, 'Are you coming out?' And I looked at them and I said, 'Fuck you. If you want me, come and get me.'

"That's all they wanted to hear. They took the padlock off and they started to open the cell door, slowly. As soon as the first one came in the door, I clubbed him. Knocked him down. I was pretty loaded so I wasn't too accurate. So when the next one came in, I missed him and I hit the floor.

"And then they piled on top of me. And they piled on top of everybody else.

"Everybody was screaming and I was trying not to scream. I was trying to let them club the hell out of me. If they killed me, I guess I wouldn't have felt it. It wouldn't have mattered. They handcuffed me behind my back and they had my face to the floor and they had my hair and they were banging my head on the floor. They pulled me up by the hair onto my feet. They slammed me all over the place with their clubs. And then one of them knocked me over. I landed on my back and my hands were cut behind my back.

"I was lucky I didn't feel the pain, I guess. 'Cause I kept right on hollering at them.

"Then they dragged me down the stairs. They had me by the feet and they dragged me down the stairs, four flights of stairs, my head banging down all these stairs. They dragged me down to the hole. Got me into the hole and they started beating on me again.

"Then the nurse came down and she was screaming at the guards to take the cuffs off my hands so she could sew me up. The guards wouldn't listen. They grabbed me and they threw me up against the wall and they were hitting me. The nurse started screaming and swinging at the guards, telling them to take the cuffs off.

"So finally this one guard said, 'Did you have enough?' I wouldn't answer him. He took the cuffs off me. And when I looked at my hands they were so swollen. Red, swollen, purple. I couldn't feel them. So I pushed one hand into a fist. I turned around slowly, and then I spun around as fast as I could and I hit that guard in the face and he fell to the floor.

"The next thing I woke up and was lying in this little cell. Handcuffed. Leg irons around my ankles. And I didn't know where I was. I hollered and the guards came down and I asked them, 'Where am I, where am I?' They laughed at me.

"After that beating they took me downtown to the hospital,

three, four times for X-rays to my head, to see if I had any fractures. And I had a skull fracture, they had to put a steel plate inside there. But there was never anything said about it. And I had my ribs fractured. I've got lumps around my chest from that.

"I was in the hole until I healed." He laughs. "It was a few months, anyway, four months.

"The guards, sometimes they would get carried away when they were beating on us. Go crazy. But it didn't matter how many marks they left on you or anything. They'd always just take you down to segregation and leave you there till you healed.

"That was my second home, was segregation. I think out of the ten years I was in prison, I spent four of them in the hole.

"Those segregation units at first are hard to handle but after you've been in there for awhile, you start getting used to it. I used to dream about a lake, forest, the animals. I used to live along that lake. There was never anybody around except myself, the lake, the animals, the water.

"And then the guard would come along and bang on the door and wake me up." Sky laughs.

"A few times down in segregation – this is when I was involved with the Indian Brotherhood – there'd be cigarette butts underneath some of the food. Or glass. It stuck in the top of my mouth when I was eating. I told the nurse about it. I even saved that piece of glass and showed that nurse. There was never anything done about it.

"I used to think, while I was in the hole, that those people were hurting a lot more inside than we are. That's why they are doing that to us. Off and on, maybe one of the prisoners would say something to one of the guards, and the guard would start swearing back and this other guard would say, 'Don't lower yourself as low as those people.' And when I heard that I would laugh. How much lower can you get than being a guard.

"I used to watch those guards walking back and forth and I'd see them picking their teeth with bones of somebody's finger. That's what I would imagine. That they were cannibals. Because they are making a living off of the prisoners.

"I would say to them, 'When you eat, you are eating a part of me because you are keeping me here.' They were building that anger inside of me so that it would stay there, so that I would be released back out into the towns, the cities, the communities, filled with that anger. So that I would go out and do something and fill their jail again. There is no way out of that system for us as long as that anger is in there.

"And these guards and the people who work in those jails, they know that. And sometimes they even come out and tell you right to your face that they don't give a damn about you. That they are getting paid for you. That you are their meal ticket."

"MY FATHER HAD passed away in September 1976, while I was in Stony Mountain. There was this phone call from the hospital that my father wanted to see me. That he had thirty-six hours to live. That he wanted to talk to me before he died.

"I went and saw a classification officer and I told him. It turned out he was the one who sent that message down to me, so he knew all about it. But he acted surprised. I told him I wanted to see my father before he passed away. And he asked me why, and he said I was a security risk and that I couldn't be trusted.

"So I told him, 'Put the leg irons on me and put the handcuffs on me, take me down.'

"And he said, 'No, I can't do that. That would look bad in the eye of the public.'

"So I left there really pissed off. I was working my way up the stairs to my cell, and this guard started laughing at me. There was a whole big circle of guards, and they were laughing at me. They started making fun of me about what was happening with my father.

"So I turned around and I hit this one guard. They all grabbed a leg or an arm. Stretched me out and beat the hell out of me all the way down to the hole. And then when they got me down to the hole, they beat on me a little more and threw me into this cage, this little cage of concrete. Four walls concrete, ceiling concrete, floor concrete. And they kept me locked in there, with one little light that burns twenty-four hours a day.

"I ended up staying in the hole about five months that time. Then they let me back out into population, saying they were sorry what happened, they didn't realize my father had passed away and all their bullshit.

"Now, off and on, I still wonder what my father wanted to tell me. Why he wanted to talk to me."

And for the only time in the years I know him, I see Sky cry.

"I GOT RELEASED from that Stony Mountain four times, I think. But each time I'd get released, I'd come out of there so pissed off. I'd come out with no support, no family, nothing. So it wouldn't take me very long to end up right back.

"One time I was out fifteen hours. One time a couple of days. Another time fifteen days. The next time I was out for about eleven months.

"That time, there were three or four girls and myself hanging around together. One evening these girls went out. We were all broke at the time. They came back and they had this guy with them. They said, 'Come on. This guy's got some beer and he's driving us around.'

"So I went riding around with them. This guy took us over to his place. We were sitting around drinking and he kept bothering this one girl and the girl didn't want him to bother her. So I told the guy to leave her alone. And he told me to mind my own business or get out of his house.

"As soon as he said that, I jumped up and hit him. And then I kicked him and then I hit him some more. I knocked him on the floor and then I beat on him until he couldn't get up. Then I took his car keys, took his stereo, wallet. Everything that I could fit in his car. Then I left the city.

"I went and found my youngest brother. I stayed with him for a few weeks and we drank. Talked about the days when I used to run out of foster homes. Talked about our aunt and uncle. Talked about all the things that had happened to us. I didn't realize these things were upsetting my brother, and that they were upsetting me. That all those things were still bothering us. The more we talked about them, the more we had to drink.

"My brother was starting to pick fights with people for no reason. He'd blow up. One day we were driving along and he hit this guy in the back seat. And he hit a cousin. And he turned around and started screaming at me.

"I told my cousin to stop the car. I got out. I dragged my brother out of the car. I slapped him a few times. And then he started swinging back. So I kicked out. Got him in the stomach and I grabbed hold of him by the neck and I pulled him to the ground. I was going to start to beat on him.

"My cousins grabbed hold of me. They wouldn't let me go. They said, 'What's the matter with you? You guys are brothers.'

"And then the police came driving by and my brother ran out and stopped them. He told the cops who I was and that I had a stolen car. That I was wanted in Winnipeg. And then when I had the handcuffs on, he tried to hit me again.

"They took us to the cells in Brandon. My brother laid a charge of assault against me. And they found out I was wanted for attempted murder, robbery with violence, assault causing bodily harm, auto theft and a whole string of other charges.

"I decided I was going to fight every one of those charges. That I wasn't going to plead guilty to any of them. That I was going to make them spend all the money I could, taking me into court, holding me in the cells, feeding me, everything.

"A lot of my charges started getting dismissed for lack of evidence, witnesses who wouldn't show up. Finally the last charge I went up on was attempted murder, assault causing bodily harm, robbery. I walked into the court room and the person who was charging me didn't know who I was. He didn't recognize me. So the charge was dismissed and I walked out of the court house.

"My friend Michael asked me one time if I ever miss my brothers. I never even think about them anymore."

"IT WAS FALL by then. I was walking around the city in summer clothes and I met these two guys who asked me if I was cold. They gave me this little leather jacket and they got me these jeans and we went out around the bars and I started to run into people I knew from the prison. And they started to give me pot, they started to give me money, started to buy me drinks. And it started all over.

"That night I ended up hurting someone else in the bar. All because he stared at me too long.

"I travelled around with these two people for awhile. This one guy used to get into fights all the time and every time he'd get into a fight, I would jump in and help him. I always stuck up for this guy.

"For some reason, this one evening, he turned on me. He came up and hit me in the side of the head. I jumped up and we had a fight. And then this other guy grabbed hold of me and this guy who was supposed to be my friend kicked me a few times.

"I got away from them. I ran down the street and I saw this tool box in the back of this truck. I took this hammer, and I went back. And I hurt those people with that hammer. This guy who was a friend, I smashed his kneecap with that hammer and I put a hole in his forehead.

"Then the cops came down. He wasn't laying charges, no one was laying charges against me and they weren't going to come to court and testify. So the cops took me underneath this bridge. They had the handcuffs behind my back. And they beat on me until they thought I was dead. I could hear them talking. I heard them say, 'Is he dead?' And then one of them checked. And he said, 'I think so.' So they took the cuffs off and they kicked me one last time and they walked away.

"I lay there and I couldn't move. I was cold. I had no shirt on. I lay there until it started to grow daylight because I couldn't get up. And then this rain started. I felt the rain. My body started to respond. Slowly I got up.

"I walked down the street to this store to buy some cigarettes. This girl started to scream and I was wondering what was going on. I looked around. I didn't see anything. She said, 'Do you want me to call the police?' I asked her what she was talking about. She said, 'What happened to you?' I didn't know I was covered in blood. I told her, 'No, the cops are the ones who did it.' She didn't believe me.

"After that I hung around the city for awhile drinking. Trying to forget all the things that happened to me. And I eventually got picked up. I ended up back in Stony Mountain."

"I WAS BEING transferred around different prisons. With each transfer there was a feeling of fear. I'd always wonder if there would be someone in that prison who'd be looking for me when I got there. If I ever hurt someone who might have a relative in this jail, or who might be there and have a lot of friends and come after me. So when I'd go into a different prison, I'd always go in prepared to die in that prison if I had to.

"They transferred me from Stony Mountain to Prince Albert penitentiary in 1980. In Prince Albert I found myself having to fight everybody, all over again. Including Indian people. That was the worst part of it.

"In Prince Albert the white people, they didn't really get along with one another, so they were broken into a lot of groups. This one group called themselves bikers and considered themselves to be really tough people. This one biker came onto one of the Indian people in the gym and this Indian guy happened to be a boxer and he was good." Sky laughs. "Before the white guy got a chance to swing, he was already on his back. He was out cold. They came down with a stretcher and carried him out.

"And from there the feelings just started to build. It built up to the point where some of the Indian prisoners decided, 'All of us Indian people are going to have a sit-down in the gym. No one is going back to their cell.' The word was spread around inside the gym that no one was going back into lock-up. And that if anyone tried to, they were going to get hurt.

"So everybody stayed out. And then the gym started to get wrecked. Everything started to get smashed.

"The administration warned us that if we didn't clear the gym, they were going to declare it a riot. There was a lot of talk about the guards hanging around by these little gun holes. All these things were starting to build up and everybody was starting to feel an excitement. No one wanted to go in and be singled out for going in, because we'd pay for it. Not from the guards, but from the other Indian people.

"So we all stayed out in the gym. And then finally the guards came shooting with their tear gas. Everybody started to panic, running around. The gas got so thick you couldn't see. It was burning the eyes. The guards came in with their clubs and with their shields. No one could really see because it was so thick with tear gas, and we were getting clubbed around and herded out the door.

"They herded us into the big yard. This was March. A really cold month. They had these dogs and these clubs and bats and shields. That was their way of terrorizing us. They were pointing these guns at us. They made us strip down and they put the handcuffs and the leg irons on us. Marched us through the cold field and up to our cells.

"It wasn't a racial thing at that point, but it turned into something racial. At the time of that incident in the gym, the Indian population was about twenty-five to thirty of us. After that incident they kept us all locked up. And the Inmate Welfare Committee was meeting with the prison administration and we had no idea what they were meeting about. No one would come down and explain anything to us. One of the Indian people was supposed to be on the Inmate Welfare Committee, but he wasn't allowed to take part in the meetings. And we were all being treated a little differently. I could feel that, even though we weren't around any of the white prisoners 'cause we were all segregated in this separate area. For some reason everything seemed kinda strange.

"Then one day they herded half the white population out into the exercise yard. And then they sent us out.

"And as I was going out, I heard about the racial riot that was coming down and how we were going to get beaten on in the yard, and how some of us might not make it back in. I was laughing about it and I was teasing a few of my friends about it. We were talking about how many of them each one of us could handle. 'I can handle a couple, how about you? You're pretty big. You can handle about ten.' We weren't really taking it all that serious.

"Then we got into the yard and we saw them. All these white prisoners were lined up along this hockey rink with their clubs and their sticks and their bats.

"Everybody was walking around in circles not knowing what to do. Some of the guys were saying, 'Well, should we go back in?' It was already too late. The other half of the white population came out. And we were sealed in there.

"Then the guards in their uniforms all surrounded the exercise grounds. They stood around on the other side of the fence. They had their M16s out, their handguns, and they were all laughing and poking fun at us. They were just waiting for someone to go over the fence so they could shoot at him.

"So we were trapped. We couldn't go over the fence and we couldn't go back the other way because we were cornered. So we decided we might as well get it over with and fight.

"We started looking around trying to find something to arm ourselves with, but there was nothing left. It had been all taken, everything. But they had this snow fence across from the diamond. And the snow fence had these iron posts stuck in the ground holding the fence up.

"We stopped at the fence and we tried to rip these bars out of the ground. All the white prisoners started looking at one another, wondering what to do next because they figured we were going to be armed when we got those posts out.

"But it turned out someone knew there was concrete holding those posts into the ground and that it would be awhile before we got them out. So they charged us as quick as they could.

"They backed us up into the corner, and then they tried to make us strip down. And everybody thought, 'To hell with that, I'm not going to strip for you or anybody else.'

"So the fight started. There was so many of them that they made it kinda hard for themselves to really hurt us too bad because, with the swinging of the clubs, they were almost hitting one another. But there were a few of the guys who got hurt pretty bad. Some of them had fractures. There was one guy, no, there was two that I know were taken to hospital.

"And one of the things I always think about off and on, when I think about it, is that I never heard anyone who was getting beat on scream out in pain or anything. Just heard a bunch of grunts, every now and then. Everybody who was getting clubbed never made a sound. They just kept quiet and took the beating.

"But it didn't seem like we really lost anything. We didn't lose that fight. The spirit among the guys after it was over, it was pretty good because everybody stuck together and took the licking without screaming. There was one guy who screamed. He ran from the group. He ran across the field and he ducked into this little sports shack and some guys from this bikers' group ran down there with their baseball bats and gave it to him. You could hear him screaming all over the place.

"He got in trouble from everybody else afterward for screaming. But I can't blame him for screaming. I wouldn't have blamed anybody for screaming. I think death went through a lot of the minds of the ones who were trapped in that corner. You had to fight for your life.

"When it ended, they cut us down in words. They threatened that if any of us were to ever act up or say anything wrong towards any of them, it would happen again.

"And with that, they turned around and left. We went back to our cells. I laid down and thought about everything that had happened. I thought about all the faces I saw, carrying those clubs. I remember them. I still remember most of those faces.

"There were a few of the Indian people who were really revengeful about what had happened. And I can't blame them. They go out of their way, whenever they run into someone who was involved in that riot, they make sure they hurt those people right back. Those people who did that to us ended up living in fear in the prison system ever since.

"And I enjoyed watching them stew in that fear. I was really bitter."

"I GOT TRANSFERRED back to Stony and I started thinking about what I would do when I got out. There was these two bars, side by side, with nothing between them but a thin brick wall. A lot of Indian people drank there. I decided I would organize all the people to go into one of the bars and tell the other guy he had to make a deal, that the people would only come back if he would share his profits with them and give the girls on the street a place to stay. And after that deal was made, I would do the same with the other guy. And after both deals were made, I'd go in and knock down the brick wall.

"I never quite got around to it.

"When I came out of Stony Mountain and I went into the city, I knew most of the people in the slums, the drag, and they knew me. Everybody sees you as tough because you've been in the prison. So you end up trying to uphold that reputation. And it just drags you right back down into the jail.

"I had no place to stay. I didn't want to go out to the reserve because I felt my relatives would be accepting me back out of pity, because they felt bad about the way I was treated when I was a kid on that reserve. And I didn't want to be pitied.

"So to forget about all that I was hanging around the streets. I had less than a hundred dollars in my pocket, I had a little bit of pot. I was walking down the street thinking about the reserve and I ran into this guy I knew from prison. He said, 'You want to come with me? We are having a party.'

"I ended up staying at his friend's place. The guy living there, him and I got along quite well. I talked to him about what it was like inside the jail, what it was like coming out. I felt kinda close with this person. So I stayed. And I drank a lot. Smoked a lot of pot.

"People used to pick on this guy because they thought he was weak, because he tried to help people out. They took his kindness as a weakness. And when people mistreated him, I would get really angry inside. I'd wait until I caught those people alone and I'd hurt them one way or another. He found out that I was helping in that way because the people who were hurting him quit. We grew together like brothers. We really respected one another in that way.

"One day these three guys started to pick a fight with this guy. I stood there and I watched while they were pushing him. Then the first guy started hitting him in the face. He gave my friend a rough time. And I got pretty pissed off and I started screaming and those guys left.

"My friend had a swollen face. I asked him, 'Do you want to get even with these guys?' And he said, 'Ya.' So I grabbed this wooden table and I broke a leg off and I gave him that table leg. I ran out the door and he followed me. We got outside and I found this two-by-four on this picket fence. I ripped it off. These guys were starting to run and I caught up to them. And I swung this two-by-four at one guy by the knees, and he went down.

"And as he went down, I started to club him. I know I broke that guy's legs. And his arms. And I broke other bones in his body.

"And while I was doing this to that guy, he never made a sound. So I just stood above him holding this two-by-four. He looked me in the eye. And I threw that two-by-four down and I turned and I ran.

"That's when I remembered what happened with us in Prince Albert. How we got beaten that day. And I thought about what had happened inside that jail. How the Indian people were beating on Indian people, checking them into protective custody. And how, when it came time for us to stand up for ourselves in that exercise yard, there was only a few of us not in protective custody, only a few of us left. All these thoughts came back after looking into that guy's eyes.

"So I went out and I got good and drunk. Tried to forget about it.

"And what I did to that guy, I guess my friend was telling his brother, cousins, he was telling a lot of people how I stuck up for him and how I beat on this guy. To him it was something. Something really good.

"My feelings were mixed. I didn't feel good about what I did, and yet I felt good about the way all these other people were starting to treat me. And I started to drink heavier and heavier and I would be really sick. I didn't like the smell of the beer and I didn't like the taste of it, but I drank. That was the way I was accepting myself, by drinking.

"I started to get worse. The anger inside me was getting to be greater and greater. I was sitting with this girl, Len's sister. We were having breakfast. She was saying she thought I should have been dead a long time ago, because of the life I was leading. Some of the things I had done. Some of the beatings I'd got. Sometimes the beatings were so bad I couldn't see. But living that type of life, you wear those beatings with your head up. They don't hurt as much as the hurt you feel from the way you are treated by people out in public, or by relatives, or by people who call themselves friends.

"While we were sitting there it came on the news that the cops were looking for someone in connection with a beating. And they mentioned a second beating and a robbery along with it. And that angered me even more because there was no robbery; that second one was just a beating.

"That beating, that time, was this white guy. I was at my friend's place and there was a banging at the door. There was this girl standing there, naked from the waist up. Her face was full of blood. I took my jacket off and told her to cover herself and I asked her what happened. She said there was this guy inside her apartment and he was trying to rape her.

"So I grabbed her by the arm and I went back to her apartment. I told her to knock. The guy opened the door a bit, and he saw her. And as he opened the door wider he saw me. So he grabbed her and tried to close the door on me.

"I threw myself against the door as hard as I could. The door slammed him in the face. He fell back against the wall. And before he could recover from the shock of being hit by the door, I was all over him. I pounded him to the floor, and while he was on the floor I kept on pounding.

"Only when he didn't move, did I stop.

"Before that the cops weren't looking for me. But now they were looking for me and I knew I was going to be taken back to jail, so nothing mattered any longer. The whole city was open to me. I was going to go out and I was going to terrorize the city. I was going to rob, I was going to do everything they were accusing me of doing. I was going to go out and do as much damage as I could before I got hauled back in.

"I went out and I drank around the city. I ran into this one guy in the bar. I knew this guy was after me. He had wanted to lay a beating on me for quite some time, years, 'cause I had gone out with one of his girlfriends once. He still had a hatred for me. And I sat there and I waited for him to do it.

"It didn't happen in the bar. He invited me to a party down at his mother's place. While we were there, they got me pretty drunk. And while I was pretty drunk, he hit me in the face with a beer bottle. Everything went blue. And he hit me again. It started. I got my licking.

"I got a severe beating that night. The cops came around. They took me to the hospital. They got me stitched up. Asked me if I wanted to lay charges. I said no. And I was surprised I wasn't hauled off to jail, 'cause I knew they were looking for me.

"The next day I got up and went downtown. I was carrying a knife. I went out looking for this guy. Finally, late in the evening, I found him sitting in this bar. He was with a few people, so I left. I went out, I got a baseball bat and I came back into the bar. And I walked over and I smiled at him. And I hit him with the bat.

"He went down. His friends jumped back. I just started swinging the bat. I went kinda wild in the bar. Hit whoever was in the way. Smashed whatever I could smash. Everybody was hollering and screaming, and I heard them hollering for someone to phone the cops. So I walked out of the bar swinging the bat.

"I couldn't stay still. There were so many things that were bothering me. So I started drinking some more. I still had this knife. And then I called a cab.

"I was talking to the cabbie while I was riding around. And then something broke out. I was arguing with him. I got really pissed off at him, and I told him to stop. He hadn't even come to a full stop and I had hold of his hair. I pulled his head back over the seat and I held the knife to his throat. I was going to cut his throat open.

"He stuck his hand in the way and held onto the knife. I pulled the knife and it cut his fingers. He sat there for a minute, facing me in his mirror. So I let go of the knife and I hit him on the side of the head.

"Then I saw these people coming so I jumped out of the cab and I ran. Through buildings. Across traffic. And then for some reason I just stopped. All these people came running at me. I didn't know whether to fight or what to do, so I just stood there.

"All these people jumped on top of me and started kicking me and hitting me. And then, when the handcuffs came out, I realized, all these people, they were the cops.

"After they put the handcuffs on me, they dragged me by the hair towards the back alley. And when they had me in the back alley they booted me, beat on me for awhile. All this time they were remarking about my being an Indian.

"Then they dragged me over to the car and they threw me in. They had a cop sitting on either side of me and two sitting in front. They were remarking how much trouble I was in. And how I would be better off dead. And I guess at the time I thought they were right. So I lifted my feet up while we were travelling, I didn't know how fast we were going or anything, and I kicked the driver of the car in the back of the head. He lost control of the car.

"I'm not really sure what happened after that. I just know I woke up in this little room with this cop sitting on top of me.

"When I was in that little room, I thought of killing myself. Then I thought, 'If I kill myself what good is it going to do? I might as well kill somebody else too.' But I was pretty loaded at that time. And I was handcuffed so there wasn't much I could do.

"Cops started coming around trying to get a statement out of me. I wouldn't make any statement. They'd beat on me, off and on, for not writing a statement. And then I guess they just got tired of beating on me 'cause they took me up to a cell and they locked me in.

"I ended up with a few more assault charges. Assaulting a police officer, a bunch of others. I ended up with about fourteen charges, total, I guess. I told the lawyer I would only fight the charges one at a time, so they wouldn't plea bargain me and send me away for a long time.

"It took about three months. I ended up getting dismissed on all but one of the charges. I got four and a half years."

"I THOUGHT TO myself, four and a half years isn't so long. I can do that. I spent the next six months trying to convince myself it wasn't such a big deal. That I'd walk out of that prison the next time and it was going to be different. That I was going to do something. Then I thought about it. That's what I'd said the first time around and the second time around.

"I started selling drugs, so there were a lot of Indian people coming around. Some would come and talk. I didn't care much for talking. I was wrapped up in myself and my drug deals. Trying to think of what I'd do when I got out. Thinking I'd have this bank account that I could rely on. That maybe I could do something different with my life.

"Then, one day, they had these posters hanging all over the prison walls. These guys were running to be on the Inmate Welfare Committee. And the names on those posters were the people who had instigated the racial riot in Prince Albert.

"I tried to ignore it. But there was no protection in that Stony Mountain, and there were a lot of Indians in there, about fifty per cent. And some of the things the Indian people were telling me bothered me a lot. I'd try not to let anyone know that they were touching my feelings when they told me how, at times, they would gather in a little group to try and defend themselves or prevent something from happening. How racial things were starting to develop in that prison.

"But something just started to burn inside me. So one day I got all these big pieces of paper together and I wrote on those pieces of paper, 'Remember Prince Albert, April, 1980.' I taped up these pieces of paper over the names on those posters. And I went back to my cell just smiling, thinking about it, thinking about the fear those people would feel.

"Then there was these two black guys I used to talk to off and on about jailhouse politics. They started telling me to get involved and take over as president of the brotherhood. I'd tell them I wasn't interested and they would ask me, 'What's the matter with you? You're involved in it whether you like it or not.'

"I ended up being sucked right into the brotherhood. I always thought I'd clear up one issue and get out. And then something would happen that would drag me a little deeper and deeper into jailhouse politics.

"I only had a grade five education but I started reading books and I started going through proposals from the brotherhood. I didn't understand the words, so I got a dictionary and I got these black guys to explain some things. Sometimes they had to go over it two, three, four times before I understood. They were kind of getting a kick out of it, kind of admiring me for trying to educate myself that way. And then they started giving me different types of books to read. Books about political prisoners in different jails and their struggles. They opened my eyes to a lot more. I wasn't really sure what I was struggling for, but everything just started to build up. The administration gave me something to struggle for each time.

"I used to kinda enjoy that fight the administration would give me. Just to know that they were scared of me. Whenever they ever wanted to do any harm to me, they would haul me off and lock me up in a little cage and say it was for the good order of the institution.

"The harder life got for me in there, the more aware of what was happening to us inside the prison I became. And the stronger they made me each time they locked me up or did something else to me. They were threatening me in different ways about being involved in the brotherhood. They threatened me with more segregation, with transfers.

"I guess it didn't matter to me any longer, because I just kept on. Because I felt a different type of respect from the people. I felt I was a better person if I was doing something. Aiming for a change.

"My belief then became that – let's say the guards dragged you off and beat on you for some reason – if no one stood up for you or spoke about what happened to you, then the same thing is going to happen to me or could happen to someone else. So that was my struggle then. If something happened to anyone, I'm going to speak up for that person.

"Then, about '83, I was locked up in this segregation. They put me down there for nine months. They thought they could break my spirit. Somehow I came across a book called *Bury My Heart at Wounded Knee*. Up until then I never really knew of any books about Indian people. All the things I heard about Indians were negative.

All of them made me feel bad about myself. And that book just sat there because, to me, it was just another put-down. I forget how long it was before I picked it up and started to read it.

"That book made me really bitter toward the system, bitter toward white people. It was late at night and I would lie in my cell and I'd remember what I'd went through in life and I'd remember what my ancestors went through. I'd see their villages being attacked and I'd see them being cut up and slaughtered. And when I'd see these things, I'd find tears on my face without knowing they were there.

"But reading that book gave me strength inside the jail. It wasn't the book, actually, it was my ancestors. I found that my suffering in that jail was nothing compared to what my people went through.

"It made me feel strong inside. I told myself there was no way in the world anybody is ever gonna make me give in, not one inch, to anything. That's where I really start to believe in myself, in my spirit. To me, my spirit is everything. If they were to break my spirit while I was in the jail, I'd have never walked out of there and I wouldn't be out of that jail today.

"And I realized there was nothing they could do to me in there. The worst they could do is kill me. And they were already doing that to me, maybe not out-and-out physically, but they were killing me spiritually. So that was my way of surviving in there. By fighting back, one way or another.

"One night I wrote a letter to one elder. I explained that I saw myself standing at these crossroads and I didn't know which way to go. I explained a lot of the feelings I was going through. And when I wrote that letter, I burned sweetgrass.

"Something happened after I sent off that letter. I was sitting in my cell and I saw these two pieces of cloth hanging on the fence. It was winter time and it was blowing but these things just hung there. At first I didn't pay attention to them. I just sat there talking to my friend. Then I turned around again. This time I didn't see paper or cloth. What I saw was an arrow. And I said to my friend, 'I know who that is. It's that elder.' I wasn't really sure what I was talking about, but I felt this chill in my body, in my spirit and I could see my friend had that same chill.

"I went down to the chapel the following day because the arrow had been pointing to the chapel, and I found out there was going to be this three-day ceremony there. And I met an elder and I took some tobacco and I let him know what I had seen the night before. And he looked at me for awhile. Not in surprise or anything. And he said, 'When you see things and you have a feeling for it, go with that feeling because those are signs that have meaning.'

"So I decided to go to that sweat lodge ceremony in the prison. I felt I had to be part of it. I had suffered long enough while I was in jail. When it came to the day the sweat was going to happen, I was there. There wasn't any thought about it, I just went. And when I went in, I was scared.

"Then when I came out, I found peace inside myself. I didn't feel anything towards anyone in jail, toward anybody. Everything seemed to be so beautiful around me, even inside the jail. I felt like I was a part of everything. I felt like I was a part of that lodge and the lodge was a part of me.

"The sweat lodge is the only place I ever felt accepted. Totally. I wasn't looked upon as a prisoner, ex-convict. I wasn't looked upon as anything but myself. And the feeling was good, so I kept going more often. And the more I went, the more I seemed to become accepted, the better I felt about myself, the stronger I seemed to grow, the more aware I became.

"When I sit among the elders in a lodge and I have my turn to talk, I call them my family. Not only them but all the Indian people. We are all related, we are all the same, whether our language is the same or not. We come from the same spot. We're all connected. It's like a spider web. We're connected through the earth, through the trees, the grass, the water, the air, the animals, the birds, the fish. We're connected to everything, 'cause all of those things sustain us. And when we pass on, our body goes back to the earth and fertilizes it. So if something new grows from the earth it is part of us, it feeds us, it gives us strength.

"In the lodge you become a part of all of that. And to be in the lodge and come out and look up at the sky and see the stars, everything is so clear and you see every star and feel everything around you. You can feel the life from the trees, the waters, the grass.

"I was told by elders that I walk alone. I know I walk alone. I grew up alone. I grew up hard. I wouldn't let anyone into my life. I was alone even when I was among people.

"Coming back and remembering the old ways, the sweat lodge, the pipe and the ceremonies, I have come to feel that I'm not alone anymore. Even when there are no people around. I'm starting to feel more freedom within myself. At times I forget that I'm really alone.

"In the lodges sometimes, some of the elders would tell me they know I've got the answers for the problems of the younger people. Because I've already made my way through the life those kids are going through. And for me to sit down and talk to the people who are going through that life, that helps those people.

"So that's one of the reasons I agreed to talk to you about working with this book. Because I don't want to damage my people, I want to help them.

"What I went through, I don't even wish that on people I sometimes feel I still hate. 'Cause there is a lot that I went through I probably missed out or didn't mention while we were talking. Because some things are a little too hard to talk about, still."

YES. SKY IS back in jail. Yes.